KONSTANTIN FEDIN

A DESCRIPTIVE AND ANALYTIC STUDY

SLAVISTIC PRINTINGS
AND REPRINTINGS

edited by

C. H. VAN SCHOONEVELD

Indiana University

LXIII

1967
MOUTON
THE HAGUE · PARIS

KONSTANTIN FEDIN

A DESCRIPTIVE AND ANALYTIC STUDY

by

JULIUS M. BLUM

1967

MOUTON

THE HAGUE · PARIS

Printed in the Netherlands by Mouton & Co., Printers, The Hague.

Dedicated to
KATHLEEN
*and the boy*s
RICHARD, MARK, ERIC and MICHAEL

PREFACE

Konstantin Fedin, Leonid Leonov, and Mixail Šoloxov have been termed by one of the outstanding American critics as "respectively the Steinbeck, Faulkner, and Hemingway of the Soviet Union".[1] Contemporary Soviet criticism considers Fedin to be "odnim iz krupnejšix predstavitelej sovetskoj literatury".[2] In the early twenties, when Fedin was just beginning his literary career, Gor'kij described him as a writer who was "ser'eznym, sosredotočennym, rabotajuščim osmotritel'no". Gor'kij added that Fedin "iz tex, kotorye ne spešat skazat' svoe slovo, no kotorye umejut skazat' xorošo".[3] Fedin's later development as a creative writer has served to confirm Gor'kij's early estimate.

Unfortunately, the works of Konstantin Fedin are still relatively unknown although they are widely read throughout the Soviet Union and the Central Eastern European satellites, and have been translated into most of the languages of Western Europe.[4] To date, the only study of Fedin published in a non-Communist country is that contained in Professor Simmons' "Introduction" to Fedin, Leonov, and Šoloxov, published in 1958, prior to the appearance of the last of Fedin's novelistic trilogy, the novel *Koster* (The Bonfire). Recently a Soviet film, based on the second novel in the trilogy, *Neobyknovennoe leto* (No Ordinary Summer), has been circulated in the United States. The latest contribution to the cause of bringing Fedin's works to the attention of American readers has been the publication, in an English language paperback, of

---

[1] Ernest J. Simmons, *Russian Fiction and Soviet Ideology* (New York, Columbia University Press, 1958), prefatory note.

[2] A. N. Men'šutin, "K. A. Fedin", *Istorija russkoj sovetskoj literatury*, ed. by A. G. Dement'ev, III (Moscow, Izd. Akademii Nauk, SSSR, 1961), p. 212. The transliteration system used here is as follows: a, b, v, g, d, e, ž, z, i, j, k, l, m, n, o, p, r, s, t, u, f, x, c, č, š, šč, ", y, ', è, ju, ja. This modification of the transliteration system used in *The Slavic and East European Journal* has been adopted as most rational for the purpose of this study.

[3] *Ibid.*, quoting *Žizn' iskusstva*, No. 22 (1923), p. 19.

[4] The 9-volume collection of Fedin's works lists translations.

Pervye radosti, under the title of *Early Joys,* with an informative and stimulating introduction by Professor Simmons.[5]

Fedin's works are worthy of study for a number of compelling reasons. Fedin was the first Soviet author to probe the psychological problems of the Revolution, rather than to confine himself to a mere description or exaltation of it. Fedin's *Goroda i gody* (Cities and Years) is the first big epic-like Soviet novel, and continues the nineteenth century tradition of the lengthy, realistic, psychological, social novel. This feature is even more apparent in Fedin's subsequent novels, particularly *Brat'ja* (The Brothers), *Pervye radosti,* and *Neobyknovennoe leto.* Fedin's works are especially significant also because of the author's ability to view the Revolution and the soul-searching of the Russian intellectual with the eyes of one with extensive residence in, and appreciation of, Western European culture. Also worthy of note is the fact that Fedin has been the winner of two Stalin prizes, awarded for his dilogy, *Pervye radosti* and *Neobyknovennoe leto.* In June, 1958, he was unanimously elected to the Academy of Sciences of the USSR in recognition of his attainments as a creative writer and literary theorist.

Fedin's works merit special study and analysis at the present time for yet another reason. His early novels were written immediately following the Civil War and the Russian Revolution, whereas his later novels were published following the Second World War. Thus the student of Soviet literature is afforded an exceptional opportunity to trace the development of a Russian novelist throughout the entire period of Soviet history. Furthermore, Fedin is unique in that, having been born in 1892, he was educated not only under the Soviet system, but also in the pre-revolutionary tradition, and was already twenty-five years of age at the time of the revolution.

There are those who would argue against the suitability of the works of a living author as a fit subject for scholarly study and analysis. This argument is invariably based on the ground that the investigator is deprived of the perspective afforded by time and the opportunity to view the author's total production, and the insight which later criticism may afford. René Wellek and Austin Warren refute this view:

But this disadvantage, valid only for developing authors, seems small compared to the advantages we have in knowing the setting and the time and in the opportunities for personal acquaintance and interrogation or at least correspondence. If many second- or even tenth-rate authors of the past are worth study, a first- or even second-rate author of our time is worth studying, too.

---

[5] Konstantin Fedin, *Early Joys* (New York, Vintage Books, Inc., 1960).

It is usually lack of perception or timidity which makes academics reluctant to judge for themselves. They profess to await the "verdict of the ages", not realizing that this is but the verdict of other critics and readers....[6]

Because of the lack of the perspective of time, this study will be primarily synchronic, with individual works being subjected to analysis in approximately the order in which they were written. The danger of such a study is recognized, namely, that the original intent of the author may be misinterpreted, and only later investigators will benefit from any refutation this may evoke from the author or others who would defend him.[7] Yet the study of Fedin's maturation as a writer, as disclosed by analysis and evaluation of his earlier novels as compared to the later novels, coupled with study of the evolution of his heroes, the recurrence of certain motifs, and the thematic and stylistic changes which may be observed will necessarily involve diachronic techniques.

The most difficult — and pleasurable — task involved in this work is acknowledging the inspiration and guidance provided by others without resorting to hyperbole. First and foremost, over a period of more years than I like to count, I am indebted to my gentle wife, Kathleen, always mindful of the importance to any would-be scholar of total immersion. By tactfully and modestly assuming the responsibilities of *pater-familias*, and creating an atmosphere of love and sympathetic understanding with generous doses of optimism and encouragement, she, more than any other individual, deserves the credit for any value which this work may have.

I am deeply grateful to all members of the "Russian side" of the Department of Germanic and Slavic Languages, Vanderbilt University, for their encouragement and forbearance, as well as for the substantive knowledge and habits of scholarship which they were able to impart. A particular debt of gratitude is owed to Dr. James W. Marchand, indefatigable mentor and guide in special problems of linguistics and in broader problems of methods, the search for fundamental principles, bibliography, and all that sound scholarship implies.

To Dr. Hongor Oulanoff, thesis director, sensitive interpreter of Russian literature, and, withal, exacting task-master, special acknowledgment is due. It was Dr. Oulanoff's investigation of the literary achievements of

---

[6]   R. Wellek and A. Warren, *Theory of Literature* (New York, Harcourt Brace and Co., 1956), p. 33.
[7]   James W. Marchand, "Prolegomena to a Theory of Literary Criticism". An unpublished, undated paper, distributed by Professor Marchand as a supplement to a series of lectures delivered at Vanderbilt University during the academic years 1961-1962 and 1962-1963, *passim*.

the Serapion Brothers which led to the choice of one of them as the subject of further study; and it was his never flagging enthusiasm and expressions of confidence which resulted in this study being carried to completion. Of invaluable assistance also was Professor Oulanoff's thorough and intimate knowledge of primary and secondary sources, as well as of their location. It was due to this motivation that part of the Summer of 1962 was spent in the Harvard University and New York Public Libraries collecting data, a task rendered both pleasant and profitable thanks to the assistance rendered by the staffs of the Slavic Divisions of both institutions.

A final debt of gratitude is acknowledged to the staff of the Joint University Libraries at Vanderbilt University, particularly to Miss Jim P. Matthews who, in less than two years, succeeded in procuring the many books and periodical sources essential to the study, many of them out of print. Her positive approach resulted in the acquisition of materials from the Lenin State Library in Moscow and the conclusion of an exchange agreement between the two libraries. Appreciation is also expressed to Dr. David Kaser, Director, for his support in initiating this project. Miss Clara Mae Brown and Mrs. Annabel Boyce were of incalculable help in locating and borrowing various materials on Inter-Library Loan. Mrs. Viola Fulghum, with no knowledge of Russian, merits special gratitude for her patience in typing these pages and in coping with the large quantities of transliteration.

TABLE OF CONTENTS

INTRODUCTION

Although Konstantin Aleksandrovič Fedin wrote his first story in 1910,[1] of the large number of articles which have dealt with his work during the past half century, only a few treat the problem of his literary craftsmanship; the overwhelming majority consist of brief reviews and political or sociological essays. Even those few articles or monographs which do purport to identify and evaluate the elements of Fedin's literary craftsmanship are so contaminated by extra-literary considerations as to be of minimal value. This is particularly true of Soviet Russian criticism.

It was to help fill this gap that this study was undertaken. Its purpose is to identify the distinguishing features of Fedin's art in an effort to contribute to a fuller understanding and richer enjoyment of his literary works. It is based on the fundamental assumption that Fedin's works do warrant reading and subjection to critical analysis and evaluation. It is recognized that if we define the object of literary criticism as the evaluated apprehension of the subject matter, then description and analysis, to which this study is devoted, are not enough. They are merely preliminary operations in a consideration of a theory of value. But the fundamental assumption of this investigation is that Fedin's works do merit study because they are of value. This stipulation is necessary at the outset, since to attempt its proof in this study would expand its scope to an unacceptable degree.

The study, then, is primarily an inquiry into what is, rather than a judgment of what ought to be. Nevertheless, evaluative terms have been used whenever it was felt that an appraisal was warranted. It has not always been possible, nor desirable, to separate and treat in order the various functions involved in the critical process: isolation, analysis,

[1] *Slučaj s Vasiliem Porfir'evičem*, which reflected the influence of Gogol's *Šinel'*. This story is not included in the nine-volume collection of Fedin's works, but is mentioned in B. Brajnina, *Konstantin Fedin* (Moscow, Sovetskij Pisatel', 1951), p. 7. Fedin's first published story was "Meloči", which appeared in the journal *Novyj satirikon* in 1913. Fedin describes the joy which he, then a student, felt on seeing his work in print for the first time: "Ja skakal i pel."

comparison, and evaluation.[2] In some cases it will be found that both description (isolation, identification) and assessment (evaluation) are contained in a single statement. This has always been done consciously.

The study is based primarily on Fedin's literary works, with major emphasis on those earliest and latest works which are most revealing of the distinguishing features of his art. Minor works, such as *Poxiščenie Evropy* (1933; 1935), *Sanatorij Arktur* (1940), and patriotic writings produced during World War II are mentioned only in passing, or not at all. A brief chapter is devoted to *Koster*, which was received too late to be subjected to the same type of analysis as was accorded the first two novels of the trilogy.

Fedin's theoretical views on literature and the process of literary creativity, as expounded in several newspaper and periodical articles and collected in *Pisatel', iskusstvo, vremja*,[3] are not discussed in detail but are cited only in substantiation of conclusions which may be based on the textual analysis. Biographical data have been kept to a minimum. They have been introduced primarily to illuminate doubtful passages or to enhance appreciation by identifying Fedin's own experience.

The original intent was to keep the literary works themselves as the center of attention, avoiding all biographical, political, psychological, or sociological analysis. As the work progressed, however, and study deepened, it became apparent that this could not be done, for two reasons. First, because of the very subject matter of the novels themselves, and second, because of the environment of Socialist Realism in which the later novels were created, demanding that Fedin, as a Soviet author, concern himself with the task of the "ideological remoulding and education of the toiling people in the spirit of socialism".[4] Some solace was derived from Austin Warren's observation to the effect that Formal Criticism (study of structure) and Ideological Criticism (judgment of philosophical attitude) will, if properly conducted, "interpenetrate".[5]

[2] These basic functions have been classified in different ways by different critics over a period of several millenia, and this particular classification is not intended to exclude any other. It is one suggested by Theodore Spencer in "The Critic's Function", *Sewanee Review*, 47 (October-December, 1939), p. 555.

[3] First published as a separate volume by Sovetskij Pisatel', Moscow, 1957, and later incorporated in the *Collected Works* as Vol. IX (1962).

[4] A. A. Ždanov, "Soviet Literature — The Richest in Ideas, The Most Advanced Literature", speech at the first All-Union Congress of Soviet Writers held in Moscow in August, 1934, reported in H. G. Scott (ed.), *Problems of Soviet Literature* (Moscow-Leningrad, Co-operative Publishing Society of Foreign Workers in the USSR, 1935), p. 21.

[5] A. Warren, "Literary Criticism", *Literary Scholarship* (Chapel Hill, Univ. of North Carolina Press, 1941), p. 151.

This work does not pretend to be a complete or definitive analysis of Fedin's style. It is intended, rather, to focus attention on those qualities which are of the essence and characteristic of his creative literary work, as well as to suggest areas for further investigation. The study is really a response to the challenge posed by Soviet criticism, where any worthwhile results of the subjection of Fedin's writings to critical analysis are obfuscated by Marxist-Leninist-Stalinist dialectic, which interferes with the application of the empirical method. This inquiry proceeded with constant awareness of the importance of following, as closely as is possible when investigating an art object, a scientific or empirical method. Every effort was exerted to avoid a dogmatic[6] or a persuasive (impressionistic) method.[7]

The scientific method in criticism is defined by La Driere as "bringing to bear upon literary judgment every item of relevant knowledge ... and restricting judgment to what is warranted or permitted by the sum of this relevant knowledge".[8] This has entailed the study of numerous secondary sources and their analysis and synthesis along with the analysis of the primary sources, Fedin's creative works. There is no indication that a similar investigation has been attempted previously. This statement takes into account the monographs and dissertations published in the Soviet Union. All those which have been examined reveal deficiencies in method, ultimately attributable to the application of irrelevant criteria, destroying the validity of the criticism, which is not what it purports to be.

The monograph of B. Ja. Brajnina warrants special mention, first because it is the pioneer in the field, and second because it is representative.[9] The greatest value of Brajnina's monograph derives from the fact that it is not merely a panegyric to an already famous and popular writer. Within the limits imposed by Soviet literary criticism, Brajnina examines the degree to which Fedin meets the requirements of the

[6] Discovery of specific qualities previously defined as valuable, which is not considered to be in contradiction with the basic assumption that Fedin's work, as a corpus, is valuable.
[7] Defined by Abraham Kaplan, "On the So-Called Crisis in Criticism", *Journal of Aesthetics and Art Criticism*, Vol. VII, no. 1 (September, 1948), p. 42, as a psychological determination that what has been discovered by analysis is valuable.
[8] J. Craig La Driere, "Scientific Method in Criticism", in *Dictionary of World Literature*, edited by Joseph T. Shipley (Littlefield, Adams & Co., Paterson, N.J., 1960).
[9] B. Brajnina, *Konstantin Fedin* (Moscow, Sovietskij Pisatel', 1951), revised in 1953, 1956, and 1962. Comparison of the four versions reveals certain changes made because of purely political considerations. Thus, certain laudatory references to Stalin in the 1951 version do not appear in the 1956 or 1962 version. It would be difficult to conceive of any other hypothesis to account for this change other than the death of Stalin in 1953 and his subsequent denigration.

doctrine of Socialist Realism, and the "partijnost', narodnost', and idejnost'" associated with it. It seems almost as if Wellek and Warren were referring specifically to Brajnina when they wrote:

Marxist critics not only study these relations between literature and society, but also have their clearly defined conception of what these relations should be, both in our present society and in a future "classless" society. They practice evaluative, "judicial" criticism, based on nonliterary political, and ethical criteria. They tell us not only what were and are the social relations and implications of an author's work but what they should have been or ought to be. They are not only students of literature and society but prophets of the future, monitors, propagandists; and they have difficulty in keeping these two functions separate.[10]

Brajnina's treatment is chronological, tracing Fedin's development from his early association with what she considers the "dekadentskaja gruppirovka", the Serapion Brethren, to the "bol'ševistski-idejnomu iskusstvu socialisticeskogo realizma". She stresses the nonliterary criteria to such an extent that only nine of the 279 pages of the 1951 monograph are devoted to "masterstvo", or literary craftsmanship. And even those nine pages, in a chapter at the end of the book titled, "O masterstve", citing such eminent literary critics as Andrej Ždanov, Lenin, and Gor'kij, make no pretense at analyzing Fedin's artistic methods — the point of view, narrative technique, linguistic structure, stylistic devices, or any of the other special problems of modes and techniques peculiar to a work of narrative prose.[11] Thus, for example, the culmination of Fedin's literary efforts (as of 1951), the two novels, *Pervye radosti* and *Neobyknovennoe leto*, are discussed only in very general terms. Brajnina herself recognized this shortcoming and attempted to rectify it in her article, "Iskusstvo slova".[12] Bearing the subtitle "Zametki o stile Fedina", the article, based primarily on material from the dilogy, contains some revealing observations on the language which Fedin uses.

    In 1959, P. Bugaenko published a monograph purporting to deal with Fedin's craftsmanship.[13] Like Brajnina, it is more of a political and sociological analysis than a literary essay. It is distinguishable from Brajnina's monograph chiefly in four respects: It was published later than

---

[10]   R. Wellek and A. Warren, *Theory of Literature* (New York, Harcourt, Brace & Co., 1956), p. 83.
[11]   A critique of Brajnina's monograph may be found in V. M. Ozerov's review in *Sovetskaja kniga*, XII (1951), pp. 79-84.
[12]   B. Brajnina, "Iskusstvo slova", *Oktjabr'*, No. 1 (1954).
[13]   P. Bugaenko, *Masterstvo Konstantina Fedina* (Saratov, Saratovskoe knižnoe izdatel'stvo, 1959).

all three versions of the Brajnina monograph; it is more fully documented, with footnotes on each page, but without any bibliography *per se*; all damaging references to Stalin have been deleted (as they have been from the 1956 edition of Brajnina); and a chapter on purely literary considerations is included.

Vera Smirnova's article, "O romanax Konstantina Fedina", is an attempt to analyze Fedin's craftsmanship as a novelist. Smirnova's basic thesis is that the central idea or theme of the novels determine their "form", and that this "form" varies from novel to novel. She stresses the unique rhythm of each of Fedin's works, the individual intonation of each of the chapters, the simplicity of the language, the author's ability to express complex thoughts, emotions, and ideas in a succinct, compressed fashion and, finally, the clarity of Fedin's own attitude and point of view.[14]

In the article, "Dva romana K. Fedina",[15] V. Ivanov provides a general treatment of the main characters of the novels, *Pervye radosti* and *Neobyknovennoe leto*.

Particularly penetrating observations regarding Fedin's craftsmanship are found in two articles by a fellow Serapion brother, N. S. Tixonov, "O Konstantine Fedine",[16] and "Neobyknovennoe leto".[17] Tixonov comments on the epic scope of Fedin's novels, calls him a "pisatelem bol'šoj temy", stresses Fedin's ability to keep the main story line sharply in the foreground and, through numerous scenes and episodes, to characterize the *dramatis personae* so that each leads his own life, separate and distinct from that of the others. Tixonov writes: "Vy s udovol'stviem čitaete každuju frazu potomu, čto eto vysokaja, čistaja russkaja reč', peredajuščaja predel'no točno, so vsemi ottenkami i živopisnost'ju, zadumannoe avtorom." Other articles containing some critical commentary on Fedin's literary style, as observed in the dilogy, are those of A. Drozdov, "Vyxod v žizn'",[18] Brovman, "Zametki o xudožestvennoj proze",[19] and Ju. Lukin, "Obrazy bol'ševikov".[20] In commenting on Fedin's language, Lukin describes the writer as a "tonkij master realističeskoj živopisi".

---

[14] V. Smirnova, "O romanax Konstantina Fedina", *O literature i teatre* (Sovetskij pisatel', 1956), pp. 5-65.
[15] *Oktjabr'*, no. 1 (1949).
[16] *Literaturnaja gazeta* (23 Feb. 1952).
[17] *Kul'tura i žizn'*, No. 35 (1948).
[18] *Novyj Mir*, no. 4-5 (1946).
[19] *Novyj Mir*, no. 3 (1948).
[20] *Novye uspexi sovetskoj literatury* (Moscow, Sovetskij pisatel', 1949).

According to P. Bugaenko[21] there are fifteen "kandidatskix" dissertations on file at the Lenin State Library in Moscow. Although that library did honor a request for several books and articles pertinent to Fedin, it refused to make the dissertations available.[22]

A. A. Fadeev (d. 1956), a leading Soviet novelist in his own right, emphasized the publicistic element in Fedin's work.

В чудесном романе К. Федина *Необыкновенное лето* с его полнокровным изображением жизни, труда и борьбы, людей из разных слоев советского общества не воплощены, однако, в художественные образы большие темы государственной политики, военной стратегии в 1919 году — этом решающем году гражданской войны; автор выразил эти темы публицический, хрониккально.[23]

The literary style of Fedin's most recent novels has been attacked by the Latvian writer, A. Upit, on the basis that the devices which he uses are not consistent with the principles of the contemporary novel.[24] Four years after his original, largely unsubstantiated allegations (as might be expected, in view of the difficulties inherent in defining the "principy sovremennogo stroenija romana"), in a letter to A. A. Fadeev on 15 October 1953, Upit wrote:

Недвумысленно, определенно я говорю, что манера К. Федина (местами) напоминает бальзаковский стиль с неизменным описанием каждого нового встречающегося в романе персонажа (*Утраченные иллюзии, Лилия в долине* и др.), по крайней мере на 2-3 полных страницах не только регистритуются мельчайшие приметы его тела, но и приключения его недавнего и давнего прошлого, судьбу его родителей, еще и части его родственников и т.д. Кажется, ясно, просто и понятно, что я говорю не об обширных скучных, устаревших прозаических описаниях вообще, а именно подчеркнуто — только о стиле романов Бальзака. Не могу пред-

---

[21]   *Masterstvo Konstantina Fedina* (Saratov, Saratovskoe knizhnoe izdatel'stvo, 1959), p. 13.

[22]   In May, 1962, a number of books, articles, and dissertations were requested by mail. In August, 1962, eight books and three journal articles were received on microfilm. As for the dissertations, B. P. Kanevskij, the chief of the library's International Book Exchange Department, stated in his letter of transmittal that "We are sorry to have to report that the rest of the publications you have asked for are not available." The non-availability of the dissertations is not surprising since internal library policies, applicable even to scholars working in Soviet libraries, frequently require special permission for access to dissertations not yet published.

[23]   A. A. Fadeev, "Za vysokoe kačestvo literatury i principal'nuju kritiku", *Literaturnaja gazeta*, No. 64 (1949).

[24]   A. Upit, "Ob èstetike socialističeskogo realizma", *Literaturnaja gazeta*, No. 64 (1949).

ставить себе, что и в наше время можно возхищаться формой бальзаковских описаний и ставить их в пример и подражание советским романистам.[25]

The few German articles which have appeared were published in East Germany, and are either translations of Soviet articles, or the same type of Marxist criticism as is found in the USSR itself. The only two English-language treatments of Fedin which warrant mention are Simmons' 78-page introduction[26] and A. J. Rolick's analysis of Soviet criticism of Fedin's earlier work.[27] Two articles in French warrant study.[28] Jeanne van der Eng-Liedmeier examines the revolutionary intelligentsia as portrayed in several early Soviet works by different authors, and analyzes Andrej Starcov, the vacillating intellectual of *Goroda i gody*. Schogt comments on the lack of color of Fedin's early positive heroes, and develops the thesis, without going into the details of Fedin's biography, that examination of the evolution of his intellectual heroes offers an insight into Fedin's own intellectual, spiritual, and even political development. Other criticism will be discussed in appropriate portions of the text.

---

[5]   A. A. Fadeev, *Za tridcat' let*, 2d ed. (Moscow, Sovetskij pisatel', 1959), p. 780.
[26]   E. J. Simmons, *Russian Fiction and Soviet Ideology* (New York, Columbia University Press, 1958), pp. 9-87. Cf. review of Professor Simmons' introduction by Francis B. Randall in *The Commonweal*, Vol. LXVIII, No. 9 (May 30, 1958), pp. 237-238.
[27]   A. J. Rolick, "Fedin and Soviet Criticism (1919-1926)". Unpublished Master's thesis, Columbia University (1950).
[28]   Jeanne van der Eng-Liedmeier, "L'intelligencija revolutionnaire vue à travers quelques œuvres soviétiques (1921-1927)", and H. G. Schogt, "Quelque héros dans les romans de Konst. Fedin", both in *Analecta Slavica*, A Slavonic Miscellany of Russian History, Language, and Literature, in the University of Amsterdam (Amsterdam, 1955).

PART I

SHORT STORIES

I

THE FORMATIVE YEARS

Fedin's literary career began during the first years of the new Soviet state. Fedin had experienced a great deal by this time, and had accumulated a fair reservoir of experiences upon which to draw for his literary production. He had spent his childhood and early boyhood in the provincial cities of Saratov and Kozlov, his school years in Moscow, and his early manhood in western Europe, in Germany. He had been a pupil in the commercial academy, a clerk in his father's stationery shop, and a student at the commercial institute in Moscow. His artistic and intellectual experience included working as musician, teacher, chorister, and actor, activities he pursued while confined in Germany during the first World War. Young Fedin experienced all this prior to his twenty-fifth birthday.

In the fall of 1918, Fedin came to Moscow. He spent eight months in Syzran', in exhausting labor in the Executive Committee of the Syzran' Soviet, editing a newspaper and the journal *Otkliki*, and writing a number of articles and short stories. This was during the stormy year 1919, when Kolčak was approaching the Volga, and when anti-Bolshevik demonstrations were flaring up in the province of Syzran' itself. Denikin's troops were approaching Tula, and Judenič was heading toward Petrograd. It was at this time that a number of the population of Syzran', including Fedin, fled to Moscow. Fedin, as a member of the Special Bashkir Cavalry Division, helped defend Petrograd. Until early 1921 he worked as an assistant to the editor of the newspaper of the Seventh Army, *Boevaja pravda*. In his autobiography, Fedin refers to the years 1918-20 as the "načal'naja škola obščestvennoj žizni",[1] the formative years in his career as writer and journalist. The articles and stories of that period "otražali vpečatlenija dejstvitel'nosti — vojnu i revoljuciju".[2]

At last the Civil War ended, only to be followed by the turbulent situation prevailing during the first years of the New Economic Policy.

[1] K. Fedin, *Sobranie sočinenij v devjati tomax*, I (Moscow, GIXL, 1959), p. 12, hereinafter referred to as *Sobranie*.
[2] K. Fedin, *Sočinenija v šesti tomax*, I (Moscow, GIXL, 1952), p. 14.

This was a period of doubt and misgiving for Fedin. Great doubt, and a sense of frustration and disappointment, are implicit in the autobiographical comment he made, along with others of the Serapion Brotherhood, in 1922: "Moja revoljucija, kažetsja, prošla. Ja vyšel iz partii. U menja tjaželaja polka s knigami, ja pišu".[3]

Fedin was faced with two problems: *how* to write, and *what* to write. Besides the war and the revolution, Fedin was disturbed by social problems of a more universal nature. He was troubled by an acute awareness, stemming from the literary heritage of the nineteenth century, from Gogol' and Dostoevskij, from Čexov and Leskov, of the "little man", the "insulted and the injured", on the fringes of life.

Prior to writing the series of stories which later appeared as *Pustyr'*, Fedin had complained to Gor'kij that the old themes were disturbing him, interfering with his addressing himself to the problems of war and revolution. "Nabrosajte ix na bumagu, zapišite. Togda oni srazu otvjažutsja", replied Gor'kij. Fedin himself later attributed his writing *Pustyr'* to the fact that, like Nikita Karev, hero of the later novel, *Brat'ja*, he considered himself a "dolžnikom uxodjaščej v istoriju staroj Rossii".[4]

In addition to this psychological motivation, there were factors operating during the period 1919-23 to explain why Fedin did not devote himself entirely to the subjects of war and revolution, as would be preferred by Soviet criticism, but dealt with pre-revolutionary, universal themes, such as love, self-denial, and sacrifice, and their effects on human character and personality. There was also a historical factor, the literary struggle which was raging in the early twenties.

A. THE SERAPION BROTHERHOOD

One of the groups which emerged during this struggle was the Serapion Brotherhood, a small literary grouping which first took shape in the Dom iskusstv in 1921. It included the poets Elizaveta Polonskaja and Nikolaj Tixonov, and the prose writers Mixail Zoščenko, Mixail Slonimskij, Venjamin Kaverin, Nikolaj Nikitin, Vsevolod Ivanov, Il'ja Gruzdev, Konstantin Fedin, and Lev Lunc. Close to the group was the literary theoretician, critic, and writer, Viktor Šklovskij. Gathering in the smoky rooms of the Dom iskusstv, or in Zamjatin's apartment, the young *litterateurs* tried to resolve the eternal question of the relation of literature

---

[3]   *Literaturnye zapiski*, No. 3 (1922), p. 28.
[4]   B. Brajnina, *Konstantin Fedin* (Moscow, GIXL, 1953), p. 49.

to life, and the problem of the subject matter and techniques of literary creation. The theoretician of the group, Lunc, formulated their position thus:

Мы собрались в дни революционного, в дни мощного политического напряжения. "Кто не с нами, тот против нас", — говорили нам справа и слева. С кем же вы, "Серапионовы братья"? С коммунистами или против коммунистов? За революцию или против революции? С кем же мы, "Серапионовы братья"? Мы с пустынником Серапионом. ... Мы требуем одного: произведение должно быть органичным, реальным, жить своей особой жизнью. ... Слишком долго и мучительно правила русской литературной общественности.[5]

The various members of the group were by no means unanimous in their thinking. Fedin recalls: "My byli raznye. Naša rabota byla nepreryvnoj bor'boj v uslovijax družby".[6] Twenty years later, Fedin insisted that he had never been fully in accord with the position expressed by Lev Lunc, and that he stubbornly defended his own point of view:

Мой приход к Серапионам сопровождался ссорой. На третьем собрании я излил отстоявшийся протест против "игры" в защиты "серьезности". Удар принял Лев Лунц. Стычка была жестокой. ... Лунц говорил: русская проза перестала "двигаться", она "лежит" ... она стала простым отражением идеологий, программ, зеркалом публицистики и прекратила существование как искусство; спасти ее может только сюжет — механизм, который ее расшевелит, заставит ходить, совершать волевые поступки; традиция сюжета находится на западе; мы должны привести эту традицию оттуда и оплодотворить ею нашу лежачую прозу. ... Поэтому наш девиз — "на Запад"![7]

V. Šklovskij also looked toward western models:

Старая русская литература была бессюжетна: писатели бытовики брали тем, что Лев Толстой называл "подробностями", действия же в русской беллетристике, "события" было всегда мало. Если сравнить русский роман с английским и даже французским, то он покажется рядом с ними композиционно бедным, новеллистическим.[8]

---

[5] *Literaturnye zapiski*, No. 3 (1922), p. 31.
[6] Fedin, *Gor'kij sredi nas* (Moscow, Goslitizdat, 1943), p. 105.
[7] Fedin, *Gor'kij sredi nas*, p. 105-107.
[8] V. Šklovskij, "Serapionovy brat'ja", *Knižnyj ugol*, No. 7 (1921), p. 20, quoted in Bugaenko, p. 19.

Fedin, although not as volatile as Lunc, was also vitally concerned with plot construction and the articulation of plot elements. Yet he felt that the first priority should be assigned to the problem of *what* to write, and then *how* to write:

Я говорил так: мечта литературы состоит не в том, чтобы размножать книжные образцу, все равно какие — западные или русские; важно к чему будет приложен механизм той или другой традиции, ибо ничего не получится, если мы ради придания подвижности русской прозе, заставим Обломова ездить на трамвае; материал литературы определит сам, какой нужен механизм для его жизни; материал литературы есть чувство, и все дело в том — обладаешь ли чувством, которое хочешь выразить; какими средствами ты этого достигаешь — безразлично — помощью прославленного сюжета или с помощью презренной риторики — все средства хороши ... и так как чувство всегда идет в ногу с временем, всегда совершенно, то нельзя себе представить в наше время писателя без страсти ко всему создаваемому революцией. Поэтому сначала нами должно быть во всей глубине понято, *что* мы хотим сказать, тогда мы найдем *как* сказать. ...[9]

But despite any differences of opinion, membership in this brotherhood did leave an indelible imprint on Fedin. He himself recognized that what was most important was not what divided the Serapion Brethren but rather that which they had in common. Fedin himself wrote:

В постоянних схватках нащупывалась цель нашего совместного плаванья, и в конце концов внутренне все признали, она у нас одна: создание новой литературы.[10]

Fedin *was*, despite the absence of any refernce to war and revolution in some of the stories in the collection *Pustyr'*, concerned with the problem of the positive hero, and the extent to which literature should treat contemporary events. Looking back after twenty years, he wrote:

В начале 20-х годов только немногие писатели вплотную садились за решение этой задачи. Едва ли не большинству представлялось, что с ней можно повременить, пока жизнь не создаст кристально сложившуюся форму современного героя. Такого решения задачи, как герои Фурманова, кроме него, тогда еще никто не дал. Растпространено было убеждение, что в развивающемся новом сознании еще не содержится будущий тип его. Я лично, например, тоже был

[9]   Fedin, *Sočinenija v šesti tomax*, VI, p. 534.
[10]   *Ibid.*, p. 109.

убежден, что пока материал зыблется, художник не способен его прочно схватить, что материал будет утекать из-под руки, как сухой песок, тем больше чем сильнее сжимаешь кулак.[11]

Even allowing for the fact that a statement made twenty years later is far from spontaneous, and with allowance made for nonliterary motivation, it remains clear that when Fedin dealt with themes other than war or revolution, it was by deliberate, conscious choice. The real question *why* he made that choice will perhaps never be answered. The fact is that Fedin did write stories with themes not related to current events and not extolling communist heroes, treating his themes and characters in a manner reminiscent of Čexov.

B. GOR'KIJ

During this period of soul-searching and groping, Maxim Gor'kij came to exercise considerable influence on the young writer:

В 1920 году я познакомился с Горьким. Нынче, когда прошло больше трех десятилетий с того памятного февральского дня, я могу сказать еще убежденее, чем раньше, что факт этого знакомства с Горьким сделался громадным событием моей писательской жизни. Первая же встреча с ним положила начало сердечному общению, длившемуся до его смерти.[12]

In the book *Gor'kij sredi nas*, Fedin recounts how he met Gor'kij, his subsequent contacts with him, and the advice Gor'kij gave him. According to Fedin's later testimony, Gor'kij criticized him during their first encounter:

Надо научиться смотреть на вещи ... отрываться от случайного, внешнего — в этом состоит искусство видеть. Во всей нашей жизни много наносного ... Вы берете голый факт, без отношения его к другому факту или к чему — нибудь большому, важному. У вас все происходит как бы в воздухе. Можно было бы подойти к рассказу иначе. Можно было бы сказать, что на смену умирающему, уходящему приходит новое. Является смерть, а в то же время происходит зачатие новой жизни.[13]

Soviet criticism bemoans the fact that in Fedin's early stories there were no signs of the "začatija novoj žizni", that Fedin's horizons were thereby

[11] *Ibid.*, p. 534.
[12] Fedin, "Avtobiografija", *Sobranie*, I, p. 13.
[13] Bugaenko, *op. cit.*, p. 25, citing the collection, *Pisateli* (1926), p. 313.

restricted, precluding his appreciating the new men, and the heroic importance of contemporary events.

Gor'kij took active interest not only in the work of Fedin, but in that of all the other Serapions. In 1922, they had published their first *Almanax*, which contained stories by Zoščenko, Lunc, Nikitin, Vsevolod Ivanov, Kaverin, Slonimskij, and Fedin.[14] Its importance lay not so much in its inherent literary value as in the fact that it signalled renewed interest in Russian prose fiction. Gor'kij, however, was concerned over the apparent interest in style at the expense of human psychology. Fedin cites K. I. Čukovskij regarding Gor'kij's comments at the gathering of the Serapion Brethren:

Горький заговорил о том, что в книге, к сожалению, нет героя. ... Человек предан в жертвы факту. Но мне кажется, не допущена ли тут — в умалении человека — некоторая ошибка? Кожные раздражения не приняты ли за нечто другое? ... А у вас герой затискан. В каждом данном рассказе недостаток внимания к человеку, а в жизни человек все-таки свою человечью роль выполняет.[15]

Such a statement would be consistent with Gor'kij's views. As D. S. Mirsky wrote in 1926, Gor'kij's work "is profoundly unlike all the work of the younger generation — first of all, for his complete lack of interest in style; and secondly, for his very unmodern interest in human psychology".[16]

Gor'kij, in his efforts to persuade Fedin to portray a positive hero, did have some measure of success. In 1922, Fedin published the drama *Bakunin v Drezdene*, whose main hero is Mixail Aleksandrovič Bakunin, Russian revolutionary and anarchist, shown at the height of his activity, when he participated in the Dresden uprising of 4-9 May 1849.

Thus, during the same period, Fedin was the creator of both "bytopisatel'nye rasskazy", full of compassion and sympathy for humble little people, and of drama, whose hero is an active revolutionary. Gor'kij influenced Fedin both in the selection of the theme and in defining Fedin's approach in the presentation:

В наших исторических сценах обязательно должно проглядывать это стремление указать на роль личности в создании культуры, творчествое начало личности, дух созидания.[17]

---

[14] Gleb Struve, *Soviet Russian Literature, 1917-1950* (Norman, University of Oklahoma Press, 1951), p. 46.
[15] Fedin, *Gor'kij sredi nas*, pp. 139-140.
[16] Struve, *op. cit.*, p. 58.
[17] Fedin, *Gor'kij, sredi nas*, p. 42.

The dramatic scenes (dramaticheskie stseny) in *Bakunin v Drezdene* are not distinguished by their outstanding craftsmanship, neither as concerns characterization nor the progressive disclosure of the basic conflict. Nevertheless, their creation did serve the purpose of compelling Fedin to concern himself, during a period of ideological soul-searching, with a revolutionary hero and theme. It might be argued that Fedin's failure to be convincing was due to his own lack of conviction. On the other hand, mere lack of literary skill is an equally plausible explanation.

Fedin continued to be besieged by doubts, by restless searching for a literary world view. His bewilderment is expressed in the article "Aleksandr Blok", published in 1921:

Волокут в холодной сыри мешки и узлы, окунают в дорожной слякоти подолы серых армейских шинелей, кидаются прихлобученные непогодью от стены к стене. Но со всякой стены вопят плакаты: — Спасайте революцию! Страшно россиянам, бегут.[18]

His aesthetic groping was shared by other young writers of the period, including others among the Serapion Brethren. Fedin looked for guidance not only to Maxim Gor'kij but also to Evgenij Zamjatin, whom Fedin respected as a literary authority. Thus, in reviews of the first issue of the journal *Dom iskusstv*, Fedin directs attention to Zamjatin's article, "Ja bojus'", calling its author "odnim iz lučšix sovremennyx pisatelej".[19] Fedin also evinced sympathy and interest in Zamjatin's experiments with language. Regarding Zamjatin's *Mamaj*, Fedin wrote: "Rasskaz interesen po priemu poperemennogo vybrasyvanija podležaščix i skazuemyx".[20]

In 1921, Viktor Šklovskij identified Remizov, Andrej Belyj, and Evgenij Zamjatin as being among the "teachers" of the Serapion Brethren.[21] Šklovskij points out that it is due to these three influences that the work of a number of the Serapion Brethren include elements of the "skaz" technique. B. Brajnina, analyzing the sylistic characteristics of Fedin's prose in the tale "Anna Timofevna", directs attention to the very noticeable influence of Remizov's literary manner. Thus Fedin's earlier works bear evidence of the literary influence not only of Maxim Gor'kij, but also of Zamjatin and Remizov.

---

[18] Bugaenko, *op. cit.*, p. 27, quoting *Kniga i revoljucija*, No. 1/13 (1921), p. 23.
[19] *Kniga i revolijucija*, No. 8-9 (1921), p. 85.
[20] Bugaenko, *op. cit.*, p. 28.
[21] *Ibid.*, citing Šklovskij, "Serapionovy brat'ja".

C. EARLY LITERARY VIEWS

During the early twenties, then, Fedin's literary views may be summarized
as follows. First of all, as will be seen in the discussion of his earlier short
stories, Fedin interested himself in the fate of the "little man", and felt
that he, with his suffering, was the most legitimate hero of the literature
of that period. "Mne kazalos', čto moe suščestvo tjagoteet k čeloveku
prostomu, k čeloveku bednoj povsednevnosti, nezametnogo truda — k
bezvinnoj kljače, perevozjaščej gruznyj voz istorii iz epoxi v epoxu".[22]
While entertaining this view, Fedin could not identify with the revolution,
and could not portray the new, positive, bolshevik hero.

During this early period, too, Fedin was reluctant to acknowledge the
tendentious role of the artist. He affirmed that "xudožnik ne tendenciozen.
Èto značit, čto on svoboden ot namerenija čto-libo nasil'stvenno pridat'
svoemu iskusstvu".[23] Gor'kij tried to rid Fedin of his compelling interest
in the "insulted and the injured", and tried to inculcate in him the sense
of tendentiousness which was later to become an essential ingredient of
Socialist Realism. Fedin recalls it in this fashion:

Он отгонял работу ... воображения прочь от традиционного в
старой литературе интереса к страданию, к обидной жизни единого
из малых сих и призывал любить существо великое и трагическое —
человека, верящего в творческие силы разума и воли.[24]

Fedin's earlier works also reflected his search for a new, original, type of
structure and unusual devices. This was a period of experimentation, of
the emergence of formalism, characterized by deliberately manipulated
composition, toying with plot, ornamental and "dynamic" prose, and
deliberately ambiguous speech.

This, then, constituted the environment in which Fedin's early stories
were written.

[22] Fedin, *Gor'kij sredi nas*, p. 126.
[23] *Ibid.*, p. 129.
[24] *Ibid.*, p. 135.

II

EARLY STORIES

A. *PUSTYR'*

Fedin's first book was a collection, *Pustyr'*, published in 1923. It included the tale "Anna Timofevna", and the short stories "Pes'i duši", "Staršij komendor", "Sad", "Rasskaz ob odnom utre", "Konec mira", and the fairy-tale "Ež". These seven stories were all written between the years 1919 and 1923. The earliest was the short story "Sad", written in 1919-20.[1]

The basic theme of the collection is found in the brief fairy-tale allegory, "Ež", which is the concluding piece in the collection. The central idea is that there exist in this world people who are needed by no one, pitiful, lonely, and unhappy. The only bright prospect in their lives is the hope of self-effacing attachment to someone, no matter whom.

B. "ANNA TIMOFEVNA"

The largest work in the collection is the tale "Anna Timofevna" (1922), the first in the book dedicated specifically to this theme. Anna Timofevna, gifted, beautiful, capable of great feeling, spends her whole life in hard work and humiliation, in unbearable labor. Hers is the life of a cur which is beaten, or a worn-out and beaten old horse. Her life is embellished only by her self-sacrificing, suffering love, first toward her drunk and brawling husband, Roman Jakovlev, then toward her idiot daughter Olen'ka, and finally toward another drunkard who provides her a short-lived, self-forgetful happiness. Fate has destined Anna Timofevna to become attached to ugly, deformed people thrust aside by society, to people who have lost their human features.

The story is written as if in affirmation of the words of the exhausted

---

[1] B. Brajnina, *Konstantin Fedin* (Moscow, Sovetskij Pisatel', 1951), p. 29. The story "Pes'i duši", which has been criticized unfavorably, is omitted from the collected works.

old woman in the fairy tale "Ež", who says that on earth man must "radost' imet', xot' raz na vsju žizn', xot' ot tli kakoj, a dolžen".

The symbolic figure of the tormented old nag pervades the entire tale:

Груженные рогожными кулями, тянулись по взвозу телеги. Суставы одной желтоспинной змеи, извитой по дороге, — подводы длинного обоза. И в каждом хомуте — покорная лошадиная шея в налитых, растянутых жилах. И глаза лошадиные красивы и добры, и от натуги ль, от обиды ль — катятся из глазниц по мордам, заползают в раздутые ноздри круглые стеклянные капли. У оглобель возов маются, пособляют возницы: бьют по лошадиным животам кнутовищами, дубинами, вопят истошно на весь берег. Жилится каждый сустав желтоспинной взвитой по взвозу змеи, глушит змея немолчным воплем: надо обозу подняться в город.
    Глянула Анна Тимофевна, подумала:
    "Притча".
    Надо обозу подняться в город — надо прожить жизнь. Груженные кладью воза-годы. Не поднять такого воза-нельзя: бьет и гонит дубьем, поленьями, кнутовищем нужда. И не отличить одного года от другого: в натуге и в обиде каждый.[2]

The image of the beaten submissive old horse is reminiscent of the nag in Raskol'nikov's nightmares in Dostoevskij's *Crime and Punishment*, or the image Ivan Karamazov evokes of Nekrasov's nag being beaten by a peasant on its "meek eyes". Those images are supplemented in the story by Anna's recollection of a small, shaggy mongrel cur, which a black-bearded peasant drags along on a rope leash.

In these early stories, Fedin keeps fixing the reader's attention on the pitiful and the sordid: a beaten-down nag, a tormented pup, a "klopovnik policejskogo učastka" (breeding place for bedbugs at the police station), a crowd of groaning cripples in the yard of a wonder-worker, a home for epileptics, and the writhing and groaning of pure Olen'ka during a seizure.

C. INFLUENCE OF DOSTOEVSKIJ AND ČEXOV

In these first stories, one cannot help noting the influence of Dostoevskij and others who followed his tradition, such as Remizov. As Harkins points out, in Dostoevskij, Remizov "finds the emotional essence of what is Russian: suffering and pity".[3] Remizov's style is characterized by his

---

[2] Fedin, *Sobranie*, I, p. 50.
[3] Wm. E. Harkins, *Dictionary of Russian Literature* (Paterson, Littlefield, Adams & Co., 1959), p. 334.

attempts to convey the purely and typically Russian flavor by means of archaic and dialect forms, folk expressions, and the peculiar syntax and intonation of colloquial speech, in the tradition of writers like Leskov and Rozanov. These qualities, along with the ornamentalism which was in vogue during this period, are also noticeable in Fedin's early stories, as in the following fragment, reminiscent of Remizov's manner:

Довольно по реке этой городов понасажено, больших городов и малых, пышных, как купецкая супруга, и убогих, точно сирота круглая.

The philosophy of self-sacrifice, self-effacement, and suffering is that of Dostoevskij's meek characters. "... samyj zabytyj, poslednij čelovek est' tože čelovek i nazyvaetsja brat moj".[4]

The influence of Čexov may also be noted in "Anna Timofevna". The entire latter part of the story recalls Čexov's laconism and muted *pointe*. This includes Anna's meeting Engel', her life with him, and her death:

Антон Иваныч пододвинул к постели больной табуретку и заглянул ей в лицо.
На нем лежал блеклый свет лампы, и оно было строго и просто, как лицо постника. Губы Анны Тимофевны шевельнулись, и ему показалось, что она спросила:
— Ты?
— Да, я, Анюта, — сказал он.
Она вздрогнула и открыла глаза. Остановила на нем свой взор, но лицо ее не изменилось, только тени на нем переместились и посветлели, и вокруг рта заблестели мелкие капельки пота.
— Посиди, — чуть внятно сказала Анна Тимофевна.
И еще погодя:
— Как ты ... без меня ... милый. ...
Потом опять закрыла глаза и часто, хрипло задышала.[5]

D. "SAD"

The tale "Sad" (written 1919-20, published 1922) is considered by B. Brajnina[6] to be the most realistic in the collection *Pustyr'*. In the very same breath, she points out that it was written before Fedin's association

---

[4] F. M. Dostoevskij, "Unižennye i oskorblennye", *Sobranie sočinenij v desjati tomax*, III (Moscow, GIXL, 1956), p. 34.
[5] Fedin, *Sobranie*, I, p. 97.
[6] B. Brajnina, *Konstantin Fedin* (1951), p. 37.

with the Serapion Brethren. Written simply and succinctly, it is the only one of the stories devoted to a revolutionary theme.

"In the summer of 1919, at Syzran'", wrote Fedin subsequently, "I was viewing some fruit orchards which had become rather run down following the war with the Czechs. The old man who was showing me around told, among other things, of the old owners: 'They fled — and took everything with them.' I asked: 'Well, and how are things with the new owners?' He replied: 'Over there, in the brick barn, not a single brick remains; there is nothing to throw to the dog!' While I was riding on horseback to town, I had prepared the story 'Sad'." [7]

The center of the story is occupied by the figure of the gardener Silantij. The former owners, landholders, have disappeared, forsaking home and orchard. Silantij is concerned only with maintaining the orchard in its former state.

After a vivid description of the garden in bloom, Fedin introduces the owner, an old lady who has lost the use of her legs a long time previously, and had to be wheeled about in a chair. She would spend entire days on the terrace, looking about her at the garden with calm observant eyes. Her son, the owner, would tramp through the garden with Silantij, sharing the gardener's pride and appreciation. The healthy hard-working peasant and the owner were friends who respected each other for his taciturnity and because each knew his own mind.

Дружба барина с садовником упрочилась издавна, когда хозяин только что принялся разводить сад и нянял здорового, работящего, неутомимого мужика Силантия, поставив ему поодаль от дачи крепкий, просторный сруб.

Уважали они друг друга, казалось, за немногословие и неуменье что-нибудь переделывать. У обоих было: сказано-сделано. А делали оба крепко, основательно, с толком. [8]

Both the owner and the gardener shared the pride of creation of the thing of beauty which the garden represented:

Были они тогда оба молодые и сильные и закладывали в этом саду каждый свою жизнь.

Бойко принялся сад, дружно стал подыматься, с каждой весной расправляя свои мощные плечи шире и шире. Переплелись ветви яблонь, груш и вишняка, и живыми щупальцами присосалась к корням, вросла вместе с ними в землю жизнь садовника. [9]

[7]   Brajnina, *Konstantin Fedin* (1951), p. 37.
[8]   Fedin, *Sobranie*, I, p. 100.
[9]   *Ibid.*, p. 101.

Then, one spring, Silantij was seized with uneasiness. The previous fall, the owner had ordered him to board up the country house, had sold the fruit as soon as it was picked, and had vanished, leaving no word as to his whereabouts. Silantij had heard from other landowners of riots in the cities and villages, but he did not like to talk about them, and ordered his wife to refrain from discussing what was happening.

Some men came and ordered Silantij to leave the garden and go to the city, but he refused, hoping vainly that the disruption would subside. The garden began to go to seed; work which in previous years had been accomplished by droves of villagers now went undone.

Надо было мотыжить, а народу не было.

Прежде об эту пору сгоняли с окружных деревень целое полчище баб и девок.

Меж рядов яблонь, если пригнуться к земле, видно было, как белые оголенные икры работниц уминали землю округ коротеньких стволов, как падали и подымались сверкавшие мотыги, отбивали такт красные хвосты подколотых юбок. Ухала земля под частыми ударами, перепрыгивали с ветки на ветку и ныряли в гущу вишняка бабьи голоса, точно перезвон:

— Машутка-а-ау! Поди нащипи мочалки-и!

... Нынче было тихо, безмолвно.[10]

Things grow worse, affecting Silantij, who becomes gloomy and morose; he scolds his wife shamefully, as he had never done before, and even beats her. Silantij's godfather, an alert, wise old peasant, describes the disorganization and breakdown in production occasioned by the Revolution:

— Хозяева, можно сказать! Мать родная наплачется! Никакого понятья. ... Поди сходи в совет-то ихний — сам убедишься. ...

Из окна видны были широкие ворота, стоявшие настежь. За ними сереи постройки не то завода, не то склада, такие же скучные и длинные, как кирпичный сарай.

— На что уж наше дело, — продолжал сторож, — не ахти какая мудрость — кирпич! А и то ничего у них клеится. Тащут тебе и днем и ночью, а воров нет! До того доигрались, что ни одного кирпича на всем заводе не осталось. В собаку нечем бросить! ...[11]

Refusing to accept the reality of the sitation, Silantij feverishly sets out to do the work himself. He is sadly disillusioned when he reaches a point where additional help is needed, but the horse and worker promised by

[10] Fedin, *Sobranie*, I, p. 102.
[11] *Ibid.*, pp. 102-3.

city authorities in response to his entreaties fail to appear. Finally he reaches the agonizing conclusion that there is nothing left to do except to let the garden perish: "— puskaj gibnet. Ne dlja kogo xoronit'."[12]

The old gardener's patience is taxed to the limit when a dozen boys, accompanied by their school teacher, a sorry young woman, all skin and bones, come to live in the country house. Noisy and active, they drive Silantij to distraction. The crowning blow comes when Silantij, panting and perspiring after chasing three boys who have broken a branch of an apple tree on which they have been climbing, is confronted by the school teacher, who demands: "— Razve možno tak pugat' detej? Vy s uma sošli!"[13]

It is at that precise moment that Silantij expresses his resolve to burn down the garden: "— Vykurju ja vas otsjuda, kak krys. ..."[14]

That same day, at long last, two peasants arrive to help the old gardener dig. But it is too late. He sends them away, sends his wife to town, and sets fire to the house and garden. When his wife returns, she joins him as he sits watching the flames. In response to her query as to what the owners will say, he replies, ending the story: "— Dura ty, baba! Razve oni kogda vernutsja."[15]

Fedin was again chastized by Soviet critics. Brajnina affirms the right of the reader to demand that the story condemn more severely and unequivocally the bear-like nature and resistance to change of the old gardener, and the possibilities inherent in the Revolution.[16] Fedin, she asserts, strives to portray good and evil without commiting himself to either; for this reason events described by him are occasionally presented in a false light, and participants in these events stand off to the side, away from the mainstream of revolutionary actuality. Brajnina would have Fedin re-write the story:

Между тем в рассказе есть прекрасная сцена, которая могла бы совсем в другом направлении повернуть сюжет, одухотворить, рассказ живой революционной идеей, сблизить его с современностью, с правдой жизни.[17]

She is referring to the scene in which Silantij, having returned from the city, determinedly sets about to do the work himself. According to

[12]   Fedin, *Sobranie*, I, p. 105.
[13]   *Ibid.*, p. 107.
[14]   *Ibid.*, p. 108.
[15]   *Ibid.*, p. 109.
[16]   Brajnina, *Konstantin Fedin* (1951), pp. 39-40.
[17]   *Ibid.*, p. 39.

Brajnina, Silantij has not only forgotten his enmity toward the Revolution, but is ready to participate in it, if this would afford him the opportunity to continue his beloved work.

В нем вдруг проснулась надежда на то, что все обойдется, стоит только похлопотать, поработать, и он рыл, копал, стучал топором, паклил желоба с таким усердием, словно хотел нагнать пропущенное за все томительные недели бездействия.[18]

Brajnina suggests that if Fedin had been faithful in his portrayal of life, the story would have ended not with Silantij's setting fire to the house and garden, but with his rebirth, since the Revolution affords every opportunity to the little man.

It was precisely concern for the little man which prompted Fedin to write *Pustyr'*. In a letter to one of his correspondents, Fedin writes:

Тематический состав "Пустыря" Вас не должен удивлять. Маленький человек — герой "Пустыря" — был предметом моего пристрастия на протяжении долгих лет. Не забывайте, что я начал свои поиски с 1910 года, а получил возможность печататься лишь в 20-х годах. Я должен был свалить с себя груз, тяготивший меня целое десятилетие. Это был плод моей жизни в старой литературе, моей замкнутой, отшельнической школы, моей скрытой мечты. Я должен был разродиться ,иначе плод умер бы во мне и отравил меня ... я должен был увидеть результаты всего предшествующего периода, ни в чем не реализованного, длительного, тяжкого, как бы бесплодного: должен был увидеть свое прошлое в книге. "Пустырь" — ето книга, которая могла и должна была выйти во время войны, но роковым образом задержалась.[19]

E.   "RASSKAZ OB ODNOM UTRE"

In 1920, Fedin shared a Petrograd apartment with the lawyer G. L. Korjakin, who had been famous in the south of Russia, prior to the Revolution, as the defense attorney in the political trials of 1908-1910. He was a talented story-teller and shared his horrible recollections with Fedin. He related to Fedin the story of the police official who carried about, "for luck", a piece of rope cut from a hangman's noose. From him Fedin also learned of a hangman-birdlover, who used to ride the circuit of the South Russian towns where the field courts-martial were taking

[8]   Fedin, *Sobranie*, I, p. 104.
[19]   *Ibid.*, pp. 402-403.

place, and of a murderer, a Don Cossack whom Korjakin had defended by direction of the court. These stories furnished the basis for "Rasskaz ob odnom utre" (publ. 1923).[20]

The figure of the repulsive hangman Savel Semenovič, who passionately loved to listen to the song of birds, represents a unique variation on the theme of suffering which lay at the basis of "Anna Timofevna". In "Rasskaz ob odnom utre", a moral and physical monster selflessly loves the beautiful, while in "Anna Timofevna" an internally beautiful person loves monsters.

Savel Semenovič, with his one eye and his deformed legs, coupled with his twisted morality, is portrayed not only as a pathological character but also as one who is romantically enigmatic. This physical and moral monster, having lost all sense of feeling toward humans, has not only come to love birds passionately, but has taught himself to pray!

Он слушал, как пели птцы, и улыбался ртом и, может быть, глазами, но этого никогда не было видно: его брови срослись в одну сплошную бровь, насевшую низко над глазами, и эта бровь не двигалась, так что улыбка была приметна только на губах.[21]

Quite in the spirit of the pre-Symbolist romanticist Bunin is Fedin's delicate, lyrical portrayal of the impression made by nature on the psychologically contradictory Savel:

Ах, осенью, когда клен высасывает из земли золото и переливает его по своим жилам в листья; осенью, когда шелк паутины щекочет печальные лучи солнца; осенью, когда земля благодарна и утомлена, как любовница, — этой осенью быть в лесу. Лежать под кустом барыни-ягоды, пощипывать красные, мясистые бусины — пряные, рассыпчатые, — лежать так и ждать, когда шустрая синица иль осанистый снегирь, нарядные, разодетые, сядут на золоченую верхушку клена и потом, не в силах устоять перед зазываньем приманки, с куста на куст, как по лестнице, спустятся на поляну к невиднимому крылу тонкой сетки. ...[22]

In this tale, even more intensely than in "Anna Timofevna", Fedin critically portrays the commonplace vulgarity of the petty bourgeois bureaucrat as he sees him. He does this by showing him in the fulfillment of his official tasks. The cossak Police Chief Askalon Ivanovič Tukmakov, Court Counsellor Tužilikin, the anonymous candidate for judicial service,

---

[20] Fedin, *Sobranie*, I, pp. 405-406.
[21] *Ibid.*, p. 113.
[22] *Ibid.*, pp. 111-112.

and Dr. Sečnikov are Philistines who are distinguished one from the other only by the degree of their baseness.

Reminiscent of the smugness and self-satisfied complacency of Gogol''s or of Čexov's characters is this description of the police chief Tukmakov:

Полицмейстер сияет. Он всегда доволен. Доволен собой, приятелями, делами, тем, что счастлив в картах и много пьет, тем, что в его городе военное положение. Он чувствует себя счастливее счастливых, и у него не два, а три румянца: два на щеках и один на подбородке, все три размером в пятачок. От пятачка на подбородке в обе стороны развеваются гроздья жирной, как кобыль, бороды, и никто не умеет расправлять эту бороду так, как это делает старшина: одно движенье руки вправо и влево — и каждому ясно, что человек всем доволен.[23]

This beaming portrait of the police chief explains how he, when attending the execution, hung the transgressor with his own hands after the young hangman, unable to go through with his first execution, had collapsed in a dead faint!

In another story of this collection, "Konec mira", the hero, Court Counsellor Porfirij Pirožkov, is a teacher in a *gymnasium*. In order to save himself and return to his family, Pirožkov becomes a traitor. During the first World War, he is captured and confined in a camp for prisoners of war, where he systematically betrays those of his countrymen who plan to escape.

Following his release and return home, in an outburst of hysterical frankness, he recounts his treasonable activities to his wife Miločka, in order to "svjazat' novym uzlom razorvannuju nitku, soxranit' svoe sčast'e, naperekor žizni, tvorivšej nad nim neščadnuju raspravu".[24]

Detesting her husband for his traitorous actions, Miločka leaves him. Pirožkov resolves to commit suicide. He writes a note to the effect that no one is to blame for his death, and that he is ending his life because his family, indeed his whole world, is destroyed. At this point Pirožkov suddenly realizes that there will be no one to read his last words except the old, senile housekeeper. He then opens his door and shouts to her that he had given her 500 rubles for groceries, but she had not returned the change.

The story ends on a note which is again reminiscent of the muted *pointe*, the unresolved conflict with which Čexov frequently ends his

---

[23] Fedin, *Sobranie*, I, p. 115.
[24] *Ibid.*, p. 115.

stories. Life goes on, disturbed and sad. In this story, perhaps more than in the others, the plot is merely a situation which serves as an excuse for the release of moods and feelings which are vague, spontaneous, and irrational, with little relation to the events of the tale. What Fedin accomplishes is to define the essence of character in terms of mood.

PART II

EARLY NOVELS

III

GORODA I GODY

A. THE NOVELISTIC GENRE

After the death of Čexov, Russian prose declined, to be superseded by the Silver Age in Russian poetry. Evgenij Ivanovič Zamjatin (d. 1937) may be credited with playing a major role in the revival of prose, having opened a studio in which he taught literary craftsmanship to aspiring writers. Among his pupils were the Serapion Brethren, who were to make a major contribution to Russian prose fiction during the early Soviet period.

During the early twenties, the short story and the novella were the most popular forms. Later, the novel became the most important genre, specifically the "realistic psychological" novel, continuing the tradition of Tolstoj and Dostoevskij.[1] Fedin was among the number of young novelists who tried to emulate Čexov's artistic economy, his avoidance of empty places in a story, and his care to charge every portion of it with equal significance and expressiveness. In this respect, Čexov remained an unattainable ideal for most of the new authors, although some, like Fedin, do manage to suggest the mood and artistic laconism which is characteristic of Čexov.

B. GORODA I GODY

Struve dates the rebirth of the novel as the dominant literary genre from 1924, the year when *Goroda i gody* (Cities and Years), the first large-scale psychological novel in Soviet literature, was published.[2] This does not mean that there had been no Soviet novels before that. There had been,

---

[1] Gleb Struve, "Leonid Leonov and his Skutarevsky", *The Slavonic and East European Review*, XII, No. 34 (July, 1933), p. 190. This journal will be referred to hereinafter as *SEER*.
[2] Struve, *Soviet Russian Literature*, p. 86.

but most of the writers of the preceding period who had treated the period of the Civil War and the Revolution had concentrated on their impressions of events, stressing incident, and deliberately avoiding the method of psychological analysis associated with the names of Tolstoj and Dostoevskij.

Some of these other novels were novels in name only, including the works of Pil'njak, Nikitin, and Vsevolod Ivanov. Neverov was in the tradition of Populist Realism, and Furmanov's *Čapaev* is really an example of documentary literature, though often referred to as a novel.

Fedin was unique in his attempt to grasp the revolution as a whole, rather than as a series of highly charged incidents. He aimed at analyzing its causes and effects, its leaders and those who were swept along by it. Fedin stressed realistic, as opposed to impressionistic, portrayal of the new mode of life, thus continuing the classical tradition of *bytopisatel'stvo* or portrayal of the details of everyday life.

Other young writers prior to Fedin were so overwhelmed by the great wealth, novelty, and variety of events and impressions of the revolution that they did not attempt to penetrate beneath their surface, to analyze them more deeply, to bring all their disjointed and varied impressions in line with each other. They contented themselves with portraying them as they saw them, and were unable to restrain their emotional agitation.

This element is, to a limited degree, also observable in Fedin's short stories and in his first novel. He, too, experimented with the so-called "dynamic", or ornamental, prose, reflecting the Revolution and the turbulent years of the Civil War, at once romantic and realistic, in which lyrical emotions and a detachment verging on cruel indifference were strangely mingled.

The novel is the most complex genre in literature. Fedin has succeeded in mastering this form, avoiding the pitfall of blind subservience to tradition, be it Russian or Western, despite his study of such masters as Turgenev, Tolstoj, Dostoevkij or Strindberg. All of Fedin's novels, as will be demonstrated, are unique in structure. Each of them, by means of a system of images, constituting their life and movement, carries within itself what has come in Soviet Criticism to be called "obrazom xydožestvennogo proizvedenija", or the form of an art product. In the theater, the form is that of a play; in architecture, that of a building; and in literature, of a book. When reading Fedin, the reader is struck by the difference in structure of each of his novels, reflecting his concern for construction.

Fedin's particular gift lay not only in the construction of the novel as a whole, but in the structure of the individual scenes and episodes, and in their unique rhythmic succession.

Early in his literary career, as evidenced by his early works, Fedin sensed the tremendous psychological power of the *mise-en-scène*, the arrangement of scenery and players, the setting or milieu, and he used it brilliantly.

In the novel, *Goroda i gody*, there is the following scene: Andrej Starcov is waiting for Mari Urbach in the Park of the Seven Ponds. He catches sight of her in the distance. She hurries toward him, smiling at him. This is their first rendezvous.

И вот, когда Мари была уже недалеко от него, он увидел лавину. Она выползала из-за поворота аллеи, в полусотне шагов от того места, где он стоял. Гул, волновавший землю, был поднят сотнями тяжелых ног.
Мари оставалось только перейти дорогу, чтобы протянуть Андрею руку. В этот момент лавина докатилась до стыка аллей. Андрей успел заметить, как глаза Мари остановились на приблизившемся шествии. Потом оно разделило их.[3]

The reader suddenly, with unusual sharpness, senses that something terrible is approaching and separating the lovers. Mari disappears, kept from Andrej by a mass of Italian prisoners blinded by gas in the war.

Тогда Андрей огляделся.
По другую сторону аллеи, прислонившись к дереву, закрыв глаза, стояла Мари, она была как будто привязана к стволу, и руки ее висели беспомощно. Андрей бросился к ней, с силой оторвавшись от куска земли, который держал его в окочененье. Мари открыла глаза, Андрей взял ее руки. Они были холодны и вздрагивали, как от озноба.
— Наша встреча ... — начал Андрей.
Мари хотела улыбнуться.
— Я не могу, — ответила она, — сегодня. ...
Потом оттолкнулась от дерева, расправила плечи.
— Я не хочу говорить сегодня ... не могу.
Она пожала ему руку.
— Я, может быть, напишу вам опять.
Она отвернулась и пошла туда, где останавливались пустые в эту пору трамвайные вагоны.
Он проводил ее взглядом.[4]

---

[3] Fedin, *Sobranie*, II, pp. 169-170.
[4] *Ibid.*, pp. 171-172.

The power of this scene derives from its dramatic foreshadowing of the tragedy which will follow. War separates people, and regardless of what happens to the heroes later, the reader now knows that they will not find happiness. They are predestined to be engulfed forever by the terrible symbol of a blind avalanche separating them.

The novel, Fedin's favorite genre — *Goroda i gody* (1924), *Brat'ja* (1928), *Poxiščenie Evropy* (1933, 1935), *Sanatorij Arktur* (1940), *Pervye radosti* (1945-1946), *Neobyknovennoe leto* (1948), and *Koster* (1962) — has evolved in his writing from the diverse lyrical monologues of *Goroda i gody* to the epic novel (the trilogy), evidencing a striving toward the continuation and development of the traditions of the Russian classical novel.

Aleksej Maksimovič Gor'kij, who carefully studied Fedin's first literary endeavors, early recognized that Fedin possessed the attributes of an "epic writer". He often cautioned Fedin about the excess of irony, the poster-like publicistic quality, and the subjective lyricism which Fedin included in his novels.

If we carefully study Fedin's works in the order in which they were written, and if we compare the tales and short stories with the novels, it immediately becomes apparent that there is a relationship between the shorter and the longer genres, with the shorter serving, as it were, as études. Thus, one of the earliest stories, *Djadja Kisel'*, was subsequently incorporated into the novel *Cities and Years*. This is not intended to detract from the independent value of these works, some of which, like *Transvaal* (1926), merit independent study. But one should not neglect the thematic and stylistic relationship. It almost appears as though Fedin attempts to develop an interesting theme, or a particularly noteworthy character, in a smaller form first, and then proceeds to make it a focal point in a full length novel.

A particularly interesting example is that of *Transvaal*, a tale about the kulak Svaaker during the NEP period in the Soviet countryside. This tale was criticized on the extra-literary ground that it overemphasized the strength of the kulak, and that Fedin failed to perceive any forces in the countryside which effectively opposed the kulaks. Smirnova, a contemporary Soviet critic, sees in this an erroneous evaluation by Fedin of the power of the peasantry, and a bias against the muzhik.[5] This point of view later finds a place in Fedin's *Cities and Years*, specifically the scenes of the kulak uprising, when Fedor Lependin is hung.

---

[5]   Vera Smirnova, *O literature i teatre* (Moscow, Sovetskij Pisatel', 1956), p. 6.

The figure of Svaaker is later expanded, assuming artistic form in the person of the Dutch lumber merchant Phillip van Rossum in the novel *Poxiščenie Evropy* (1933, 1935). Even externally, van Rossum reminds the reader of his predecessor Svaaker. But it appears as though some of the earlier uncertainties and doubts existing in Fedin's mind have been resolved. No longer does Fedin portray what the Soviet critics are fond of terming contradictions. Now the shades of gray have been eliminated, leaving only the black.

Also quite clear and explainable is the genetic relationship between a work like *Ja byl akterom* and the novel *Goroda i gody*, which preceded. The tale *Ja byl akterom* was first published in the journal *Novyj mir* in 1937. In a letter to one of his readers in 1948, Fedin called *Ja byl akterom* a gayer counterpart of *Cities and Years*.[6] He called it "the same Bischoffsberg (Cittau), seen through laughing eyes".

By virtue of its details, *Ja byl akterom* is even more autobiographical than *Goroda i gody*.

The basis for the novel *Goroda i gody* consists of facts and events from real life, either witnessed by Fedin, or in which he actually participated during his four-year stay in Germany, from the spring of 1914 to autumn, 1918. The novel also draws on facts and events observed by the writer in the first years of the Civil War in Russia.[7]

This by no means means that the novel is based exclusively on autobiographical material. In a letter written to one of his correspondents in 1948, Fedin states:

Your conclusion that the majority of the episodes, scenes, pictures and the like were seen, heard, or experienced by me (of those included in *Goroda i gody*), is false. One cannot speak of the majority, inasmuch as the majority, beyond any doubt, is the fruit of my imagination. The scenes developed and grew out of facts of observation in a soil of impressions of what had been experienced.

For example: Being a civilian prisoner, I, like the other foreigners interned in Cittau, occasionally received permission from the police and the *stadtrat* for a stroll outside the city. This is fact. I develop the episode of the meeting with Mari in the mountains on the basis of this external fact. Andrej received permission for a trip outside of the city and saw Mari. Further, he takes advantage of this permission for an escape attempt. Further, this permission "rehabilitates" Andrej in the eyes of Zur Muellen-Schoenau. This is invention ....[8]

There is considerable documentary material in *Cities and Years*. Monsieur

---

[6] Fedin, *Sobranie*, VI, p. 505.
[7] *Ibid.*, II, pp. 433-434.
[8] *Ibid.*, II, pp. 433-436.

Percy's diary is based on extracts from German newspapers, which Fedin brought from Germany. "Nedelikatnyj fel'eton" and "Jagody" are also authentic. The telegrams of the Berlin university and the camp administration are invented.

For Fedin, literature was a means of cognition of the world about him, the contemporary world. All of his works exhibit the same tortured doubts and reflection about the meaning and purpose of life, the clash of ideas. For Fedin, every new book is an attempt to resolve some basic problem of life, an obstacle to be overcome before he could proceed further. Thus his books reflect his own growth, as well as provide a picture of contemporary events, shaped by his artistic consciousness.

The novels *Goroda i gody*, *Brat'ja*, *Poxiščenie Evropy*, and *Sanatorij Arktur* are not a direct continuation one of the other, but they are related. The events portrayed in them present a definite time sequence. Also, the evolution of the figure of the main hero and the development of the same theme dominate these works.

These internal and external ties between separate works are very characteristic of Fedin. They are particularly noticeable in his novels, and permit us to understand the nature and the direction of Fedin's development as an author.

In *Goroda i gody*, the first novel, the years are explicitly stated, constituting the titles of the various chapters: About the years 1919, 1914, 1916, 1917, 1918, and again about 1919, about 1920, and preceding them all, "about the year in which the novel was finished", 1922, actually the year in which Fedin began to write the novel.

In *Brat'ja*, the time is not stated explicitly, but the scope of the novel is broader. It includes the events of 1905, the childhood of the hero (which corresponds to the childhood of the author), the war of 1914-1918, the first years of the Revolution, the Civil War, and the beginning of the industrialization of the country.

The events described in *Poxiščenie Evropy* occur during the first Five-Year-Plan, 1928-1932. In *Sanatorij Arktur* there are no direct references to time, but the reader is made to sense the oppressive atmosphere existing in Europe prior to the outbreak of the second World War.

Even after only a cursory examination of the works written by Fedin during the period between the two world wars, it becomes apparent that for almost twenty years, year by year, Fedin was attempting to reflect the spirit of his time.

Particularly interesting in Fedin's works is the evolution of the figure of the main hero, the young Soviet intellectual, who occupies the center of the stage in all Fedin's novels, being the focus of his attention. One may speak exclusively of the evolution of the hero, or one may focus on the ever-expanding background as portrayed in the successive novels, in terms of both time and space. In the latter event, by virtue of the changing situation, the portrayal of the character of the hero also changes. Yet it may be argued that it is not so much that time and place are changing Fedin's hero so much as the fact that Fedin's relationship to his hero, his own personal attitudes, are undergoing change. In any event it appears that an insight into the artistic development of the author may be formed from an analysis of the evolution of his hero, which will be done below.

C. ANDREJ STARCOV, VACILLATING INTELLECTUAL

The novel *Goroda i gody* brought immediate fame to its author. In the USSR alone it was published in fourteen editions, over a period of sixteen years, until the outbreak of the second World War. Soviet readers were particularly impressed by its novelty, originality, and freshness, which resulted from the fusion of Russian and Western themes, motifs, settings, and characters, combined with its unique construction.

Goroda i gody was known in Germany and, in the thirties, was consigned to the bonfires along with other proscribed works.[9] The novel portrays, among other things, Germany as it was under the Kaiser during the years immediately preceding the first World War. It reflects Fedin's attitude toward German militarism and chauvinism, expressed with an incisive irony. Although leading roles are assigned to that personification of Prussian militarism, Count von zur Muellen-Schoenau, and to the German communist Kurt Wahn, the central and main hero of the novel is a Russian, the young intellectual Andrej Starcov.[10]

---

[9] Cf. B. Brajnina, "Konstantin Fedin", *Novyj Mir*, No. 11 (1947), p. 129, in which she says: "Fedin seems to foresee the bloody abomination of fascism; he portrays the sources of the catastrophe into which the Nazis plunged the world. It was for good reason that the German translation of *Goroda i gody* was greeted with hostility by the German conservative press in the 1920's, and that, in the 1930's, the Nazis burned the novel in bonfires.

Militarism, national arrogance, war-like intolerance towards all non-German nationalities, the stupidity of the petit-bourgeois, and the fetishism of discipline — these attributes of Germany under the Kaiser proved to be favorable, nutritive soil for the microbes of fascism."

[10] German names will not be transliterated from the Russian. Umlaut will be indicated by vowel plus -e-.

In the novel *Goroda i gody*, the theme of Germany and war is closely
interwoven with the theme of Russia and the Revolution. This is of
course unavoidable, since the war ended with revolutions in both Russia
and Germany. As concerns structure, the whole central part of the novel
is devoted to Germany and the Germans. But the most important events
take place in Russia, to which the hero, Andrej Starcov, returns after
confinement in Germany. It is in Russia that we observe the full development of the German communist Kurt Wahn, and the Prussian von
Schoenau, each in his own way, with the latter leading a counter-
revolutionary uprising of Mordvinians in a remote Eastern town.

Although the novel encompasses a broad expanse of events, in both
time and space, it has been criticized on ideological grounds by Smirnova,
Brajnina, Bugaenko, and other Soviet critics for the contradictions in the
thoughts and feelings of the main hero, Andrej Starcov, and the shortcomings in his personal life.

The actual chronological sequence of events, inverted in the novel, is
as follows: The war, which breaks out in 1914, disrupts the friendship of
Andrej Starcov, a student in Germany, and Kurt Wahn, who leaves for
the front. It also interrupts Andrej's love for Mari Urbach, inasmuch as,
in 1917, Andrej and other prisoners are returned to their Russian homeland. Earlier, Andrej had undertaken an unsuccessful escape attempt,
from the consequences of which he is saved by Lieutenant von zur
Muellen-Schoenau, former fiancé and lover of Mari Urbach, which
Andrej does not know. After returning to Russia, Andrej meets Kurt
Wahn and, under his influence, Andrej joins in the work of the Communists during the Civil War. He unexpectedly meets von Schoenau who
now, in his turn, demands that Andrej help him return to Germany with
a party of prisoners. Andrej, considering himself obligated to von
Schoenau for past services, and desiring to send a letter to Mari Urbach,
for whom he yearns, steals an incriminating document from Kurt Wahn,
which facilitates von Schoenau's successful escape. Later, in Leningrad,
Andrej again meets von Schoenau, who has come for the letter to Mari;
von Schoenau learns that Rita is living with Andrej and is expecting his
baby. After making his way back to his estate, von Schoenau maliciously
imparts this news to Mari. Mari does not believe him, and sets out for
Leningrad, where she verifies that Andrej is married. But Andrej does
not love the girl he has married, Rita. In despair, he finds himself crushed
by a twofold force with which he is unable to contend — the revolution,
and his love for Mari. While in this disturbed condition, he encounters
Kurt Wahn, and confides in him. And Kurt, like the dedicated Com-

munist which he has become, does "everything which should be done by a comrade, friend, and artist" — he kills him.

The distraught irony of Andrej's monologues, the gloomy pictures of the cave-like daily existence in Leningrad, the scenes of counterrevolution in the countryside, and Fedin's obvious lack of complete sympathy and identification with the Bolsheviks, contribute to the feeling of complete upheaval in the life of the nation. The atmosphere of complete reorganization — perhaps disorganization is a better word — not only in the political, but also in the philosophical and intellectual life of the country pervades the entire novel. This mood, apparently present in Fedin, is transmitted to the hero Andrej. But, for him, it becomes the source of tragic doubts and misgivings, which lead to his destruction.

Andrej Starcov says about himself:

Я всю жизнь старался стать в круг. Понимаешь, чтобы все в мире происходило вокруг меня. Но меня всегда отмывало, относило в сторону.[11]

Who is this man, occupying the central position in the novel, and claiming the exclusive attention of the reader?

Недавно я хлопотал о каких-то бумагах. Мне задали вопрос: "Ваша профессия?" Я не мог ответить. Мне вдруг пришло в голову: к какой профессии готовился я прежде? Я сбился, вышло глупо.[12]

The reader has no idea what type of work Andrej was doing prior to the Revolution, or for what type of career he was preparing himself. In short, Andrej is deprived of any *vorgeschichte*. The reader knows only that Andrej was a student and, further, one who had not completed his studies, had not found a place in the world. In fact, he reminds the reader of Turgenev's Rudin, also a student, a man of high ideals, who lacks the will to put his principles into action. He, too, wins the love of a worthy young girl, Natalja (perhaps more worthy than Mari Urbach, who had had a previous liason with von Schoenau), but is too weak and ineffectual to risk his fate with her, and gives her up. The absence of the *vorgeschichte* may be attributable to the hero's superfluity in the given context. Čexov also dealt with the problem of man's adjustment to the world. But Fedin sets this problem in a concrete historical context, that of revolution and civil war, whereas Čexov puts it on a universal level, applicable at any place and time.

Andrej Starcov acknowledges his failure to harmonize with the world,

[11]   Fedin, *Sobranie*, II, p. 13.
[12]   *Ibid.*

his confusion and lack of identification, what today's writers — in the Soviet Union as well as in the United States — term alienation. Like a character in one of Čexov's short stories, he is tortured by awareness of his position, and cries:

Если бы можно было начать жить сначала. ... Раскатать клубок, дойти по нитке до проклятого часа и поступить по-другому. Совсем по-другому. ...[13]

This is not only a fleeting onslaught of despair. Andrej Starcov later sinks lower and lower. Not too long prior to his demise — and this was in 1922 — he feels that the world has become for him an endless waste-land, and that everything within him has already died. He has become alienated from the world because of his vacillation.

A. M. van der Eng-Liedmeier, analyzing the revolutionary intelligentsia as portrayed in some early Soviet novels, has applied the term used by Russian critics, "vacillating intellectual" (*koleblju*š*čijsja intelligent*), in referring to these complex characters who may accept Communism in theory, but vacillate when they are confronted with the practice of a revolution. This type abhors violence and feels compassion toward the victims of the Revolution. The opposition between intellectual convic-tion, which assures them of the need for change, and emotional revulsion, occasioned by abhorrence to violence, leads to inner uncertainty.[14]

Soviet critics interpret the aversion to violence on the part of the intellectual as a typical class phenomenon and attribute it to egotistic motives. The vacillating intellectual is often characterized as a coward, unreliable not only politically, but also morally.

Fedin, however, at this juncture merely a fellow-traveler and not an ardent apologist for the new order, expresses an entirely different view. He attributes Starcov's conflict and vacillation to a moral conviction which is opposed to the Bolshevik theory that good may be attained by evil means.

Andrej Starcov, still a student at the outbreak of the war, is a lonely, withdrawn man. He loathes war, and the inhumanity which man inflicts on his brother man. He attempts to embrace Communism in an effort to right some of the wrongs existing in the world, and also in an effort to rid himself of his individualism, but he fails. He admires the com-munists, who work not like humans, but rather like "Rumkorff induction

[13]   Smirnova, *op. cit.*, p. 14.
[14]   A. M. van der Eng-Liedmeier, *Soviet Literary Characters* (The Hague, Mouton & Co., 1959), p. 72.

coils". But he protests against their cruelty, although he is unable to muster convincing arguments to prove that even a moral end does not justify immoral means.

Although Andrej has admitted to Kurt Wahn that he could never kill, because he would have to live with the knowledge that he had killed, he does volunteer to fight in the Civil War and to kill anonymously. He feels tremendous elation after his first encounter with the enemy. Starcov feels strongly that, like Dostoevskij's heroes, he shares responsibility with all of mankind for the suffering and horror which man frequently visits upon himself. He is prepared to accept death personally, rather than to permit that responsibility to be assumed by others. Now, for the first time in his life, he feels free.

When the anonymous enemy no longer confronts him, however, he loses his sense of identification, with its consequent sense of satisfaction. When he helps von Schoenau escape, his twofold motives being his sense of gratitude for von Schoenau's help earlier, coupled with his desire to have von Schoenau serve as courier in delivering a letter to Mari back in Germany, Starcov dooms himself to his tragic fate. Andrej is completely shattered when Mari Urbach forsakes him because of his affair with Rita, and he is tormented by the consciousness of his guilt. He works himself into a state of mental confusion, and is already a broken man when Kurt Wahn finally finds him and kills him.

Fedin himself adopts a somewhat ambiguous attitude towards the hero. In some comments he sides with Kurt Wahn; yet it is felt that his sympathies are really with Starcov who, of all the characters, is most credible and most convincing. Fedin ascribes Starcov's conflict not only to moral objections, dislike of violence, and pity for the enemy, but also to a deeper metaphysical cause. Starcov is not so much the victim of his failure to support the Communist Revolution as he is to himself. His tragedy lies in his wavering, in his incapacity to choose in any situation, because he has not been able to discover the purpose of life. In this respect he is related to the *Lišnij Čelovek*, portrayed so often in the Russian literature of former times, the superfluous man who also could not find out where he stood in life.

D. KURT WAHN, POSITIVE HERO

A comparison of Starcov and the vacillating intellectual portrayed by other Communist authors reveals a certain similarity. Invariably the indecision of these figures is represented as a trait of character which is also found in their personal lives. In the work of Communist writers, this inner uncertainty is attributed to class and is based on egotistic reasons: the vacillating individual turns out to be a coward who feels no pity for the victims of the Revolution, only for himself. But Starcov is not depicted as a coward, for ultimately he prefers being killed himself to killing others. Fedin advances motives other than that of self-preservation to explain his hero's indecision. Starcov is troubled by a metaphysical consciousness of human deficiency. He is unable to embrace any ideal, including the Communist vision of perfection. His tragedy is rooted not only in a philosophical, but also in a moral base. Starcov is unable to sanction the pursuit of any aim, no matter how moral, by immoral means.

The question of Fedin's attitude toward Starcov is one which merits attention. Non-party writers, like Fedin, Kaverin, and Oleša, dealt sympathetically with the tragic maladjustment of the pre-revolutionary *intelligent*, unable to comprehend the disorder of a world in revolution. This type of hero, including Starcov, continues the long line of super-fluous men who keep recurring in nineteenth-century Russian literature, but who, by 1929, are clearly disappearing, with the "new Soviet man" establishing himself at the center of literature. The term has been used to designate heroes who are aware of the social, political, economic, and ethical problems of their time, but who fail to take any positive action because of personal shortcomings, repression by the political or social order, or both. Invariably these superfluous men have been opposed by strong resolute characters, often feminine (like Tatjana in *Evgenij Onegin*, or Natalja in *Rudin*), but also masculine, like Stoltz in *Oblomov*. Indeed, Kurt Wahn, the German didactically-inspired positive hero, may be considered a literary descendent of Gončarov's Stolz or of Turgenev's Insarov, the Bulgarian radical hero of *Nakanune*.

In this sense — the confrontation and juxtaposition of characters — Fedin preserves the older novelistic tradition with its attention to structure. The absence of any real plot in *Oblomov* does not detract from this assertion since, as Professor Poggioli points out, the absence of plot does not mean absence of structure.[15]

Fedin opposes Kurt Wahn to Andrej Starcov, but presents him as a schematic, conventional character. It was intended that he personify the strength of will of the Revolution, which stands in opposition to the

[15]   R. Poggioli, "On Goncharov and his Oblomov", *The Phoenix and the Spider* (Cambridge, Harvard University Press, 1957), p. 37.

searching of the intelligentsia. The strong friendship of Kurt Wahn and Andrej Starcov, depicted in pre-war Germany, accentuates the difference in their natures.

The artistic and ideological characterization of Kurt Wahn is not at all agreeable. There is no internal logic in his development, nor is there any psychological motivation for the transitions from one phase to another. Actually, there are three Kurts in the novel, united only by the external thread of the plot.

The reader meets the first Kurt in the very first chapter of the novel, in the section, titled "Formula perexoda". The chapter itself is titled "Chapter about the year in which the novel is completed", which is 1922. Kurt Wahn, in this section, is informing the tribunal of Andrej Starcov's "crime" and how he, Kurt, killed him:

Сомнений не оставалось: по личным мотивам он спас жизнь нашему врагу и предал дело, которому мы все служим. Как человек он мне стал ненавистен, как друг, — я был его другом, — отвратителен. Я убыл его.[16]

Seven men are listening to Kurt:

На председательском месте сидел человек в толстых очках, фокус которых ни разу не переместился, пока Курт говорил.
Курт стоял прямо против председателя, уткнув кулаки в стол и коротко потряхивая головой в конце каждой фразы. Говорил он без запинки, будто читал по книге; и речь его была книжной.[17]

The glassy face of the chairman, and the mechanical man with the soulless, bookish speech, remind the reader of the preceding section of the same chapter, titled "Pis'mo", and the reader cannot help agreeing with Andrej, who calls people of Kurt's ilk *rumkorfovymi katuškami*.

The author accepts Kurt as a Bolshevik and vainly attempts to convince himself and the reader that the activity of this man is not only predetermined by fate, but is also necessary and justified.

The reader later meets Kurt a second time, in Germany, in the "Chapter about the year 1914", and learns what type of person Kurt was in the year when war was declared. This is a different Kurt, in no way resembling the first.

Before the reader is a modest young artist, all of whose output is purchased by the German Count von zur Muellen-Schoenau. Young

[16] Fedin, *Sobranie*, II, p. 15.
[17] *Ibid.*, p. 14.

Kurt vainly struggles to free himself from von Schoenau's domination. He reacts to von Schoenau with undisguised hate, but is powerless. Count von Schoenau is the typical representative of Prussian militarism. Then, when Germany declares war, Kurt Wahn himself is suddenly and unexpectedly transformed into an ardent militarist and chauvinist.

The reader meets a third, completely different Kurt in Russia in 1918, when Kurt is taken there as a prisoner of war. Kurt has been transformed into a revolutionary this time. Fedin treats him with undisguised sympathy, admiring his energy and the zeal with which he plunges himself into his new activities. But there is one trait, of major import, which is repugnant to Fedin. Kurt is incapable of feeling; he does not know the meaning of love. Friendship, too, he ridicules as something "mystical".

Kurt himself acknowledges these personal shortcomings. This partly explains why he is drawn toward Starcov, saying, "Ty dopolnjaeš' menja".

Fedin fails to portray any human sympathy or warmth in the Bolshevik character, and the humanism which is so highly vaunted in the new Soviet man is missing from Kurt's characterization. Fedin portrays Kurt as impoverished and schematic. Kurt's shortcomings are intensified artistically by the contrast with Starcov's humanism and the depth of his feelings. Soviet criticism attributes this characterization to the fact that Fedin had not reached a point where he was ready to view, evaluate, and portray artistically the new Soviet hero in accordance with Socialist principles.

Федин еще не раз будет пытаться механически дополнить больевист-скую енергию, волю интеллигентским гуманизмом, пока факты социалистического опыта не помогут писателю правильно увидеть, оценить и художественно выразить нового героя новой действитель-ности.[18]

There is another character in *Goroda i gody* who attracts attention as embodying, to a greater extent than Kurt Wahn, the qualities of the new Soviet man. However, this individual is a secondary character, appearing only episodically. He is the chairman of the Semidol executive committee of the party, Semen Ivanovič Golosov. In contrast to Kurt's flatness, Golosov is portrayed as a three-dimensional figure. Unforgettable are his round face, his ready laughter, the way in which he tugs at his upper lip, and other physical details consistent with his personality.

Unlike Kurt Wahn, Golosov does not remind the reader of a "Rumkorff

[18]   Brajnina, *Konstantin Fedin* (1951), p. 73.

coil" and nature has not denied him the capability of feeling. He is able to love woman, to become ecstatic over nature, to experience compassion, to feel affliction, and to rejoice.

In short, Golosov possesses the positive qualities which Fedin later embodies in Peter Ragozin, the positive hero of *Pervye radosti* and *Neobyknovennoe leto*. In a letter to Fedin, Gor'kij praised the figure of Golosov, noting that he considered his characterization a particular success.

It is apparent, then, that Fedin has preserved his independence as a writer up to a point. Fedin does not extol the revolution but, from a purely pragmatic viewpoint, considers it right because it is inevitable. It is equally inevitable that the man who is unable to adjust to its demands will necessarily end up as its victim, apart from the question of the rightness or wrongness of his views.

As Mathewson points out, this is a viable formula, avoiding political commitment, yet affording Fedin the latitude he requires for the psychological probing. This formula has never become the prevailing characteristic of Soviet literature, and stimulated a great deal of controversy when it was applied as the central motivating principle of *Tixij Don*.[19]

E. INVERSION OF CHRONOLOGY

One of the questions which has interested both Soviet and American critics has been the unusual structure and chronological displacement in the novel *Goroda i gody*. A hypothesis not previously suggested is offered below, based on an idea developed by Professor Davidson of Vanderbilt University in a study of the "inversive method" of narration in the works of Joseph Conrad.[20]

Every novelist must concern himself with fixing the attention of the reader on the inner meaning of incidents, and their relation to his theme or characterization, rather than on the mere narrative interest inherent in the unfolding of events. Fedin restricts the dominance of incident by tampering with the chronology. In some instances, an author may subdue

[19] R. W. Mathewson, Jr., *The Positive Hero in Russian Literature* (New York, Columbia University Press, 1958), p. 254.
[20] Donald Davidson, "The Inversive Method of Narration in the Novels and Stories of Joseph Conrad". Unpublished Master's thesis on file at the Joint University Libraries, Vanderbilt University, Nashville, Tenn. (May 15, 1922). Professor Davidson discusses five well-known inversive devices: the story within a story, the pluperfect summary, parallel narratives, the detective or mystery story, and the newspaper story.

excitement by disclosing the result of an event, even though it be of critical importance, prior to narrating the incidents leading to it. Joseph Conrad does this in *Nostromo*.

Fedins begins *Cities and Years* with Andrej's deranged harangue through the window of an apartment house. This is followed in the first chapter by his letter to Mari, in which he looks back at his life as though it is already ended, which indeed it is. In the final scene of the first chapter, the reader learns from Kurt Wahn's statement to an investigative tribunal that he has shot his former friend, Andrej.

Now the reader is motivated by a higher type of interest, which transcends the mere fact of mental derangement and physical death. The reader now seeks the *how* and *why*, rather than the *what*. He turns his attention to an analysis of motivation of conflict, and evaluates the justice and import of events. The reader knows the outcome of the tragedy in advance, and now seeks the revelation of human character, and the arousing of the emotions of pity and terror which he knows will be forthcoming.

At the outset Fedin establishes Starcov as a tragic hero, possessing the qualities established by Aristotle in his delineation.[21] Judging by the content of his hysterical outburst, Starcov evidences a deeper vein of feeling than the ordinary man. He is of noble nature, but like the reader in elemental feelings and emotions. He is idealized, but retains so much humanity that he enlists our eager interest and sympathy. He is tragic in his fall, which is attributable not to deliberate wickedness, but to some great frailty. Starcov undergoes the suffering which was so important in Aristotle's theory, and is involved in "an incident of a destructive or painful sort, such as violent death, physical agony".[22] For the suffering to evoke pity, Aristotle recommended a hero neither superlatively good nor bad, but "brought low through some error of judgment or short-coming". In Starcov's case, it might be either or both, if one were to apply Marxist criteria. In fact, in modern social drama the "tragic flaw", or *harmatia*, may exist more strongly in the milieu or society than in the hero, who may then become the victim of external circumstances. This is not the case with Starcov, who does have the option, as did every intellectual, of accepting or rejecting the revolution. Starcov's flaw was that he did neither, lacking the will and firmness of purpose.

[21]   S. H. Butcher (ed.), *Aristotle's Theory of Poetry and Fine Art* (New York, Dover Publications, Inc., 1951), p. 317.
[22]   J. T. Shipley, *Dictionary of World Literature* (Paterson, Littlefield, Adams & Co., 1960), p. 420.

It appears, then, that Fedin does accomplish, at the very beginning, what Aristotle considered to be the effect of tragedy, "to arouse the emotions of pity and fear in the audience".

The device of inversion also results in technical advantages to the novelist, mainly economy. Fedin's plot contains a mass of informative material which does not readily submit to conventional treatment. By re-arranging chronology, Fedin is free to introduce material where, in his judgment, it is most pertinent and significant.

The device of inversion is as old as narration itself. The narrator may begin, "You have heard of Starcov's death, haven't you? ... Well, this is how it happened." And then, having disclosed the dénouement, the narrator relates the events leading up to it. The final event, or some event precipitating it, is presented at the beginning.

By depicting Andrej's disturbed impressions at the very outset, Fedin arouses the reader's interest and expectations in an abrupt and forceful fashion. The reader is at once curious to learn the motivation for this first outburst, and the identity of the person calling Andrej's name.

Another effect of this displacement is to impart dramatic convincingness to the action. At the very beginning the actors and the reader are placed in direct confrontation with each other, and the author has vanished completely. In this method, all information must be contained in the action and dialogue of the characters already at the footlights. In the first section, "Reč'", Fedin provides the dénouement to one of the *noeuds*, Andrej's mental derangement. In the second section, "Pis'mo", additional dénouements are presented. Kurt finds Starcov in Petersburg, and Starcov is aware of the fact that he has come to the end of his superfluous life. In the next section, yet another dénouement appears, at which time the reader learns that the staunch Communist Kurt Wahn has served as the executor of revolutionary justice and has murdered his former friend.

This pattern of a series of successive dénouements is followed in the next chapter, dealing with the year 1919. The perspective continually broadens during these two chapters, and it is only in the third that the reader is transported back to the actual chronological beginning in 1914. Events then move foreward in a generally proper chronological sequence until the last chapter, 1920, which ends at the moment of maximum impact on the reader. Thus, what would ordinarily be a point of weakness is transformed into a point of strength.

This construction reverses the sequence of events postulated in

Freytag's pyramid.[23] In that pyramid, intended to portray the development of a five-act play, but with some applicability to the novel as well,
the action is diagrammed as rising from the inciting moment, through the
exposition and complication, to the climax. Then it falls, the reversal
taking place, to the dénouement and the moment of last suspense.

Fedin moves the dénouement from the end to the beginning, placing
it at the beginning of the period of rising action. The moment of last
suspense is also shifted to the beginning. Thus, the structural composition
is strengthened as concerns the period of rising action and continues
toward the climax. But the period of falling action is correspondingly
shortened, so that the book ends almost as the climax is reached, leaving
the reader while his emotional expectations are still at a high level. In
fact, the reader may be so aroused that he is impelled to return to the
beginning and to re-read the first two chapters, thus himself completing
the pyramid.[24]

F. EARLY NARRATIVE STYLE

When *Goroda i gody* was first published, Soviet critics engaged in violent
polemics regarding Fedin's toying with structure and with plot. V. Percov
had written that he experienced "irritation because the plot was twisted
to excess and because events were presented not in the order of the internal logic of their development, but following the capricious trans-
position of the years — either backwards, or one step forward and two
backward, which permits the author to display his compositional artfulness, inasmuch as the threads of the narrative, tangled and broken by the
author, are finally joined in the mind of the reader. Nevertheless, this
results in cheapening this device, though declaring it to be literariness."[25]

Brajnina criticizes Percov for categorizing as literariness the very thing
that Fedin was allegedly combating, namely literariness. Fedin was
searching for a new form of literary expression. According to Brajnina,
he was impelled to seek this form to express the new, unusually complex
material of life, meaning, of course, the war and revolution.[26]

Other Soviet critics also saw in the unusual composition a reflection of
the mental and spiritual derangement of the hero. Vera Smirnova takes

[23]   Shipley, *op. cit.*, p. 189.
[24]   Cf. Hongor Oulanoff, *The Theory and Practice of the Serapion Brothers* (= *Slavistic Printings and Reprintings*, 44) (The Hague, Mouton & Co., 1966).
[25]   V. Pertsov, *Ètjudy sovetskoj literatury* (Moscow, Goslitizdat, 1937), p. 118.
[26]   Brajnina, *Konstantin Fedin* (1953), pp. 84-86.

exception to this view, seeing in the chronological re-arrangement a conscious and deliberate effort by Fedin — feeling a secret sympathy and compassion toward Starcov — to find some means to temper the stern judgment against him. It is for this reason, says Smirnova, that Fedin selects and sorts specific episodes, rather than to present the affair in the order in which it developed.[27] But, Fedin's attitude toward Starcov is much more complex than mere compassion, which is essentially an emotional manifestation.

The last section of the last chapter of the novel, titled "My kvity, tovarišč Starcov" provides the key to the meaning of the novel. The section title is a quotation from the letter which von Schoenau sends to Andrej, in which he cruelly informs him that he, von Schoenau, had been Mari's lover. The irony of the situation is shown to be even more tragic when Andrej reads in the letter that Mari loved him, Andrej, so much that she had married a Russian for the sole purpose of gaining entry into Russia so that she could join Andrej!

Fedin precedes the letter with a lyrical digression, noteworthy for the insight it provides into Fedin's attitude towards Andrej Starcov, and the meaning of the tragedy which is his lot.

Вот мы кончаем повесть о человеке, с тоскою ждавшем, чтобы жизнь приняла его. Мы оглядываемся на дорогу, по которой ступал он следом за жестокостью и любовью, на дорогу в крови и цветах. Он прошел ее, и на нем не осталось ни одного пятна крови, и он не раздавил ни одного цветка.

О, если бы он принял на себя хоть одно пятно и затоптал бы хоть один цветок! Может быть, тогда наша жалость к нему выросла бы до любви, и мы не дали бы ему погибнуть так мучительно и так ничтожно.[28]

From the foregoing, Soviet critic Smirnova concludes that Fedin had no liking for his hero, only pity, otherwise he would not have permitted him to die such an inglorious death. Smirnova also concludes that the reader must likewise feel an aversion for Andrej, for the same reason. It appears that the question of like or dislike is hardly pertinent to an analysis of Goroda i gody. According to Aristotle's dictum, tragedy is intended to arouse the emotions of pity and fear in the audience, and to arouse it in such a way as to cause that special purging and relief (catharsis) which is characteristic of tragedy. Tragedy, then, provides experience which enables the spectator — and the author — to discharge

[27]   Smirnova, op. cit., p. 15.
[28]   Fedin, Sobranie, II, p. 407.

these emotions, thus relieving the soul. Modern psychoanalysis explains this phenomenom as the patient's reliving unconscious experience, bringing it into the open, and evaluating by the intellect consciously what had been unconscious, and therefore inhibiting and painful. Beaumarchais points out that "the nearer the suffering man is to my station in life, the greater is his claim upon my sympathy".[29] Thus does the problem of the effect on the reader, or on the author, resolve itself more into one of sympathy and pity than of liking or disliking. And even Smirnova does not deny that Fedin did feel pity for Starcov, as evidenced by the text quoted above.

There is a certain inconsistency in Fedin's characterization. On the one hand, Fedin strives to convince the reader of the "purity" of the hero, a purity which is carried to an unusual degree. He bemoans Andrej's not being besmirched by a single spot, the fact that Andrej has not crushed a single flower, nor taken any action whatsoever. But in point of fact, Andrej has besmirched himself, has crushed flowers, as evidenced by his liaison with Rita, whom he does not really love, and which, in fact, contributes to the tragic dénouement of his love affair with Mari Urbach.

Again it appears that Andrej's tragic flaw is his inability to commit himself wholly, in the personal as well as in the public spheres, emotionally as well as intellectually. The motivation for his love for Mari is not strong enough to preclude his liaison with Rita, and does detract from the sympathy which he arouses in the reader.

Since literature is, in effect, the art of the word, it is well to turn to a preliminary examination of Fedin's use of language, an examination which will be conducted in greater detail in conjunction with the analysis of Fedin's later novels.

There is a traditional line of development in Russian classical literature, which can be traced back to Puškin, which is founded on the trinity "jasnost', četkost', prostota": clarity, precision, simplicity. Anton Čexov wrote to young Gor'kij:

Красочность и выразительность в описаниях природы достигается только простотой, такими простыми фразами, как "зашло солнце", "стала темно", "пошел дождь", и т.д., и эта простота свойственна вам в сильной степени, как редко кому из беллетристов.[30]

Čexov cautioned Gor'kij against the use of words which were in the language only fleetingly, rather than as part of the permanent stock. He

---

[29] Shipley, *op. cit.*, p. 421 quoting Beaumarchais, *Essai Sur le Genre Dramatique Sérieux* (1767).
[30] B. Brajnina, "Iskusstvo slova", *Oktjabr'*, No. 1 (1954), pp. 156-166.

also advised against the use of words of foreign, as opposed to Slavic, origin, on the ground that they detracted from the clarity and expressiveness of the written word. In the early twenties, Gor'kij wrote the following on the manuscript of Fedin's *Sad*: "Očen' xorošo, no mestami vstrečajutsja lišnie ili nemnogo vzjatye slova." Following the precepts of both Čexov and Gor'kij, Fedin continually strove toward precision and clarity in his later works.

In his earliest works, Fedin deliberately complicated the sentence, being attracted to so-called "ornamentalism", and "rhythmic prose". The language of *Pustyr'*, Fedin's first collection of stories, is multi-colored, with words seemingly selected primarily because of considerations of sound, such as the requirements of measure or because of an overall rhythmic effect. At this early stage, Fedin had not yet found his own characteristic language, and was still groping.

This was still a period of literary experimentation, even for Fedin, and he was drawn more to the succinctness of Čexovian laconism and Čexovian grace. Čexov himself defined the latter as follows:

Когда на какое-нибудь определенное действие человек затрачивает наименьше количество движений, то это грация.[31]

To Čexov, literary creation was unthinkable without this grace for, in his own words, "kratkost' — sestra talanta". Brajnina noted that in Fedin's style may be found a number of peculiarities which are also characteristic of the language of Lev Tolstoj and Anton Čexov. "In his work on poetic language", she writes, "Fedin strives to combine on a new foundation the traditions of Tolstoyan detailed psychological analysis with the traditions of Čexovian laconicism. This laborious and creative work yielded brilliant results."[32]

As for Fedin's syntax, particularly prevalent in *Cities and Years*, *The Brothers*, and the dilogy is the reinforcement of an action expressed by a verb with an adverb, answering the question "how?", preceding the verb. In Fedin, such a combination of adverb and verb becomes one expression, an integrated action better imparting the visual image. Some examples follow:

сосредоточенно прожевывает; насупленно молчал; остро усмехнулся; обиженно ушел прочь; торопливо вышел; резонно советовал; молча засмеялась; озорно, подевичьи взглянула на него; грузно

[31] B. Brajnina, "Iskusstvo slova", *Oktjabr'*, No. 1 (1954), p. 164.
[32] *Ibid.*

опустился в кресло; осторожно, одним глазом выглянул в окно; круто обернулся к жене; коротким, злым рывком выдернул из ее рук полу куртки.[33]

Fedin thus makes the action concrete, presenting it as visual, plastic movement, a gesture expressed by a verb. This is why his portraits, which always show the character in motion, reproduce the pose, the gesture, so plastically.

This is evidently achieved as a result of the most painstaking, almost anatomic, study of men and of human movements, like that of a sculptor or painter. Here Fedin follows Turgenev's dictum, as recorded in a letter to K. N. Leont'ev in 1860: "The writer must be a psychologist, but a secret one: he must know and sense the roots of phenomena. ... The psychologist must disappear in the artist, as the skeleton is concealed in the warm and living body, for which it serves as a firm but invisible support."[34]

Fedin would agree with Turgenev that just as a painter studies anatomy to have a better structural idea of the human form, so the novelist must investigate human feelings, traits, attributes, and gestures, recognizing them as continually undergoing modification. This anatomical study, then, is conducted on two levels, the psychological and the physical.

A classical example of the detailed exposition of a person's movements on the physical level is offered in *Cities and Years*, where Fedin shows how little Mari Urbach, nine months old, is learning to walk. This is the description:

Девяти месяцев Мари научилась ходить. Отец случайно видел, как это произошло. Ребенок, окруженный игрушками, сидел на полу. Няня вышла. Посмотрев ей вслед и точно убедившись, что в комнате никого нет, Мари потянулась ручонками к стулу. Кряхтя и тужась, она привстала и начала переставлять непослушные, тсеплявшиеся

друг за друга ножки. Обойдя вокруг стула, Мари решилась сделать несколько шагов без опоры и двинулась к кровати. Но тотчас упала и стукнулась затылком об пол. Герр Урбач невольно шагнул вперед. Мари с трудом приподнялась, попыталась дотянуться ручонкой до ушибленного затылка и потереть его, не дотянулась, пролепетала что-то себе под нос и осмотрелась. Стул стоял позади нее, кровать — перед нею. Для того чтобы ухватиться за стул, нужно было сделать два-три шажка. До кровати было дальше. Мари

[33] Smirnova, *op. cit.*, p. 61.
[34] S. D. Baluxatyj (ed.), *Russkie pisateli o literature* (Leningrad, 1939), I, citing as its source *Russkaja Mysl'* (1886), no. 2. It is quoted in translation in A. Yarmolinskij, *Turgenev* (New York, 1926), p. 194.

решила достичь кровати. Сначала она встала на коленки. Потом, с большим усилием, подставила коленки под живот и немного отдохнула, стоя на четвереньках. Поднять голову и в то же время оторвать от пола руки было труднее. Мари могла бы с легкостью доползти до кровати на четвереньках, но она решила встать на ноги, и она должна была добиться своего. Одна ручонка оторвалась наконец от пола и заболталась в воздухе. Зато вся тяжесть маленького тела навалилась на другую. Встать было невозможно. Тогда Мари присела, передохнула и начала всю работу сначала. Опять коленки были подведены под живот, опять была сделана передышка, опять одна рука заболталась в воздухе. Но тут неожиданно ножки подогнулись в коленках сами собой, и Мари очутилась на корточках. Тогда она оперлась ручками о колени, натужилась выпрямилась и, не отнимая рук от коленок, переставила сначала одну, потом другую ногу. Уверившись, что она может передвигаться, Мари выпятила одну ручонку вперед, еще больше выпрямилась и заковыляла вперевалочку вперед, вперед, почти до самой кровати. Здесь она оторвала и другую ручку от коленки, всплеснула радостно в ладоши, крякнула по-утиному и упала на постель, вцепившись пальцами в одеяло.[35]

This fragment brings to mind Stanislavskij's book *Rabota aktera nad soboj*, particularly the chapter on "xarakternosti", in which Stanislavskij describes teaching an actor, who had to play the part of an old man, how to sit down in a chair:

Изучите сначала самую природу старости. ... У стариков все делается не скоро. ... Проверьте, под каким градусом у вас согнулись коленки ... вам, как старику, позволено сгибать не больше, чем под углом в двадцать градусов ... не забывайте, что у старика полуслепые глаза. Ему необходимо, прежде чем класть руки на локотники, рассмотреть и понять, куда он их кладет, на что опирается. ... Медленнее, а то будет прострел. Не забывайте, что сочленения заржавели и заедают. ...[36]

Fedin recognized that this type of detailed study of the nature of old age is the *sine qua non* not only for the actor and painter, but also for the writer. Only then would he be able to offer a plastic portrayal of man, harmonizing form and movement.

---

[35] Fedin, *Sobranie*, II, pp. 119-120.
[36] Smirnova, *op. cit.*, p. 62. Cf. K. S. Stanislavskij, *On the Art of the Stage*, translated with an Introductory Essay on Stanislavskij's system by David Magarshack (New York, Hill and Wang, 1961), 154ff.

IV

BRAT'JA

A. COMPARED WITH THE FIRST NOVEL

Fedin's second novel, *Brat'ja*, was published in 1927-1928. Contemporary critics immediately noted its similarity to its predecessor novel, *Goroda i gody*. The events constituting the basic setting of the novel are also war and revolution, and the main characters of the novel are members of the intelligentsia with the same background as Andrej Starcov. The basic theme concerns the problem of the artist and the Revolution, a refinement over the basic conflict of *Goroda i gody*, which was the conflict of the intellectual in general, and the Revolution.

Nikita Karev, like Andrej Starcov, is beset by torturing doubts. He reacts to the Revolution not as a tremendous social and political force for the betterment of the lot of the Russian masses, but rather assumes a romantic, idealized position, seeing its tragic overtones. This tragic quality of the Revolution, in the consciousness of Nikita Karev, is the basis for the tragic character assumed by his artistic creation. The last chapter of the novel bears the expressive title "Utraty", and ends with the following:

Мир отвергал Никиту Карева, чтобы принять. Обогащал одну его судьбу опытом несчастья и утрат в другой.[1]

In *Brat'ja* it is not only the intellectual, unable to identify with the Revolution, who attracts the main interest of the author. Fedin devotes considerably more attention to the characterization of his Communist *personae*, of whom the three outstanding figures are Šering, Rostislav Karev, and Rodion Čorbov. These three come to embrace the Revolution by various paths. Fedin does impart to these characters certain positive qualities. But the characterization of these Communists still lacks psychological depth, and they are not too convincing. Even a contem-

[1]   Fedin, *Sobranie*, III, p. 416.

porary Communist critic like Bugaenko recognizes the schematic nature of their portrayal, especially in the case of Šering.[2] Fedin just does not seem to have been capable at this time of creating a worthy Communist hero who would have measured up to his artistic capabilities.

Fedin's true capabilities as a craftsman, as concerns the creation and portrayal of character and personality, are observable in the figure of Nikita Karev, whose spiritual and mental world Fedin portrays in all of its complexity. It is this characterization which offers the most convincing proof of the strengthening and maturation of Fedin's craftsmanship, and of his increasing power of psychological analysis.

The sense of the unfolding of historical events is conveyed in this novel to an even greater degree than in the first, and with even greater attention to detail. This novel is also based, to a significant degree, on Fedin's own autobiography, on the impressions of his own childhood and youth.

В городе учился на скрипке ... на концертах скрипачом и чтецом выступал ... погромы с матерью в погребе отсиживал (дверь на погребицу тоненькой веревочкой завязал), страшно было. Пожаров, стонов и того, как с иконами в руках у ворот стояли, чтобы отвести погром; и того, как на глазах поляка разорвали, а я топал ногами и плакал; и того, как своего учителя скрипача (Гольдмана) в кухне под лестницу спрятал и луком прикрыл, — никогда не забуду.[3]

These bitter memories of his early youth were sharply etched in Fedin's consciousness, and provide the basis for the material presented in the third chapter of *Brat'ja*.

The novel *Brat'ja* has many features in common with Fedin's first novel, especially as concerns structure. Particularly noticeable is the complex composition, the same inversion of the chronological sequence of events, and the same features of language usage.

B. EVOLUTION OF THEMES AND CHARACTERS

In his second novel, Fedin continues to develop the same type of hero first encountered in *Goroda i gody*, deepening and changing his features. Apparently Fedin did not concern himself with a search for a new hero. Rather he was seeking a place in the new society for the old one, seeking a means for the hero to assert himself. Fedin was seeking a variation in both the hero and in the circumstances in which he could exist.

[2] Bugaenko, *op. cit.*, p. 40.
[3] *Literaturnye zapiski*, No. 3 (1922), p. 27.

Fedin frankly makes use of material from his first novel, even preserving some of the plot relationships. Nikita Karev, like Andrej Starcov before him, lives and studies in Germany, where he meets and falls in love with Anna.

Returning to Russia following the revolution, he wanders about, visiting cities where he has lived in his youth. Eventually he finds himself in Petrograd, where he is lonely and leads a miserable existence. He loves Anna and, after her death, Irina, who resembles her. (This same motif is later repeated in *Poxiščenie Evropy*.) Like Andrej Starcov, Nikita lives with another woman whom he does not love as deeply, Varvara Šestobitovaja, and she is expecting his child.

Nikita Karev belongs to the same generation as the hero of *Goroda i gody*, but Fedin has invested him with a great deal which is lacking in Andrej Starcov. First of all, Nikita has a profession; he is a musician. Music is not merely his profession but his grand passion, his vocation, his *raison d'être*. But music is also the source of conflict with life, particularly with the revolution. Like a slave chained to the piano or violin, he forsakes all other interests and activities for his art. He stands apart from the revolution, his family, friendship, and even love. The genuine artist, according to Nikita Karev, is a tragic and solitary figure.

But Karev does recognize that the aim of art is to afford pleasure to man. He experiences great satisfaction seeing the effect which his symphony has on the most unexpected of audiences, sailors who have come to his concert. It is specifically through art, through his music, that he is able to identify with the Revolution. Thus does he find that essential contact with life, a justification for his existence, a place in life. But how agonizing is his road to the heights of art, how many mistakes does he make, and how fleeting is the joy of success!

The novel ends with a manifest parallel to the last chapters of *Goroda i gody*. In that novel, Andrej Starcov wandered in terror, at night, through the wasteland: "Over him hung the black sky, and there were no human dwellings, and there were no roads." In *Brat'ja* the desert extends over the earth, and Nikita walks through the wasteland, reviewing all his mistakes in his mind. He, like a man on a melancholy island at night, "did not see a single living soul". He saw only the poster proclaiming his concert.

The central thematic problem which continues to occupy Fedin is that of the relationship of the Revolution to art. This problem shapes the main characters of Fedin's novels: the Bolshevik, representing the Revolution, and the painter, musician, writer, actor or dramatist, representing art. This problem pervades *Goroda i gody* and, even more so, *Brat'ja*. It is also a central problem in the first two novels of the trilogy. In order to observe how Fedin approaches this problem, it would be well to compare the first two and the last two novels.

In *Goroda i gody*, the Bolsheviks are Kurt Wahn and Golosov. The reader cannot help sensing that Fedin is attracted to, and aroused by both men, although to different degrees. Fedin admires these strong-willed, resolute, stubborn types, but he is not too successful in delineating their characters, personalities, and motivation. They puzzle Fedin himself, and consequently remain a puzzle to the reader.

Fedin never explains how the German artist Kurt Wahn became a Bolshevik. One possibility is that he was motivated by his hatred toward such people as von Schoenau, who was stifling his talent. But the reader is never shown how this came about. Equally obscure is the reason why Rostislav Karev became a Bolshevik. Actually the reader learns very little about him and his activity. The reader does learn that Rostislav Karev is not a bad soldier, and that he has a stable personality, but he does not learn much more. We learn only that, while still a boy, Rostislav finds himself on the German front. Then, several years later, he turns up as a commander of a Red detachment on the Volga. "Ja bol'ševik", he announces during an unexpected encounter with his brother Nikita.

Nor does the reader learn how Rodion Čerbov became a Communist. While yet a boy he acquired a revolver from a seaman and used it when the need presented itself. Then he turns up, with no apparent motivation, in a fighting detachment, and, later, in jail. Then, following the revolution, we see him as commissar aboard the flagship in Šering's flotilla.

Fedin's bolsheviks all remain essentially lifeless, schematic outlines. The cause does not lie exclusively in the fact that Fedin was not conversant with the nature of an honest-to-goodness Bolshevik. It may also be attributed to Fedin's scepticism, and at times clearly expressed irony, both of which are felt by the reader *vis-à-vis* the views and objectives of the Bolsheviks.

This is especially evident in the portrayal of Rodion Čerbov, who is not only semi-literate, but a man of extremely limited intelligence and imagination. This is demonstrated, among other things, by his relationship with Varvara Mixajlovna, who is a copy of Dostoevskij's infernal beauties. She is an unusual type of merchant's daughter, whose destiny soon becomes intertwined with that of Rodion. But she soon grows disillusioned with him and, when they quarrel, the reader finds himself sympathizing with Varvara. Even the Communist reader must involuntarily side with her, so shallow and unworthy is this Bolshevik.

In the scene in which Rodion clashes with Nikita, the loser is again Rodion. He is unable to govern even himself, and Fedin leaves the reader wondering why such a sensitive and poetic young lady like Irina should show any interest in him.

C. SUMMING UP

H. G. Schogt, in an article in a collection reviewed by Georgette Donchin, notes, as a characteristic of Fedin's early work, that his early positive heroes are colorless.[4] This represents a link between old and new Russian fiction. Indeed, there has never been in Russian literature a really convincing positive character.

But in his later novels Fedin succeeded in drawing at least the ideal hero of Socialist Realism. Kirill Izvekov, the hero of *Pervye radosti* and *Neobyknovennoe leto*, always acts in exemplary fashion. He belongs, of course, to the new generation. The psychological problems of the super-fluous man are alien to him. This does not mean that he never hesitates or makes mistakes, but he always finds the right way in the end. Fedin's own mental evolution can be traced in this difference between his earlier and later heroes. Andrej Starcov, Nikita, and Rodion, give way to Kirill Izvekov and Petr Ragozin, and Mari Urbach and Varvara Mixajlovna to Anočka. Good and bad, right and wrong, are now clearly distin-guished. Doubts, proper not only to the old times, but also to youth itself, are abandoned.

Fedin's last two novels are retrospective. What at the beginning of the revolution was merely a disquietening chaos becomes order in the eyes of the later observer.

Continuity? Yes. No literature can be entirely new, not even when tradition is disparaged.

The two salient aspects of the old literature of the intelligentsia — social idealism and interest in the human soul — have both been retained. The emphasis alone has been shifted.

---

[4] Georgette Donchin, review of *Analecta Slavica*, in *SEER*, XXXIV (1955-56), pp. 556-557.

V

TRANSITIONAL WORKS

In his autobiography,[1] Fedin mentions that, following his extended stay in Germany during World War I, he was able, in the 1920's, again to visit Western Europe. After finishing *Brat'ja*, Fedin, in 1928, toured the Scandinavian countries, Germany, and Holland. Looking back in 1957, Fedin somewhat bitterly refers to this period between the wars as one of "stabilizacii", and accuses the West of being concerned only with its own enjoyment, indifferent to the grief of the rest of the world.

In 1931, seriously ill, Fedin traveled to Switzerland. He expresses his gratitude to Gor'kij who again, as he had done in Petersburg when Fedin was ill in 1921, helped him to get the prolonged treatment which was needed. Gor'kij also arranged for Fedin to meet the French writer Romain Rolland, who invited Fedin to visit him at Villeneuve, on Lake Geneva, when he had recovered sufficiently in 1932, in the midst of a period of international economic and political crisis. Fedin again visited Germany at the end of 1932, and witnessed the last free election in that country prior to Hitler's takeover.

A. *POXIŠČENIE EVROPY*

Fedin's visits to the West in the late twenties and early thirties provided the motivation and subject matter for one full-length and one shorter novel, *Poxiščenie Evropy* (Vol. I in 1933, Vol. II in 1935) and *Sanatorij Arktur* (1940). In the first novel, Fedin wanted to contrast the USSR, in the midst of its feverish drive to build Socialism under the Five Year Plan, with the West which, observed from the point of view of a Soviet journalist, Rogov, appeared as a decadent, capitalist, bourgeois society. *Poxiščenie Evropy* has been characterized as Fedin's weakest novel. "... it is disjointed, its plot is slim, its motley episodes are poorly

---

[1] Fedin, *Sobranie*, I, pp. 16-18.

integrated within the general framework, and the characters lack depth";[2] Gleb Struve has commented on the lack of dynamic power of the novel, its excessive meditations and descriptions, and the "thin" characterization.[3]

Yet the construction of the novel *Poxiščenie Evropy* is clearer than that of the previous two novels. There is less place for shadows, and Fedin's judgment of the representatives of the upper strata of society becomes more incisive. Fedin exhibits very little, if any, compassion for his characters. The wealthy lumber merchants, the van Rossums, hide their predatory instincts behind a facade of civilization. Their hearts are dried out, and human sentiments are crowded out by cold calculation, the striving for profit, and the law of mutual destruction. The principal character, Philipp van Rossum, a Dutchman, is hostile to the Soviet Union although he demands that his government extend diplomatic recognition.

Life in Amsterdam during the economic depression of 1930 forms a cruel background for the first part of the novel. Of the entire van Rossum family, only Frans, the firm's representative in Leningrad, makes any claim to Fedin's sympathy. He is more open, more frank than the rest of the family. His wife, Klavdija Andreevna, a very beautiful refugee, deceives him with Rogov, and with Philipp. In Klavdija, Fedin tries to personify what he conceives representative capitalistic women to be like. Seductive and spiritual, but inane and egoistic, she is incapable of anything positive or constructive. Her moments of lucidity reveal the impasse in her life, and she is unable to make amends. Russia is closed to her forever, of which she becomes sadly aware when she leaves Leningrad in the company of Philipp van Rossum after Frans' death at the end of the second part of the novel. This part does not merit comparison with Fedin's previous works, the main themes now being Socialist construction and the industrial and economic development of the Soviet Union.

Fedin now portrays the new generation which continues the revolution. It does not miss the luxury which it has never known, and the psychological problems of the superfluous man are totally unknown. Its enthusiasm is stimulating, although it is counteracted by the monotony and sameness, which are somewhat oppressive. Rogov, the journalist-

[2] M. Slonim, *Modern Russian Literature* (London, Oxford University Press, 1953), p. 309.
[3] G. Struve, *25 Years of Soviet Russian Literature* (London, Geo. Routledge & Sons, 1946), p. 41.

intellectual who stands out among the crowds in Leningrad because of his half-European clothing, refers to the typical physiognomy which he meets with increasing frequency throughout the country: the determined expression, serious, calm, and with quiet joy, the prominent chin and cheekbones, and the clear, blazing eyes, just like a Majakovskij poster!

The communist Sergeič, the oldest of the active members in the little port in northern Russia from which lumber is exported, corresponds well to this description, although his individuality is not expressed at all. Rogov himself is like his clothing, divided between two worlds. His love for Klavdija is largely explained by his need for luxury and well-being, which could not be satisfied in the Soviet Union. Yet he, unlike Nikita, is able to reconcile himself to the new socialist way of life. An unfortunate love experience, which he has in common with Andrej of *Goroda i gody*, does not defeat him, and the positive elements of his character prevails.

As concerns Fedin's artistic development, the most significant conclusion to be drawn from both *Poxiščenie Evropy* and *Sanatorij Arktur* is that he appears to have overcome his objections to the Soviet regime, despite Communist criticism for showing Rogov overly absorbed in his own, personal, love interest.

B. *ISPYTANIE ČUVSTV*

During the Second World War, Fedin wrote a number of smaller works. These included several sketches and short stories, the most significant of which were included in the collections *Neskol'ko naselennyx punktov* (1943), and *Svidanie s Leningradom* (1944). He also wrote a play, *Ispytanie čuvstv* (1942), obviously intended to intensify wartime patriotic sentiment.

The play may be summarized briefly as follows: In a small town on a navigable river, a woman is visited by her daughter Valja and her husband, Aleša, a young architect. Valja has just been graduated from a *vuz*, an institution of higher learning.

The joy of their reunion is suddenly destroyed by the war. On the morning following their arrival, a German airplane bombs a passenger ship in the river. Among those wounded is a friend of Valja, Aglaja. Her appearance serves as the *noeud*, the initial dramatic shock introducing the plot elements built around the personal drama of Valja and Aleša. Five years previously, Alesa had been close to Aglaja.

Subsequent events develop rapidly: the town is occupied by the

Germans. Aleša hides, and both girls help him. The strong personal feelings of the main characters must be subordinated to the unselfish, sacrificing call of patriotism, requiring selfless dedication to the task of defending the motherland. Their highest feelings are subjected to the most severe test and emerge victorious.

There are nine characters in the play, all related psychologically to the theme of "ispytanija čuvstv". In the background, continually attracting the attention of the spectator or reader, is the horror of war. The characters, caught up in the events of the war, disassociate themselves from their personal and intimate experiences with varying degrees of success.

There are two basic dramatic *pointes* in the play, constructed like a complex poetic work. In the first, the old machinist Lukaškin is repairing a damaged locomotive. When the Germans enter the town, the repair work continues, but now it is under German direction. In order to preclude the locomotive falling into German hands, Lukaškin blows up the machine shop. The second highly dramatic moment occurs as follows. Aleša, who has joined the underground which has been organized in the town, shoots a German officer who plays a leading role in the play. Aleša then hides, accompanied by his wife and a group of his fellow conspirators. Aglaja, wishing to save Aleša and Valja's mother, who is also implicated in underground activities, puts herself in a position in which she is shot, sacrificing her own life to save theirs.

One of the central moments in the development of the play is the psychological "duel" between Aglaja and the German officer, a typical Prussian stereotype.

Fedin's aim was to glorify Russian heroism in the face of the hardship and suffering of war. But even from this brief resume it is apparent that Fedin develops his theme in a psychological manner, highly personal and intimate, relegating the war theme somewhat to the background.

The wartime patriotic message of the play is summed up in the comments of Anna Pavlovna, Valja's mother, who, at the conclusion of the play, expressed the following sentiments concerning love and hate:

Все мы любим, у всех у нас женское сердце. Но пусть злой враг побоится нашего женского сердца! Любовью своей оно напитает ненависть к нему. ... И мы идем, идем воздать врагу за все, без пощады![4]

---

[4]   K. Fedin, *Sobranie*, V, p. 228.

The heroism of Russian women during World War II was a theme which particularly interested Fedin. For this reason the figure of Aglaja was to play a leading role, and Fedin originally considered calling the play *Aglaja*.

Nemirovič-Dančenko, who approved the play for presentation by the Moscow Art Theatre (although it never was staged), considered the role of Aglaja as one of the best, one of the most enticing for an actress to play. Nemirovič-Dančenko wrote to Fedin:

Между прочим, от этого образа веет романтизмом дореволюционной эпохи. Он как-то заведомо театрализованный и по поведению, и по стойкости и четкости всех переживаний, и по некоторой драматической взбаламученности, душевности, и по изощренности языка. При постановке можно будет проследить, чтобы актриса больше опиралась на все живые черты, какие отмечают этот образ, не слишком увлекалась внешней красивостью их — куда роль легко может потянуть. В то же время прекрасная работа для актрисы. Я понимаю, почему, как мне сообщили, автор одно время даже думал назвать пьесу *Аглая*. Хотя, конечно, это решительно снизило бы содержание пьесы с огромного явления до частного любовного эпизода.[5]

Illustrating the high regard which Nemirovič-Dančenko had for the dramatic structure of the play is the following:

... В драматургической структуре пьесы, в ее архитектонике, проводится прием, один из самых сценичных и интересных, как бы сказать, двойного содержания пьесы: одно, составляющее атмосферу ее, чисто фактическое, более внешнее выражение ее частей, которое в то время находится в непрерывном динамическом движении, как бы является фабулой пьесы, ее сценарием; и другое — столкновение человеков, их переживаний, их взаимоотношений, их страстей, что тоже идет по линии динамического развития. И два эти содержания неразрывно слиты. Очень хороший и благородный драматургический прием. ...[6]

Although *Ispytanie čuvstv* was never produced by the Moscow Art Theatre, it was staged frequently in provincial theatres during the war years.

C. *GOR'KIJ SREDI NAS*

It was also in the 1940's that Fedin published his volume of literary reminiscences, *Gor'kij sredi nas*. Although Gor'kij is the central figure,

---

[5]   Fedin, *Sobranie*, Vol. V, p. 441.
[6]   *Ibid.*, p. 442.

the book is a literary memoir of an entire period, although not an exhaustive one. The first volume was published in 1943, the second in 1944, and both are included in the latest edition of this collected works in nine volumes, in the ninth volume.

The first volume treats Fedin's acquaintance with Gor'kij and their meetings during 1920-21. It also touches upon the life of the writers of the time and the various schools of literary thought which were then contending for domination.

The second volume covers the period 1923-28. It contains Fedin's correspondence with Gor'kij and a description of his return to the Soviet Union in 1928.

In 1943, the year the first volume was published, and also the year Fedin celebrated his 30th anniversary of literary activity, the Presidium of the Writers' Union sent Fedin a letter stating in part: "You are an example of that eternal restlessness which is the quality of great artists and men of action. Your last book about Gor'kij, whom you knew well and intimately, is undoubtedly one of the best books written about the great writer on the basis of personal reminiscences. ..."[7]

When the second volume was published in the summer of the following year, Fedin was immediately subjected to a barrage of criticism in the press[8] and in the Presidium of the Writers' Union. In the second volume, Fedin had devoted several pages to the description and characterization of Aleksej Remizov, Fedor Sologub, and Akim Volynskij, a novelist, poet and critic. All were prominent literary figures in pre-revolutionary literature and in the early 1920's. Sologub and Volynskij died in the Soviet Union within a decade after the Revolution while Remizov emigrated to Paris, where he continued his literary activity.

Fedin's references to these authors in his personal reminiscences is perfectly normal. All three were active in the first two decades of the century, the period about which Fedin was writing. Among other things, Fedin was criticized for his apolitical treatment, for his-so-called "dispassionate objectivism". One critic, V. Višnevskij, criticized Fedin in the following terms:

The writer has come forth with a book about Gor'kij, about the stormy years of the revolution. But there is no storm in the book. Only the quiet of salons and literary cabinets. The author fences himself off from battles, political passions and the great seekings. ... You see each gesture of these diseased persons –

---

[7] G. Reavey, *Soviet Literature Today* (New Haven, Yale University Press, 1947), p. 121.

[8] L. Dmitriev, "Contrary to History", *Literature and Art*, 5 Aug. 1944.

Sologub, Volynskij, etc. You see how they are dressed, but you hear no word of how these gentry conducted themselves politically. ... Astonishing is the almost complete absence in this book of the historico-political background. Somewhere outside the frame of the literary world a great struggle is taking place, but it is not introduced into the book. ... Fedin's book is a sort of defence of a displaced literature that knows no right or wrong, and accepts manifestations "quietly", "objectively", and in the fashion of a chronicle. ... How can one be outside politics in the time of the Patriotic War? What will that lead to? [9]

I. Ležnev, another Soviet critic, considers Fedin one of those who,

... not having freed themselves from the burden of old conceptions and among whom are to be found such as, not putting two and two together, have begun to delve into the heritage in the wrong place. ... In their enthusiasm they have lost their sense of proportion. ... Hence their readiness to submit to revision the very foundations of our world outlook. This tendency towards a re-valuation of values, so fashionable in the circles of people who are cut off from life, has been clearly expressed in Fedin's book. ...

Ležnev concludes that the cause of Fedin's "crude mistakes" is his "toleration, dispassionate relation to the reactionary ideas of the past, and disintegrating scepticism". [10]

Fedin was also criticized by M. Šaginjan, who reminded Soviet readers that "Truth is always concrete and historical. ... The atmosphere of soft benevolence in which Fedin presents his memoirs disorients the reader and distorts the past." Tixonov goes further and accuses Fedin of misconstruing Gor'kij's fundamental ideas:

If we speak of the heritage of Gor'kij, then the whole simplicity and boldness of Gor'kij's relationships lies especially in the further transformation of the world, and not in that chaotic self-wilfullness, which will only confuse all manifestations and lead us far away from the important questions of the present moment. The artist, who attempts to restore individualism in general, will have nothing in common with the growth of socialist individuality, and the manifestations of life will lose for him that completeness and truth, which is being consolidated in art for a long time to come. [11]

Fedin was accused by another critic, L. Dmitriev, of

... defending and justifying his false point of view regarding the place of the artist in relation to reality and the purpose and significance of art. ... Fedin's book is an obstinate, thought out defence of the position of the contemplative

---

[9] *Literatura i Iskusstvo*, 9 September 1944.
[10] Translated by G. Reavey, *Soviet Literature Today*, p. 122.
[11] Reavey, *op. cit.*, p. 122.

artist, the defence of apolitical art. ... Fedin has clearly taken up a position contradicting the testament of Gor'kij.[12]

The scope of this work has not permitted detailed analysis of the two books. Their contents are summarized here in the hope they will stimulate further study. The contents of the section devoted to the year 1920 include: Gor'kij persuades Fedin to write a one-act drama; Gor'kij is always ready to help; Fedin praises the symbolists and Aleksandr Blok; Fedin refers to Gor'kij as his "pomoščnik i osvoboditel'"; Fedin plastically portrays Gor'kij; Gor'kij cautions Fedin against the Dom literatorov, praising the Dom iskusstv; Fedin observes Tynjanov and Šklovskij at the Dom literatorov, which he describes ironically; Gor'kij advises Fedin to join the circle of young writers at the Dom iskusstv, and to become acquainted with Aleksandr Blok; Gor'kij praises Blok, Čukovskij, and Zamjatin; Gor'kij advises Fedin to leave the newspaper and to become a litterateur; Fedin discusses Blok; Gor'kij considers that the peasant has sometimes been overrated in Russian literature, a tendency which Čexov and Bunin tried to correct; Gor'kij advises Fedin to write a great deal, and to do so every day; Gor'kij impresses Fedin with the importance of women characters; Gor'kij considers Russian literature to be in a state of decline and crises; Kornej Ivanovič Čukovskij analyzes Fedin's work at the Dom iskusstv; Fedin speculates on the nature of art; Gor'kij, as a teacher and mentor in literature, stresses its greatness, with matter more important than manner; Gor'kij cautions Fedin to listen to the critics, but not to subordinate himself, "Slušajte, no ne slušajtes'"; Fedin tells Gor'kij of the themes bothering him, and Gor'kij counsels him to put them on paper; Gor'kij introduces Fedin to Vsevolod Ivanov, who relates Civil War atrocities in Siberia; Fedin evaluates Vs. Ivanov as one of the boldest writers of the post-revolutionary period; Gor'kij writes to the paper recommending that Fedin be released so that he can devote himself to belles-lettres.

The year 1921 is summarized as follows: Gor'kij continues to urge Fedin to join the group of young authors at the Dom isskustv and to associate particularly with the Serapion Brethren; Gor'kij influences Fedin without dictating; Fedin, in explaining the views of the Serapion Brethren, makes them sound like those of the Russian Formalists; Fedin stresses his opposition views; Gor'kij compares literature to a trade or craft, with masters, journeymen, and apprentices; Gor'kij criticizes Fedin's manuscripts, and those of four of the Serapion Brothers; in-

[12] *Ibid.*

fluences on the Serapion Brothers include Ol'ga Forš, Marietta Šaginjan, Kornej Čukovskij, and Viktor Šklovskij; the period of the New Economic Policy (NEP) begins; Fedin assesses Lev Lunc; the Serapions stage impromptu live "films" for children, directed by Lunc; Fedin stresses that declarations by Lunc do not represent unanimous Serapion thinking; Gor'kij's obituary for Lev Lunc; Gor'kij counsels beginning Russian writers to read great French literature, by authors like Stendhal, Balzac, Flaubert; "Na zapad"; Gor'kij was proud to write like the French; Gor'kij's search for new forms; Gor'kij makes various observations on how to write; Gor'kij criticizes Šklovskij's preoccupation with "sjužet" but praises Vsevolod Ivanov; Fedin wins a prize for a short story at the Dom literatov, without Gor'kij's knowledge; Gor'kij criticizes the language of *Sad* and *Molčal'nik*; Fedin therefore does not publish *Molčal'nik*; Gor'kij assesses the Serapions' *Almanax*; death of Blok and, in Fedin's opinion, the end of an era; Gor'kij's fondness for the Serapion Brethren.

PART III

THE TRILOGY

VI

HOW FEDIN WORKS

Professor Marchand, in his *Prolegomena to a Theory of Literary Criticism*, opposes synchronic study of the art product (in literature, the symbolic expression of the intuitive experience of the artist) to diachronic study. He defines the first as "... the observation of the art product and its communication at one time, e.g., the present", and the second, diachronic study, as "... observation of the art product through time, being conveniently broken up into three parts: 1. the pre-natal history of the work of art; 2. the discussion of the various post-natal versions of the art product; 3. the effect of the work on various generations of readers."[1] Professor Marchand stresses the value of all three parts in affording the reader an insight into the intuitive experience which the author is attempting to communicate.

The pre-natal history of the novels *Pervye radosti* and *Neobyknovennoe leto*, comprising the first two novels of the trilogy, provided the subject matter for a Candidate's dissertation written by A. G. Berezkina, which she defended in Moscow in 1954. In it, she makes extensive use of materials in Fedin's personal files, rough drafts and preliminary outlines of various chapters of the dilogy, correspondence, and personal conversations with Fedin.[2]

The Lenin State Library in Moscow provided a microfilm copy of a

---

[1] James W. Marchand, *op. cit.*, pp. 7-8.
[2] One of the chapters of the dissertation, "Stanovlenie zamysla dilogii K. Fedina *Pervye radosti i Neobyknovennoe leto*", was published in *Učenye zapiski*. Kujbyševskogo gosudarstvennogo pedagogičeskogo instituta imeni V. V. Kujbyševa, Literaturovedenie, Vypusk 19 (1958), pp. 359-387. The remainder of the dissertation, titled "Tvorčeskaja istorija romanov K. Fedin *Pervye radosti i Neobyknovennoe leto*" was "not available". The "Candidate's" dissertation is equivalent to the Doctoral dissertation in this country. In the USSR, two advanced degrees are awarded by academic institutions of higher education. The degree of "kandidat nauk" is awarded after three years of graduate study, plus defense of the dissertation. A higher degree, *doktor nauk*, is generally awarded on the basis of considerable additional teaching or research. Cf. B. I. Gorokhoff, *Publishing in the USSR* (= *Indiana University Publications, Graduate School, Slavic and East European Series*, Vol. 19) (1959), pp. 21-22.

published chapter, which served as the basis for the material which follows.

"Every book", says K. Fedin, "has its own biography. This rule applies to all writers, in all countries. ... Every book, while reflecting the social ideas of a given period, simultaneously reveals, as it were, the individual history of the author himself — his development, as it is related to the particular period."[3]

The novels *Pervye radosti* and *Neobyknovennoe leto* likewise have their individual biographies, related to a specific period in the history of the Soviet Union, as well as to the personal development of the author himself. The 1930's were a particularly significant period in Fedin's literary development, as indeed they were for most other Soviet littera-eturs. For Fedin, they were years of intensive ideological and artistic development. This was the period of the Five Year Plans, the adoption of a new constitution and, of perhaps even greater significance, the announcement of certain guiding principles at the First All-Union Congress of Soviet Writers, held in 1934.

During the twenties, Fedin was able to stand apart from contemporary events, and to treat universal themes and motifs in his writings. But during the thirties, he wrote a series of publicistic articles: "Tema najdena" (1934), "Moja rabota nad romanom *Poxiščenie Evropy*" (1934), "Avtor i tema" (1936), and others in which he affirms that "bol'šie voprosy sovremennosti stali voprosami našej literatury".[4] In the twenties, Fedin had asserted the right of the artist to write about whatever he pleased, rather than to be obligated to treat contemporary problems. But a decade later he was writing of the obligation of the author to teach his readers about life.[5] Fedin's views that literature must be didactic and tendentious are evidenced in such major works and articles as the novels *Poxiščenie Evropy* (1934-35), which Fedin called "opytom raboty nad materialom gluboko sovremennym";[6] "Reč' o xudožestvennoj proze leningradskix pisatelej", in which he speaks of the need to create "razvernutyx kartin dejstvitel'nosti", dealing with "našu istoriju, geroičeskoe nastojaščee";[7] and articles concerning foreign writers, developing Gor'kij's theme "S kem vy, mastera kul'tury?"[8] It was in the

[3]   K. Fedin, Zapis' ot 6 Oktjabrja 1948 goda. Arxiv pisatelja.
[4]   K. Fedin, "Tema najdena", *Pravada*, 23 Aug. 1934.
[5]   K. Fedin, "O našej professii", *Literaturnaja Gazeta*, 26 June 1940.
[6]   K. Fedin, "Svidetel'stvo sovremennosti", *Literaturnyj Leningrad*, 20 Oct. 1935.
[7]   *Literaturnyj Leningrad*, 11 Apr. 1934.
[8]   K. Fedin, "Zapadnaja tragedija", *Izvestija*, 1 May 1934; "O Romen Rollane", *Literaturnyj sovremennik*, no. 4 (1938).

thirties that Fedin began to refer to the decisive influence of "idejnogo zamysla" on the "texnologičeskie priemy povestvovanija",[9] and to state that "našej literature svojstvenno ponimanie formy xudožestvennogo proizvedenija kak metoda razrešenija idejnoj zadači".[10]

It was during this new stage of Fedin's development that he began work on the novels *Pervye radosti* and *Neobyknovennoe leto*. Fedin's work is remarkable for the certainty and conviction of his creative impulses. His workshop was devoid of any manuscript variants of the novels, preliminary drafts are rare, and the manuscript bears little trace of changes. Only one draft was made of the final manuscript. "Na perepisannom èksempljare rukopisi ispravlenii očen' nemnogo, a na grankax korrektur ix počti net", Fedin wrote in 1930 when describing his manner of work.[11]

Yet the actual writing was always preceded by intensive preparation. Fedin's archives contain three large envelopes of draft materials. These include the plans for the two novels of the dilogy, the plans for several of the chapters, fragments of episodes, and brief notes containing "obryvki dialogov ... načal'nye frazy opisanij, xarakteristik".[12] Among the draft materials are to be found extracts from documents which served as source materials, correspondence with various persons, and only two manuscript variants of two unfinished chapters of the novels *Pervye radosti* and *Neobyknovennoe leto*. There is no other evidence that Fedin labored to revise his initial drafts as did, for example, Tolstoj, whose wife copied portions of the *War and Peace* manuscript five or six times. Many of the episodes in Fedin's novels lack any trace of preparatory work. Thus, ideas which impinged on the imaginative consciousness of the author were recorded in written form only during the actual writing of the single manuscript.

Study of the draft materials disclosed that Fedin begins to write only when the images which have taken shape in his imagination "ne dajut pokoja",[13] as Tolstoj phrased it. Fedin himself explained that the preparatory phase of his work varies, but it is always "... dovol'no dolgo. S momenta pojavlenija načal'nogo zamysla pervogo obraza do raboty nad samim tekstom proxodit mnogo mesjacev (*Transvaal'*, *Brat'ja*),

[9] K. Fedin, "Ne snižat' urovnja svoego iskusstva", *Literaturnyj Leningrad*, 8 Apr. 1936.
[10] K. Fedin, "Jazyk literatury", *Literaturnaja učeba*, 1933, no. 3-4, p. 111.
[11] K. Fedin, "Kak ja rabotaju", *Literaturnaja učeba*, No. 4 (1930), p. 114.
[12] *Ibid.*, p. 116.
[13] L. N. Tolstoj, Letter to A. V. Žirkeevič, 30 June 1890, *Literaturnoe nasledstvo*, Vol. 37-38 (Moscow, Izd. Ak Nauk SSSR, 1939), p. 418.

inogda god (*Narovčatskaja xronika*)."[14] The preparatory period for the novels *Pervye radosti* and *Neobyknovennoe leto* was of particularly long duration. From the moment when Fedin was first consciously aware of the idea for these novels until the writing of the first outline of *Pervye radosti* three years elapsed.

A. PRE-NATAL HISTORY OF *PERVYE RADOSTI*

The idea for the dilogy first came to Fedin, and matured, during the latter 1930's. The initial stimulus impelling Fedin to begin work on the new novels was a trip which he made to Minsk in February, 1936.

Я был в 1936 году в Минске, городе, который я совершенно не знаю и не знал тогда вовсе. Этот город удивил меня тем, что он состоял из двух противоположностей. Тогда в 1936 году, он был довольно типичным для наших больших городов: новые какие-то постройки, новая жизнь, построенная очень разумно и выразительно, а рядом как-то стихийно облепили все это мелкие домишки, дышащие старинным укладом. ... Была, изумительная зима. Снег лежал фарфором, обливающим весь город. Высились Дом Правительства, университет — очень эффектно — и тут же занесенные снегом мелкие флигелечки. Они гармонично вживались друг с другом. Была какая-то гармония противоположностей. ... Мне казалось, хорошо бы в таком городе позелить какую-нибудь молодую девушку, которая росла бы вместе с ростом этой новой жизни. ...[15]

In 1955, Fedin returned to a discussion of how he created the dilogy. Again referring to his 1936 visit to Minsk, he stated:

Я сделал тогда первые записки к будущему большому роману, который представлялся мне романом об искусстве, скорее всего о театральном искусстве, вероятно о женщине, актрисе, о ее развитии с детских лет ́до славы и признания. Ее родина, ее страна, ее искусство меняются, а с ними меняется она сама.[16]

In 1939, Fedin advised a correspondent of the magazine *Rezec*:

Начат большой роман в трех частях. Это — 1910, 1919, и 1934 годы. В романе будет отражен русский театр разных исторических этапов. Театр дореволюционной провинции, театр гражданской войны, театр наших дней.[17]

---

[14] K. Fedin, "Kak ja rabotaju", *Literaturnaja učeba*, No. 4 (1930), p. 118.
[15] From a speech by Fedin at the Central'nyj Dom Sovetskoj Armii, 26 May 1949, Stenogramma, Fedin's personal archives.
[16] K. Fedin, "Po povodu dilogii", *Oktjabr'*, No. 8 (1955), p. 156.
[17] S. Rom, "Pisatel' i èpoxa, Beseda s pisatelem K. A. Fedinym", *Rezec*, No. 11-12 (1939), p. 33.

B. CONCEPTION AND ACTUALIZATION

Attesting to this concept are the first two names of the novel, which are found on the title page of the manuscript: (1) *Šestvie akterov. Trilogija.* (2) *Aktery.*[18]

The main characters of the new work were to be actors. The central hero is a woman, an actress. Fedin intended to portray the fate of an actress from birth to maturity. It was for this reason that the image of Anočka impinged itself so forcefully on his artistic consciousness. Fedin's personal experience in the theatre played a crucial role in the choice of this theme.

Актерство, театр, я хорошо знаю и помню, а знакомый материал сам напрашивается, чтобы его ввели в сочинение. Легче всего писать о том, что знаешь, что имеется в собственном орыте.[19]

While selecting his *dramatis personae*, Fedin was also faced with the problem of choosing a suitable milieu in which they might live and act. For his setting Fedin chose the provincial city of Saratov, where he had lived during his youth and which he had visited in later years. But the choice of Saratov as the setting was not dictated only by biographical considerations.

В русской литературе сравнительно мало прикреплений к месту. Классики в большинстве избегали изображения конкретного города. Были изображены Москва, Петербург, Урал, у Мамина-Сибиряка и Волга у Горького. Провинция была всегда зашифрована. Читатель так привык не видеть конкретно названной провинции, настолько в русской литературе нет традиции этого рода, что как только изображается провинция, читатель ищет прототипов, что, конечно, неверно.[20]

Fedin had already written about Saratov in the novel *Brat'ja* and in the tale *Starik*, but only in general terms, characterizing it merely as a city on the Volga. Now he was to present Saratov in concrete terms, striving to portray precisely "každyj ugolok Saratova".[21]

[18] Fedin's own archives.
[19] From an address by Fedin at the Saratovskij gosudarstvennyj universitet im. N. G. Černysheskogo, 9 March 1949, Stenogramma, p. 2. Cf. Fedin's story "Ja byl akterom".
[20] From a conversation on 27 April 1951, reported by A. G. Berezkina, "Stanovlenie zamysla dilogii K. Fedina *Pervye radosti i Neobyknovennoe leto*", *Učenye zapiski kujbyševskogo gosudarstvennogo pedagogičeskogo instituta im. V. V. Kujbyševa*, Вур 19 (1958), p. 364.
[21] K. Fedin, Address at Saratov State University, 9 March 1949, Stenogramma, p. 4, from Fedin's own files.

Fedin considered setting the first novel in the early 1900's, since he was especially interested in the sources of the war of 1904-05. The progressive development of his work on *Pervye radosti* is attested in the following materials preserved in Fedin's personal files: (1) An early reference to the theme, (2) an outline of the nature of the theme of the proposed novels, in draft dated 31 August 1939, (3) an outline of the novel made in 1939, (4) a 1943 outline, (5) an outline of a group of chapters, 10-22, (6) a variant outline for chapters 12-25, (7) a variant outline for chapters 18-38, (8) a final outline of the novel — "razmetka glav", (9) rough outlines of various episodes, sketches and reflections of the author on the behavior of his heroes.

An early rough draft, written prior to 1939, reads as follows:

Старому актеру 63-64 года. Саратовский театр. Антреп. 1904-05 года (?) Молодой талант. Поклоники. Купчик Шубников. Очкин-Открыт-сцена. (Война с Японией?) Госдума? Извозчики-лихачи. Потом (годы реакции) Петербург. Слава. Тогда Н-мальчик. Детство-приют (или Н. приходское). Юноша агитатор-ссылка. Его подруга учительница. Ее миссия: работать для него.
Два характера   Мешков-смерть в 1919
    1919   Шубников 1910-1919, затем 1923
    1934 Шубников (Неп Козлов, 1926, Нижный 1930-32 — ссылка.[22]

The draft notes cited refer to the pre-revolutionary theatre in Saratov. Named as primary characters are an old actor, an entrepreneur, and a young talent. The time is indicated as the early 1900's. There are references to the Russo-Japanese War, the State Duma, and the "years of reaction". The first draft outline indicated that Fedin did not intend to confine himself to the milieu of the theatre. Among his heroes is listed a young agitator who, because of his revolutionary activity, will be exiled. Also listed is his girl friend, a teacher.

Of interest is the earliest reference to the girl friend of the future Izvekov: "Her mission is to work on him." In the role assigned to this heroine may be clearly seen reflections of the motif of sacrifice which was so characteristic of Fedin's earlier period.

The early draft refers to two characters from the merchant class, Šubnikov and Meškov, who later occupy a significant place in the novels. The first rough outline of the figure Šubnikov closely resembles the character who takes final shape as work on the novel progresses. In the early draft he is already a merchant, an habitué of the open stage in

---

[22] K. Fedin, Rough outline of the novel *Pervye radosti*, contained in the author's personal files.

Očkin's garden, later to be described by Fedin more fully in *Pervye radosti*.[23]

Also referred to in this early outline is Šubnikov's fate. Having lived through the 1917 revolution, he strives to adapt himself to the new life and to profit from it, which leads to his exile in the thirties.

Meškov's future is not yet revealed. Fedin only notes the date of his death — 1919. From this early draft outline, it is evident that Fedin planned to write a work in three parts, with the action unfolding during the first decade of the 1900's, in 1919, and finally in the 1930's.

During the process of development, the theme assumed greater depth. As Fedin himself says, he gradually came "K idee sozdanija kartiny nravov",[24] an idea which had become fixed by 1937, and is recorded in a note Fedin wrote in March, 1937.[25] The draft note of 31 August 1939 (item 2 above) is significant for it provides the outline of the theme of the proposed novels. It furnishes evidence that in the thirties Fedin had already determined to treat the "tema istorii", which was to be a distinctive feature of his work in the forties.

The 31 August 1939 note demonstrates that Fedin was thinking of creating a large epic canvas, a novel in three parts, depicting the life of Russian society in its historical development. Fedin characterized the theme of the new work in the following manner:

Замысел романа возник сравнительно давно. План романа подготовлен настолько, что, вероятно, сохранится без перемен, до конца работы. Книга будет состоять из трех частей. Действие первой относится к 1910 году, второй — к 1919, третьей — 1934 году. События, изображаемые в первых двух частях, протекают в богатом провинциальном городе. Я даю большое число действующих лиц, разнообразные круги общества начинающего подпольную жизнь юношу — революционера, рабочего жв депо, грузчиков, торговца, актеров губернского театра. Театр вообще будет занимать в романе существенно-важное место, потому что коллизия искусство и жизнь является одной из основ замысла.

В 1910 году протекает ранняя юность героя романа-революционера и детство героини-будущей актрисы. Здесь завязываются первоначальные отношения главных фигур романа — на фоне торгового русского города с его нелепыми богатствами и отчаянной нищетой. Театр с вечным своим стремлением отразить действительность будет показан здесь в образе российской провинциальной сцены и ее актерства. Героический год 1919-й будет дан в романе

---

[23]   K. Fedin, "Pervye radosti", *Izbrannye proizvednija* (Moscow, GIXL, 1947), p. 544.
[24]   Berezkina, *op. cit.*, p. 366.
[25]   *Ibid.*

как картины гражданской войны. Город обороняется от белых ... революцию защищают на фронтах. Все средства мобилизованы для защиты красного знамени, в том числе искусство. Баталии перемежаются тетральными представлениями в перерывы между боев. Самое жаркое и жизненное биение сердца сменяется отважной смертью. Героиня романа начинает свою большую судьбу в битвах против контрреволюции, в беззаветной службе Красной Армии и в первом волнении сердца на подмостах фронтового театра. Позади фронта ждет своей участи обороняемый город и в нем-глухая, подавленная надежда прошлого и непреклонная вера будущего.

Наконец — третья часть романа. Ее действие относится к 1934 году, и в ней я хочу дать синтез больших человеческих судеб нашего времени. Далеко позади осталась гражданская война, шествует, второе пятилетие побед социализма. ... Но последнего боя еще не было, враг таится по щелам, его укусы смертельны. Нити переплетенные когда-то в провинции, связаны временем и в Ленинграде. Путь замечательной актрисы по-новому пересекается с жизнью выдающегося большевика, со старым актером и былым провинциальным драматургом. Большая сцена ищет художественного выражения действительности. Искусство изучает жизнь как ученик, и в то же время поучает ее как учитель. ...

Я стремлюсь наполнить этот роман большим движением, связать его четким сюжетом, дать много характеров. Это должен быть роман нравов, в котором реалистические картины будут сочетаться с романтикой героизма.[26]

It is apparent that Fedin's ideas underwent a profound change during the thirties. He was no longer interested primarily in the theatre, but rather in a "kartina nravov". From his notes it appears that the idea of drawing a picture of the "čelovečeskix sudeb našego vremeni" matured in 1939. Fedin referred to this in print for the first time five years later.[27]

The central roles of the novel are no longer played by actors, but by a young revolutionary and a would-be actress. The first two parts of the novel were to portray epochs "kontrastnye po soderžaniju i tonal'nosti", as Fedin himself phrased it.[28] In order to portray the "kollizija iskusstvo i žizni", one of the basic themes of the novels, Fedin elected to portray a worker in a railroad depot and a young revolutionary on the one hand, and artists on the other. At first, Fedin only conceived the actor Cvetuxin as the representative of art. In his preliminary rough draft outline, there is as yet no reference to the theory of "iskusstvo dlja iskusstva", to be

---

[26] K. Fedin, Zapis' ot 31 avgusta 1939 goda, arxiv pisatelja, quoted in Berezkina, *op. cit.*, pp. 366-67.

[27] K. Fedin, Predislovie k glave romana *Pervye radosti*, "Na krasnuju gorku", *Literaturnaja gazeta*, No. 4 (25 Nov. 1944).

[28] Berezkina, *op. cit.*, p. 368.

personified by Pastuxov. The problem of the interrelationship of art and life was to intrude later.

Having decided to make his novel a portrayal of "nravov", Fedin felt compelled to include a portrayal of the "galax-gruzčik" Parabuxin, whom the "smešannyj poezd žizni privel v tupik, v meškovskij nočležnyj dom".[29]

"Parabukina ja izobrazil po dvum pričinam", said Fedin in 1951.

Саратов был похож на Самару (Недаром, всегда шел спор о том, кто является столицей Поволжья — Саратов или Самара). Выл похож и рисунок жизни этих городов. Саратов, как и Самара, был наводнен грузчиками. И в 900-е годы мне запомнились живописные фигуры грузчиков, галахов, оборванцев. Мог ли я уйти от изображения такого типа, задавшись целью дать картину нравов?[30]

In his early draft outlines of 1939, Fedin referred to his intent to depict "kartiny prošlogo", and these were to constitute the "sjužetnyj" skeleton of the first 13 chapters of the novel, *Pervye radosti*. A comparison of the outline with the published novel reveals that the draft outline of 1939 was composed when Fedin's concepts had already matured and crystallized. Thus most of the material committed to writing in the early outlines, or thoughts jotted down by the author on separate slips of paper and retained in his personal files, were, in fact, included in the final form of the novel.

In the draft outline of 1939, Fedin had so precisely delineated the roles and relationships of his heroes that further definition was not needed. Fedin's heroes, from the very beginning, were placed in characteristic and consistent settings and situations, with definite mutual interrelationships. Thus, in the draft outline, Kirill Izvekov is shown alongside Nataša (Liza) Meskova ("Vesna. Natasha končaet gimnaziju, Izvekov v poslednem klasse texničeskogo").[31] Nevertheless, Kirill also assumes the role of Anna's defender. He participates in revolutionary underground activity and falls ill with a "strannoj bolezn'ju". According to this outline, Kirill Izvekov is supposed to reveal his secret to his mother, since he suffers from lead poisoning. But in the novel itself, his mother does not learn his secret until Kirill is arrested. The lead poisoning serves as evidence for incriminating Kirill in the clandestine printing of revolutionary proclamations, which are found during a search by the authorities.

In the first outline Izvekov's mother is already conceived as a contrast

[29] K. Fedin, *Pervye radosti*, p. 328.
[30] Berezkina, *op. cit.*, p. 369, reporting a 7 Apr. 1951 conversation with Fedin.
[31] Outline of the novel from the personal archives of the author, cited by Berezkina, *op. cit.*, p. 370.

or opposition to Nataša Meškova's mother. Next to the entry in the draft outline in which Kirill admits to his mother that he "nabiraet v podpol'n. tipograf", is the entry: "Mat'. I drugaja mat' — Nataši Meškovoj."[32] Anočka's role is also clearly defined in the outline. She is shown in essentially the same situations, and she behaves in basically the same manner as in the corresponding chapters of the published novel. In the outline, for example, the following entry is found: "Anočka. Nočl. dom. Priezd Cvetuxina s dramaturgom. Vstreča s Pastuxovym. Dvugrivennyj."[33] "Dvugrivennyj za ščekoj u Anib. Poboi otca. Presledovanie. Izvekov — zaščitnik. Anja u Izvekovyz. Spor iz-za Ani (sud'ja, policija?)." "I vdrug ... Anja sama vosvraščaetsja v nočležku , k mame i k bratiku. ..."[34] In the process of further work on the novel, Fedin removed only such details as the "poboi otca", interference of the authorities in the quarrel between the Izvekovs and the Parabuxins over Anočka, and Anočka's admission to Izvekov in 1919 that he appeared to her "ne nastojaščim".

The figure of Cvetuxin as it appears in final form is similar to that of the original preliminary draft. He strives to get to know life itself so that he might properly portray it on the stage. In the outline, as in the beginning of the novel, Cvetuxin visits a lodging house, a "nočležnyj dom", where he meets the Parabukins. Then he rehearses his role in Gor'kij's play "Na dne" and, having become interested in Anočka whom he first saw in the wings, he "nabljudaet za nej". Only the figure of Pastuxov is missing from the early draft, although he appears in the first chapter of the novel.

As in the novel, the outline presupposes a separate chapter on the Meškovs. Fedin sets himself the task of portraying the development of this family: "Meškovy. Istorija materi i otca. Nataša."

Also referred to in the draft outline of 1939 is the "sjužetnaja linija", or story line, of Liza Meškova (Nataša), Izvekov, and Šubnikov. The thread of their interrelationships is the same as in the novel. Liza loves Kirill Izvekov, but she marries Šubnikov, whom she neither loves nor finds compatible. But in the draft outline Šubnikov woos Liza Meškova prior to Kirill's arrest, and on the same "noč', kogda u Meškovyx svad'ba", Liza "uznaet, čto Izvekov arestovan, i kogda ostaetsja s Šubnikovym-vse o nem, Izvekove-Sobač'i Lipki, vesna. ..."[35]

---

[32]   *Ibid.*, citing the outline in Fedin's personal files.
[33]   *Ibid.*, cf. *Pervye radosti*, Ch. 1.
[34]   Berezkina, *op. cit.*, p. 370, citing outline. Cf. *Pervye radosti*, Ch. 4, 8.
[35]   Berezkina, p. 371. Cf. *Pervye radosti*, Ch. 18, 22, 28.

In the outline, Fedin recorded his intent to portray Šubnikov's leave-taking of his friends prior to his marriage: "mal'čišnik" and "noč' ožidanija, slez Lizy". Later Fedin was to deepen the content of this collision and make it more dramatic. In the novel, Šubnikov's courtship and his marriage to Liza occur after Kirill is arrested. This change in the chronological sequence motivates Liza's experiences more effectively, and deepens her entire characterization.

The outline also fails to mention Petr Ragozin, Polotencev, or Oznobišin. The figure of Ragozin was introduced only after the idea of portraying a "kartinu nravov" had matured. Then the process of development of the primary characters, the communists Kirill Izvekov and Petr Ragozin, led to the creation of new, secondary characters, Polotencev and Oznobišin, who, in turn, motivated the development of new plot elements and situations.

Thus the analysis of the first draft outline reveals the nature of the process of artistic transformation as it applies to Konstantin Fedin. It appears that before Fedin actually began to commit his thoughts to writing, his consciousness had already transformed the raw material of life into the artistic form which it was to assume in his novels. Before writing, Fedin was able to visualize his heroes and their development through various situations. Konstantin Paustovskij, referring to Fedin's work on *Neobyknovennoe leto*, wrote in 1955:

Да простит меня Федин, что я решаюсь писать об этом. Но мне кажется, что манера работы каждого писателя, особенно такого мастера, как Федин, интересна не только для писателей, но для всех людей, любящих литературу. ... Невольно наблюдая за Фединым, я узнал, что он садился писать только в том случае, если очередная глава была строго обдумана, выверена, обогащена размышлениями и воспоминаниями, если она складывалась в сознании вплоть до отдельных фраз.

Федин, перед том как писать, очень пристально всматривался в эту свою будущую вещь, всматривался под разными углами и писал только то, что ясно видел, и притом в законченной связи с целым. Ясный, твердый ум и строгий глаз Федина не могли мирится с зыбкостью замысла и воплощения. Проза должна быть, по его мнению, отработана до безошибочности и закалена до стальной крепости.

Вся эта работа шла у Федина не во время писания, а заранее. Поэтому черновые рукописи Федина отличаются чистотой и малым количеством поправок.[36]

[36] K. Paustovskij, "Zolotaja roza. Kniga o pisatel'skom trude", *Oktjabr'*, No. 10 (1955), pp. 67-68.

After compiling his first outline in January, 1939, Fedin devoted a lengthy period to clarifying and refining his conception of the main heroes and situations. During this period Fedin did not concentrate exclusively on *Pervye radosti*. He wrote a number of other works testifying to the scope of his literary ability. Thus, while his ideas for the new novel matured, he wrote the following: 1937, the narrative *Ja byl akterom*; 1940, the short novel *Sanatorij Arktur*; 1940, a number of new short stories; 1941, the first part of the book *Gor'kij sredi nas*; 1942, the play *Ispytanie čuvstv*; and 1943, the second part of the book *Gor'kij sredi nas*.

World War II interrupted Fedin's work on the new novel. Then, in 1943, after having drawn up a second outline, Fedin began to write *Pervye radosti*, working uninterruptedly until its completion on 19 August 1945. On the title page of the manuscript are recorded the exact dates that Fedin began and ended the novel: "Vtorično. Načata 2 maja 1943 goda. Moskva (Pervye četyre glavy) ... Okončen 19 avgusta 1945 goda." [37]

It was during the war years that Fedin conceived and brought to maturity the idea of projecting the action of the third novel to the period of the war, 1941-45, rather than merely to 1934, as he had intended earlier.[38]

Konstantin Fedin writes about his efforts to make "vremja ... glavnym dejstvujuščim licom",[39] to portray "obraz vremeni".[40] Fedin later characterized his work during this period in the following manner:

Тема истории, выдвинувшись как главная, расставила кому по новым местам героев, перераспределила их вес и показала, кому где быть. Она поставила впереди других героев-людей, содержанием жизни которых было будущее нашей страны. ...[41]

In the second outline, drafted in 1943, Fedin opposes the life of the Meškovs and Šubnikovs to that of the Parabukins, Izvekovs, and Ragozins. As in the first outline, the majority of episodes involve Kirill Izvekov, to whom Fedin assigns the leading role. Fedin devotes a great deal of detail to the unfolding of the main story lines or sjužetnye linii: Kirill-Liza and Kirill-Petr Ragozin. The other characters occupy a subordinate position, emphasizing the social character of the novel.

[37] Berezkina, p. 373, citing Fedin's personal archives.
[38] Berezkina, p. 373. Cf. Fedin, "V Jasnoj Poljane", *Lit. Moskva* (Moscow, 1956).
[39] Fedin, "Naši plany na 1940 god", *Oktjabr'*, No. 1 (1940), p. 225.
[40] K. Fedin, *Sočinenija*, Vol. 1 (Moscow, GIXL, 1952), p. 18.
[41] Fedin, "Po povodu dilogii", *Oktjabr'*, No. 8 (1955), p. 157.

The 1943 outline also refers to the sjužetnaja linija "Cvetuxin-Liza" and to the first conflict of Liza with Šubnikov arising from their differing attitudes toward art, complicated by Šubnikov's jealousy. "Teatr v den' svad'by. Osen'. Šubnikov i Liza v lože: iskusstvo dlja nego i dlja nee-Cvetuxin."[42]

The problem of the relation of art to life makes its appearance in various forms in the outline. In the second outline, Pastuxov is cited as a partisan of the idealization of art, and the beginning of the polemic about art is recorded. The figure of Methodius also appears: "V gostjax u Mefodija (Parabukin i Meškov). Prixodit glava." It is during a visit to Parabukin that the reader first meets Meškov as a "glava", and also Parabukin, who is living in Meškov's lodging house. It is here, during the course of the dispute about the nature of art, that the figures of Cvetuxin and Pastuxov are delineated sharply.

Appearing in the second outline for the first time are the pictures of city life, depicting the general level of cultural development of a pre-revolutionary provincial city. Thus, in the outline, is the comment: "Universitet-tramv. (Nekotoryj pod'em v gorode, rost značenija)." Fedin intended to compose an entire chapter titled "Dvory, Ulica" and one titled "Dvor u Meškova".[43] In the novel, "Dvor Meškova" is portrayed in two chapters. It is shown circumstantially in Chapter 6, devoted to Meškov, and in Chapter 11, supplementing the earlier characterization. Fedin's personal files contain several drawings of Meškov's property, in which are portrayed the courtyard and buildings located thereon. These include Meškov's own home, the wing occupied by Petr Ragozin and Methodius, the wing with the clerks, and the lodging house. Also sketched are the school located nearby, and the Izvekovs' quarters, with a view from the yard to the docks, the Volga, Sobač'i Lipki (the boulevard Dogs Limes) and the other places in the city which are mentioned in the novel. This again demonstrates how thoroughly and in what detail Fedin thought out his material and how clear was his mental image of what he would portray in final written form.

The third outline of *Pervye radosti* includes the plot elements found in Chapters 11 to 21. This outline was compiled after the first ten chapters had already been written. Except for two references, the entire contents of the third outline were incorporated into the novel. Fedin rejected his original impulse to portray Cvetuxin as a skeptic (Znakomstvo s Cvetuxinym ... Raz'edajuščij skepsis uma ...). He also discarded one of

---

[42] Cf. *Pervye radosti*, Ch. 28.
[43] Berezkina, *op. cit.*, p. 375.

the aspects of the sjužetnaja linija involving Izvekov and Ana which he had recorded as early as 1939 ("Izvekova beret Anočku").[44] In these chapters, more than in the earlier ones, Fedin connects the fate of the individual characters to their participation in revolutionary activities. He also exalts the activist side of the revolution, as did Gor'kij.

The last two chapters of the novel are also referred to in this outline, demonstrating that Fedin had not only decided upon the skeletal structure, but also on its "sjužetnaja tkan'".[45] Thus the outline includes this comment:

Предпоследняя: следствию конец. Смерть Т-го. Последн: Кирилл в ссылке-зима, Лиза читает письмо из ссылки, плача. Беременна. ...[46]

Another comment reads: "poslednjaja: tjuremnaja bol'nica. Ksana Afan. rodila syna."

Fedin's wavering in the choice of the final scene was not without its motivation. In 1930, in the article "Kak ja rabotaju", he wrote:

Как драматург заботится о том, чтобы каждая картина пьесы была наделена постепенным драматическим ростом и кончалась каким-нибудь сильным заключением, точно также романист строит главы и книги своего романа, никогда не забывая об эффекте 'занавеза'.[47]

While working on the dilogy, Fedin did not forget this principle, but the "èffekt zanavesa" could not be achieved at the expense of the ideological theme of the novel, to portray the new superseding the old. In his desire to portray the positive side of his new heroes, Fedin wavered in his choice between Kirill's letter from exile, demonstrating that his will had not been broken, and the death of Ksana, carrying with her to the grave the secret of her fugitive husband's location, again testifying to the moral courage of the new.

In the final outlines, and in the novel itself, Fedin structures the last few chapters in such a fashion that they bring the fate of the main characters to a logical conclusion. Thus, in Chapter 35, he portrays the unsuccessful interrogation by Polotencev of Ksana, who is dying in the prison hospital. The outline, fully expanded in the novel, reads as follows:

---

[44] Berezkina, p. 376.
[45] Ibid.
[46] Ibid.
[47] Literaturⁿaja učeba, No. 4 (1930), p. 16.

"У Ксан. Аф., когда у нее послерод. горячка Полотенцев явл. в тюрем. больницу. Он обещает Кс. Аф. сделать все для ребенка. ... Спек ... на мечте Рагоз. о сыне. Знает о смерти первого сына — 1906 г."[48]

Chapter 36 furnishes a picture of the "bala-loterei", in which the prosecutor orders the termination of the Pastuxov affair due to the absence of incriminatory evidence. At the same time Fedin stresses Ragozin's role as the head of the underground revolutionary organization, still evading capture and continuing his clandestine activities. The next to the last chapter, Chapter 37, brings to a culmination Kirill's relationship to Liza, who has now reconciled herself to her destiny. Chapter 37 also reaffirms Kirill's readiness for further revolutionary activity. Chapter 38, the last chapter, is referred to in the two last outlines as follows: "Finale. Cvetukhin repetiruet. Anočku lovjat v zritel'nom zale ..."[49]

In Chapter 38 of the novel, Fedin portrays the "ot'ezd na pervyx sankax Pastuxova" to Petersburg, and his parting conversation with Cvetuxin at the railroad station, demonstrating that Pastuxov, as before, still remained firm in his resolve to stand aloof from politics. The chapter ends with the scene in which little Anočka is discovered in the theatre while furtively watching a rehearsal in the "samom bol'šom", "samom krasivom" building "iz vsex, kotorye videla Anočka".[50] Thus, in the last chapter Fedin united the motif of Kirill-Ragozin, that is, of the Revolution, with the motif of Anočka, who would personify the new art.

C. PRE-NATAL HISTORY OF *NEOBYKNOVENNOE LETO*

According to the title page of the manuscript, the second novel of the dilogy, *Neobyknovennoe leto*, was begun 2 October 1945 and completed on 27 August 1948. The pre-natal history of the novel may be studied in the following draft materials:

1. An outline consisting of four parts:
   a. "Načal'nye glavy", dated 2 October 1945.
   b. "Seredinnye glavy"
   c. "Predfinal'nye glavy"
   d. "Finale" (Ch. 32)

---

[48] Berezkina, *op. cit.*, p. 377, citing a variant of the outline of *Pervye radosti* in Fedin's personal file.
[49] *Ibid.*
[50] Fedin, *Pervye radosti*, p. 590.

2. A variant of the outline for the group of Chapters 19-29.
3. A variant of the finale in 7 chapters.
4. Another variant of the finale.
5. A rough draft outline of the "Finale finalov".
6. An outline "Razmetka glav romana".
7. Rough draft outlines of individual chapters and episodes.[51]

A change in the conception of the overall theme of the trilogy led Fedin to change the theme of the second novel long before he began to work on it uninterruptedly. For this reason the draft materials pertaining to *Neobyknovennoe leto* reflect that Fedin had decided to relegate the problem of art, originally conceived as central, to a subordinate position.

Fedin came to conceive of *Neobyknovennoe leto* as an epic work concerned with the birth of a new Russia, a work about a decisive period in Russian history. Examination of the draft materials discloses that Fedin was now concerned with breadth of theme, the significance of recent historical events selected for artistic portrayal, and concern with capturing the essence of the new Soviet man. According to Berezkina, Fedin's draft materials now show a preponderance of interest in the Revolution. "Krestjane protiv pomeščikov za svoju zemlju"; "Rabočie — protiv xozjaev za svoju sud'bu — osnova dviženija i fon vsego romana ..."; "Tema nadežd"; "Nadeždy večnogo mira"; "Nadeždy na to, čto narody ne pozvoljat, ne zaxotjat, ne dopustjat"; "Sjužet. Dviženie na Vostok (na Volgu) ot nemcev: bežency. Ranenye. Plennye nemcy (avstrijaki). Vozr. russkie plennye. Pobedy nemcev. Ix poraženie, ix krax."

Other motifs are "Intelligenty v rassloenii (Cv. Past.)"; "Učitel' v revoljucii (Izvekova)"; "Besprizornye" (Pavlik, Paška Parabukin); "Deti (syn Lizy, syn Ragozina)"; "Belye. Byvšie (Pastuxin, Meškov, Oznobišin, Šubnikov)".[52]

Fedin's interest in the portrayal of the positive Communist hero is reflected in these notes included in his draft papers:[53] "Bol'ševizm — kak otbor sil'nyx ... i žadnyx do žizni, sposobnyx povesti Rossiju ... k buduščemu"; "Geroj poslan v 1919 godu v Moskvu i popadaet v Kreml' k Leninu." In later drafts are comments which are closer to the novel as it appeared in final form: "Katorga i ssylka na svobode. Revoljucionery za delom — berem, čto nužno dlja buduščego. Kirill, Ragozin."[54]

Fedin felt a strong desire to portray a war hero returning from captivity

---

[51] Berezkina, *op. cit.*, p. 379.
[52] *Ibid.*, p. 380.
[53] *Ibid.*, p. 381.
[54] *Ibid.*

in 1919. Fedin proposed to begin the second novel with such a portrayal. "Nepremenno voennye! Oficer russkoj armii, tradicionnyj, geroičnyj, tragičeskij-perexodjaščij k krasnym ... (tema prisjagi, vernosti — v kollizii s temoj istorii naroda, kak istorii sem'i). Komy prisjagali, togo net. Ignat'ev." [55] Thus did the figure of Dibič originate.

The following notations are found on individual sheets in the early outlines:

I. "Начало. 1919. Герой возвратился из плена от немцев и учится понимать происшедшее и происходящее. Он ранен был при попытке бегства из лагеря, выздоравливает."
II. "Великая болезнь и перерождение, второе рождение каждого."[56]

Fedin proposed to make the "new man" the central hero of *Neobyknovennoe leto*.

III. "Новый человек — центральная фигура второго романа, им начинается вторая книга (офицер из плена)."

While working on the novel, Fedin discarded and re-emphasized much of his draft material. Thus he omitted references to those mutilated in World War I, and to German prisoners, and he did not develop the motif of the "učitel' v revoljucii". In its final form, Fedin made the central heroes of *Neobyknovennoe leto* the Communist Ragozin and his pupil in the ways of revolutionary underground activity, Izvekov. Fedin does not confine his portrayal of the "vtoroe roždenie každogo" to the officer Dibič only, but also portrays such a rebirth in Ipat Ipat'ev, Nikon, Strašnov, and others.

Ipat Ipat'ev plays a particularly significant role, symbolizing the people in a manner which recalls Lev Nikolaevič Tolstoj's glorification of the peasant in the person of Karataev. In the beginning of the novel, in the confused scene at the railroad station, Ipat, backed by the crowd, declares to Pastuxov: "Teper' bez našego učastija ničego ne rešaetsja, esli želaete znat'." [57] Pointing to Pastuxov and Dibič, Ipat announces to the railroad authorities: "Narod somnevaetsja", to which someone asks: "Vy čto že-narod?" Ipat seriously replies: "Narod ... Byl v bojax. ..." [58]

In an early draft, Ipat's role is defined as follows: "1919. Ipat. Dux bespokojstva-večnoe neterpenie neset v sebe na protjaženii vsego dejstvija

[55] Berezkina, *op. cit.*, p. 381, citing Fedin's personal archives.
[56] *Ibid.*, p. 382.
[57] Fedin, *Neobyknovennoe leto*, p. 14.
[58] *Ibid.*, p. 15.

(soldat, otvoevavšij na Karpatax ... izgonjavšij nemcev iz Ukrainy, etc.), tot geroj vremeni, s kotorym Pastuxov stalkivaetsja v pervoj glave i kotoryj v nem podozrevaet izmennika, perebežčika i, konečno, buržuja. (Trebovanie aresta, vmešatel'stvo oficera iz plena etc.)." [59] Ipat thus symbolizes the mass of "restless soldiers" who helped make the revolution and with whom Pastuxov finds himself in conflict.

Fedin also recalls Tolstoj in the way he introduces massive battle scenes into the novel. This is treated in the draft outline in the following fashion:

Церем марш вплоть до Царицын. Неудача под Царицын. Матросы в действии. Катастрофа отхода — Бой и ранение. Страшнов выносит Р-на. Дивизион прикрывает огнем отступление. [60]

In *Neobyknovennoe leto* can be perceived Fedin's deepened sense of history. By 1946, Fedin speaks not only of his striving to portray "kartiny nravov, kartiny byta kak slagaemye istorii", [61] but also of his consideration of the trilogy "kak na proizvedenie istoričeskoe". [62] Also, in 1946, when the *Literaturnaja gazeta* had published an extract from *Neobyknovennoe leto*, Fedin submitted the following preface: "Sud'by ljudej na fone istoričeskix javlenij — not kak bliže vsego možno vyrazit' avtorskij zamysel." [63]

On 22 April 1947, Fedin wrote:

Я ... представлял себе вся коллизию как политическую. Мне важно преломление сознания героев на фоне и под воздействием событий. Поэтому без знания исторических фактов я ничего не мог бы сделать. [64]

This striving to combine the personal fate of his heroes with historical events (the element of "historical concreteness" required by Socialist Realism) is apparent in all of Fedin's draft outlines. It is this approach to the problem of characterization which helps impart an epic quality to *Neobyknevennoe leto*.

[59] Fedin's personal files. Cf. *Neobynovennoe leto*, Ch. 26, p. 340.
[60] *Ibid.*, p. 384.
[61] Fedin, "Naši plany na 1940 god", *Oktjabr'*, No. 1 (1940), p. 225.
[62] Berezkina, *op. cit.*, p. 385, quoting the manuscript of Fedin's autobiography, dated 15 June 1946, contained in Fedin's personal files.
[63] *Literaturnaja gazeta*, 14 Dec. 1946.
[64] Letter to V. V. Višnevskij, from his personal file, quoted by Berezkina, *op. cit.*, p. 386.

VII

THE DILOGY

The novel *Pervye radosti* was first published in the journal *Novyj Mir*, Numbers 4-9, in 1945. Extracts from the novel, under the title "Na Krasnuju Gorku", were published in *Literaturnaja gazeta*, Moscow, Number 4 (1944), and in the Saratov *Kommunist*, Number 45 (1946). Another extract, "Na Volge", was published in the journal *Leningrad*, Numbers 10-11 (1945).[1]

The experiences which Fedin lived through in the war years, and his patriotic writings during that period influenced the development of *Pervye radosti*. The theme of art, which had been central in the original concept along with the fate of the actress, was subordinated to the story of the development of a new hero, Kirill Izvekov, Communist and "inžener buduščego".

Fedin writes that

... первоначальный замысел не умер, а, претерпев огромные изменения, остался жить в особом мотиве, в особой судьбе, тесно связанной с главным героем. Это судьба девочки, которая становится актрисой. Это мотив искусства. Мотив чистого, солнечного, снежного города, в котором новая действительность бурно проникает в ткань прошлого, уничтожая ее.[2]

Having expanded the scope of the novel from the portrayal of the personal life of an actress to an attempt to capture the spirit of the time, its historical significance, Fedin showed himself to be a mature artist and a master of prose, capable of creating epic literature. But it is obvious that he has undergone a transformation, accomplishing what Andrej Starcov was incapable of achieving in *Goroda i gody*, "načat' žit' snačala, raskatat' klubok, dojiti po nitke", returning to the beginning in order to "postupit' po-drugomu. Sovsem po-drugomu". Fedin again dealt with some of the problems which had troubled him earlier, but this time he

---

[1]   K. Fedin, *Sočinenija*, VI (Moscow), p. 507.
[2]   *Ibid.*, p. 509.

resolved them (or at least discussed them) in a somewhat different fashion, more in keeping with the demands of Soviet literary criticism and Socialist Realism.

This does not mean that he changed his literary method. On the contrary, the distinguishing features of his literary creativity become even more pronounced in the dilogy than in his previous works.

A. THE AUTOBIOGRAPHICAL ELEMENT

The question constantly arises as to the degree to which a novel like *Pervye radosti* or *Goroda i gody* expresses the actual experiences of the author, or, to phrase it differently, the extent to which the author and his characters coincide. Fedin addressed himself to this question in 1948, in a letter to a doctoral candidate who had inquired as to the proportion of fact and invention in Fedin's novels:

Ваш вывод, что большинство эпизодов, сцен, картин, и т.д. было видано, слышано и пережито мною ..., не верен. Нельзя говорить о большинстве случаев, лишь точка приложения силы, которую мы зовем фантазией. Вы, кажется мне, переоцениваете значение жизненных (фактических) познаний писателя по сравнению с его работой, 'сочинитля'. Вы умаляете вымысел. Сейчас, после окончания огромной дилогии, в общей сложности в 60 печатных листов, я оцениваю соотношение вымысла и факта, как 98 к 2-м. Конечно, я много знал и знаю жизненных фактов из русской действительности 1910 и 1919 годов. Но только оттолкнувшись от них в простор воображения, я мог сочинить людей, в жихни никогда мною не виданных, не встреченных, но как бы безусловно живших.[3]

Fedin points out that the novel is hardly the best genre for autobiography, adding that the center of the novel is not any particular character but rather its aim, its central theme. The author, he continues, "razdaet svoj žiznennyj opyt, vospolnjaemyj domyslom, gerojam romana, kak kompozitor razdaet golosa instrumentam orkestra".[4] Smirnova suggests that, from his own person and experience in life, Fedin extracts the essential features of the four heroes of the dilogy: Kirill Izvekov, Dibič, the writer Pastuxin, and the actor Cvetuxin. But, once conceived and having been assigned certain characteristic attributes, they begin to live their own life,

---

[3] K. Fedin, "Pis'mo aspirantu", *Pisatel', iskusstvo, vremja* (Moscow, 1957), pp. 509-510.
[4] Vera Smirnova, "O romanax Konstantina Fedina", *O Literature i Teatre* (Moscow, 1956), p. 29.

shaped by the historical past, and differing from Fedin's own, personal development.

Although much of the material for the dilogy was conceived or gathered prior to the second World War, it appears reasonable to assume that the advent of the war, with the resultant upsurge in the patriotic feeling of the Russian people (as of all participants, on both sides), had its effect on Fedin. The huge outburst of national feeling must have stimulated him to think in epic terms, to glorify the Soviet nation, and to portray its heroes as fighters for the Revolution.

B. AN OVERVIEW

When one reads a novel by a contemporary author dealing with the past. the question naturally arises as to why he chose a particular epoch, what was it that he had seen, heard, or read of an era now past which compelled him to re-create it for others. In some cases, the author may write in the spirit of historical research, or antiquarianism, creating a period novel which is a detailed re-creation of a past epoch, motivated by the author's sentimental fondness for the period. Others may write historical romances, as an escape from the humdrum, often baffling, present to the exploits of the heroes of the past. Some authors portray the past as a historical parallel to the present, and yet others stress the conflict between the old and the new.

Fedin's dilogy does not fit into any of these categories, although he does treat the past, discussing actual historical events. The reader cannot avoid the feeling that Fedin introduces the past to illuminate the present, and even the future. Fedin does not try to circumvent reality, but intensifies it. He abstracts the essential and enduring problems from mere contemporaneous circumstances. He does not favor the past over the present, and actually minimizes the use he does make of recent historical events and personages, thereby underlining his true sense of history.

When, immediately following the war, Fedin first published *Pervye radosti*, some Soviet critics greeted the novel as an escape into the past.[5] These critics failed to consider Fedin's overall plan for a trilogy, which, beginning in the past, would extend to the war years. Thus *Pervye radosti* was in effect a prelude to the epic which Fedin intended to write This explanation serves to clarify the selection of the name of the first novel, which was somewhat of an enigma to contemporary critics.

[5]   Smirnova, *O Literature i Teatre*, p. 29.

In it Fedin portrays Russian provincial life in the year 1910 in the old commercial center of Saratov on the Volga, a dusty, tasteless city. It is characterized by its merchants, its restaurants situated in the harbor or in the city where sterlet is featured, drunken Volga stevedores, clergy, actors, a visiting Petersburg writer, a theatre decorated in red velvet, the "fashionable" play *Na dne*, a philanthropic ball, and a "maevka".[6]

A student at the technical academy, Kirill Izvekov, a young man of strong character, upright, pure, and serious, lives in Saratov. But in the opinion of the city fathers and those in authority, he is an "isporčennyj mal'čik", one who holds revolutionary views.

The youth, with all of the agony and ecstasy accompanying such an attachment, is experiencing the "first joys" of love. The object of his love is the *gymnasium* student Liza, daughter of the prosperous hardware merchant Meškov. But there is unrest in the city, with the police investigating the activities of the professional revolutionary Ragozin. Searches are conducted throughout the city, and a search of Kirill's quarters leads to his arrest. He is first imprisoned, then exiled. Meškov forces Liza into marriage with the young merchant Šubnikov. Liza receives a letter from Izvekov, but by that time she is already expecting a baby and is unable to leave Šubnikov, whom she does not love.

This is the basic plot of the novel. Social, economic, political, and religious forces buffet the young lovers, extinguishing the flame of the "first joys". On balance, judging only from the external features of events, this first novel of the trilogy represents a triumph for the merchant Merkurij Avdeevič Meškov, the Old Believers, the procurator and police officer Polotencev. Kirill, at the end of the novel, is still in exile, the roustabout Parabukin is still living in ignominious poverty, and the fastidious playwright, Pastuxov, has the same outlook on art and life as at the beginning of the novel.

Nine years later, in the second novel of the trilogy, his freedom and his love are restored to him. Nine years later the reader meets him, and the other characters of *Pervye radosti*, in a completely different setting.

Neobyknovennoe leto is the story of the spring, summer and fall of 1919 which was, as Fedin explains in the epilogue to the battle scenes, "vysšaja točka naprjaženija v bor'be Sovetov ... na frontax graždanskoj vojny".[7] But the second novel is by no means merely a military history of the year

---

[6] In pre-revolutionary Russia, this was an illegal revolutionary gathering of workers on May 1st. S. I. Ožegov, *Slovar' russkogo jazyka*, 4th ed. (Moscow, 1960).
[7] K. Fedin, *Sočinenija*, Vol. VII (Moscow, 1961), p. 676.

1919, although many parts are devoted to an analysis of military actions, reminding of Tolstoj's analyses in *War and Peace*. Fedin seems to have been more concerned with the effect of contemporary events, of the Revolution and the Civil War, on individuals, on the development of the "new" Soviet man, on the conflict which resulted from the replacement of the old by the new, and the paths by which different individuals reached some sort of reconciliation with the new order, a struggle which was waged in every city, home, and individual.

The action of *Neobyknovennoe leto* takes place on and along the Volga, in Saratov, Voronezh, Kozlovka, Xvalynsk, and Tsaritsyn (later Stalingrad, now Volgograd), in the southwestern part of Russia. Here, in the 1670's, Cossacks, peasants and local non-Russian tribes under Stepan Razin revolted against the central government in Moscow, and, in 1918-19, Denikin's Volunteer Army, taking advantage of the widespread revolt of the peasants against the Soviet government, engaged the Bolshevik troops in the South and directed an offensive against Moscow.[8]

Fedin stresses the strategic importance of the southwest early in the novel. But even earlier, on the very first pages, he transmits to the reader a feeling for the *time*, the historical period when the action takes place. In the spring of 1919, one of the heroes of the novel, the former lieutenant in the Tsarist army, Dibič, returns from four years captivity in Germany. It is from his point of view that the reader first becomes acquainted with Soviet Russia in the third year following the Revolution. It is specifically for the purpose of having the reader sense the spirit of the time that Fedin makes him perceive all events and people through the eyes of one who, due to circumstances beyond his control, has been away from his homeland for four years. This is a classical example of "ostranenie", estrangement, a device in which the "author 'refuses to recognize' the familiar objects and describes them as if they were seen for the first time".[9]

Dibič is an honorable, straightforward, and loyal soldier, ready, without vacillation, to give his life for his country. But he is now faced with the problem of to which side to be loyal, to which cause to dedicate the remainder of his life.

Dibič is a member of the intelligentsia, and Fedin almost immediately confronts him with representatives of two other species of the intelligentsia; the old Russian intelligentsia, personified by the writer Pastuxov,

[8]   G. Vernadsky, *A History of Russia*, 3rd revised edition (New Haven, 1951), pp. 79 283.
[9]   V. Erlich, *Russian Formalism* (The Hague, 1955), p. 151.

and the new Soviet intelligentsia, in the person of the secretary of the city soviet, Kirill Izvekov. At first, as was to be expected, Dibič finds himself drawn to Pastuxov and his attractive family and, conversely, is somewhat skeptical of Izvekov. Pastuxov finds himself interested in Dibič as new material for literary creation. Izvekov, though, is portrayed as perceiving the raw material of the new Soviet man in Dibič, which motivates him to make an active effort to indoctrinate him with the principles of the Revolution.

Dibič is one of the few new characters in *Neobyknovennoe leto*, the majority having been introduced earlier, in *Pervye radosti*. In the second novel, those who had formerly been the masters of the situation become *byvšie ljudi*, former people, to use the title of one of A. M. Gor'kij's earlier (1897) works. They are deprived of their former influence and belongings, and are portrayed as enemies of the Revolution, hoping and conspiring for the return of the old order. Fedin depicts their end in rather gloomy terms. Typical is the capture and identification of the disguised police official Polotencev, who is unmasked and destroyed by the very same young man with whom he had played cat-and-mouse nine years earlier. The former merchant and patriarchal head of his household, Meškov, is also reduced to an ignominious situation when he is deprived of his wealth and finds himself a mere boarder in his own home. The merchant's son Šubnikov and the adjutant Zubinskij also lose their possessions and social status, while the former procurator's assistant Oznobišin is forced to take refuge in the protection provided by Liza, in her love, as he strives not to attract any attention to himself. Now it is the new element in society, the Bolshevik, who occupies the central position in the novel, and who monopolizes Fedin's attention and sympathy.

Fedin portrays various revolutionary types and various generations. Among them is the secret sympathizer, the non-party member of the intelligentsia, Dorogomilov, and old man who dreams of a better life, is ready to help the revolutionaries, an unselfish lover of books, art, and of every form of beauty, a companion to children, and even somewhat of a child himself. Fedin did not wish to temper the severe judgment of life against this solitary lover of books, and the old man dies amidst the books which served as a barricade, a shelter for both his apartment and for his life. "Ves' mir ego veščej, mir ego knig byl mirom neokončennym, slovno večnym. I nel'zja bylo ponjat' — začem že teper' èta večnost' končalas'?" But the words of Ragozin, pronounced over his grave at the cemetery, justify his existence. When the boys are engaged in a discussion as to a suitable inscription for his tombstone, Ragozin decides for them: "Nado prosto: Arsenij Romanovič Dorogomilov, revoljučioner."

Ragozin himself is a revolutionary of a different type. The Revolution is the basic fact of his life, his vocation and profession, and he gave himself unstintingly to it, as well as everything and everyone whom he held dear: his beloved wife, and his son who had been born in prison and whom he had not seen in many years.

Having been educated in the exacting school of underground revolutionary work, the Bolshevik-worker Petr Ragozin is a type which is not new in Soviet literature. Fedin portrays Ragozin as a simple, intelligent, resolute person, amazingly wholesome, movingly tender, and completely selfless.

While lying in the hospital after having been wounded at the front, impassioned by concern over his newly-found son, Ragozin says to Kirill Izvekov:

Думаешь ты о человеческих отношениях в будущем? ... Так вот, ты ищи такое в нынешней жизни, чтобы сейчас в тебе хоть немножко зажило из будущего, понял? Как бы тебе сказать? Ну, вополоти, что ли, свой план в живом человеке. В отношении своем к человеку. ... Чтобы практика была. А то ты будешь поклоняться своему желанию, скажем, коммунистического общества, когда еще общества такого нет. И привыкнешь поклоняться — желанию. А от человека отвыкнешь ... А ты его сейчас найди. Хоть немножко в человек найди от будущего. ... Тогда будет кое-что закрепляться из наших желаний будущего в нынешней жизни. Посев будет, понял?

Thus there arises within Ragozin a paternal interest in people, in whom he sees "nemnožko ot buduščego". Ragozin behaves like a father towards Kirill Izvekov, Strašnov, and the soldiers and sailors. Only in his relations with his own son does Ragozin find himself somewhat perplexed as to the proper way to conduct himself. As a positive hero Ragozin unites within himself the qualities of humor, interest in people, love for nature, simplicity, perceptivity, persistence combined with tenderness, intelligence, and the expressive speech of the Russian workingman.

In the person of Kirill Izvekov, Fedin attempted to portray the characteristics of the new generation of Soviet revolutionaries. Smirnova considers the portrayal of Izvekov to be the greatest success of the entire novel.

От этой небольшой крепкой фигуры, ... веет такой победоносной любовью к жизни, к ... родной земле, к людям, такой верой в будущее ... что невольно скажешь: вот это надежная опора! ... Этот молодой человек несет в себе уже какие-то новые черты — черты новой советской интеллигенции.[10]

It is indeed as a member of the new Soviet intelligentsia that Fedin portrays Kirill Izvekov and makes of him the central hero of *Neobyknovennoe leto*. There is nothing equivocal in Izvekov's characterization. He is shown as a young party worker, a fighter and a thinker, with broad vision, demanding the best of himself, subjecting his will to the most severe of iron discipline. In all of his activities he shows himself to possess the same monolithic character, whether at work or in combat, during a wolf hunt or at the theatre, before a revolutionary tribunal or possessed by a strong love for Anočka.

The future about which the communist heroes of *Neobyknovennoe leto* are so often thinking is personified in the novel by four boys, coming from varying parental backgrounds, but thrown together by the levelling influence of the Revolution: Aleša Pastuxov, Vitja Šubnikov, Pavlik Parabukin, and Vanja Ragozin. Despite the different social status of each of their fathers, and their sometime conflicting relationships, the boys are all close friends.

It is with particular brilliance and optimism that Fedin feelingly portrays this band of youngsters, their fights and their friendship, their playing at "kto dal'še dopljunetsja", their uninhibited childish views as to the life of their elders, their solicitous tenderness toward Dorogomilov, and their fearless relations with adults and with the symbols of authority.

Some of the most wonderful pages of the novel are those treating the activities and adventures of the children: the discovery of the Volga by little Aleša, Dorogomilov's garden, and the fishing expeditions. Here Fedin was doubtlessly stimulated in his portrayals by the memories of his own childhood, by the myriad sensations and the most detailed recollections of disconnected incidents from everyday life, which, taken together, provide the raw material for literary transformation such as are found in the accounts of boyhood of such Russian authors as Tolstoj, S. T. Aksakov, and Gor'kij.

Three types of women from the intelligentsia are portrayed in *Neobyknovennoe leto*: Izvekov's mother, the teacher Vera Nikandrovna; Liza Meškova, Kirill's first love; and Anočka Parabukina, the young actress who was to become Izvekov's wife. In opposition to them stands Asja Pastuxova, representing the woman of the past.

---

[10]   Smirnova, *O Literature i Teatre*, p. 36.

Fedin assigns a difficult task to Anočka, that of typifying the characteristics of the "new" Soviet woman. Fedin made her an actress, endowing her with talent, and then showing how she shared her talent, making it available to her audiences even though it meant lengthy separations from Kirill.

Problems of talent and of art always interested Fedin, and he tried to resolve them even in his earlier novels. But in *Neobyknovennoe leto* he poses the question in a somewhat different fashion, showing its inextricable relation to life and reaching conclusions consistent with Soviet ideology. Fedin does not present the "uncommitted" artists, the actor Cvetuxin and the writer Pastuxov, in a very favorable light. Cvetuxin is depicted as the type of artist who loves himself rather than art, and who thinks of other people only in terms of their constituting a public, an audience for his acting. His own wife, Agnija L'vovna, says that all the rest is "pritvorstvo i čush', Prosto on staryj lovelas! I bol'še ničego!".

Aleksandr Vladimirovič Pastuxov is a more noteworthy and complicated character than Cvetuxin. In him are found features considered by Fedin to be typical of many Russian writers at the beginning of the 20th century. Among these was an awareness of social shortcomings, but a reluctance to do anything about them, or even to admit their existence. Some writers simply remained aloof from the problems of the day, devoting themselves entirely to their art. "On sam inogda divilsja — oberegat' sebja ot neprjiatnogo: glaza ego ne ljubili smotret' na to, čto omračalo." In the novel *Neobyknovennoe leto*, this quality has crystallized to the point that Pastuxov consciously characterizes himself as "vne politiki", "nezavisimym xudožnikom".

Fedin does not portray Pastuxin as a very agreeable or sympathetic character. Pastuxov is clever, cold, and calculating, and, for the most part, devoid of inspiration. Fedin never shows Pastuxov at work, and in neither of the two novels does he create anything significant. He spends his time meditating about life, amassing impressions, analyzing his feelings, and engaging in similar "duševnaja gimnastika", as Smirnova calls it.[11] Pastuxin is rather secretive, not even disclosing his thoughts to his wife, despite the fact that he is fond of, and skilled in, conversation. Smirnova considers Pastuxov's wanderings and the course of his mental development since being uprooted by the Revolution to be a case study of, to borrow a phrase from A. N. Tolstoj, a "xoždenie po mukam" of the "internal emigration".[12] Pastuxov goes to such lengths to avoid

[11]   Smirnova, *O Literature i Teatre*, p. 39.
[12]   *Ibid.*

involvement in the Revolution that the Reds consider that he is one of the Whites, and the Whites, mistaking him for a Red, put him in jail. All his life, Pastuxov was concerned with maintaining appearances, that is, an air of accomplishment. But when he is thrown into a cell which is so crowded that one must await one's turn merely to sit on the floor, Pastuxin soon comes to doubt that he has ever achieved anything worthwhile.

Когда-то он слышал о занятиях в тюремных камерах: заключенние преподавали друг другу языки, проходили целые курсы наук. Проверяя себя: чем мог бы он поделиться, Пастухов обнаружил что, несмотря на разнообразие своих знаний, он ничего не знал до конца.

Pastuxov failed to see how he could help or be needed by anyone.

His perceptive wife Asja, who involuntarily reveals her husband's shortcomings every time she speaks, reaches the following conclusion:

Как блудный сын, когда он вернулся в отчий дом, мы с тобой тоже вольны вернуться. С повинной головой. Повинную голову не рубят.

VIII

THE THEME OF ART IN THE DILOGY

Fedin was always attracted by the question of the portrayal of the process of artistic creation. Treatment of this question necessarily involves such subsidiary questions as: How is the creative idea first born and how does it develop? What conflicts serve to stimulate the original idea?

Fedin's novel, *Brat'ja*, may be considered to be devoted to this theme of "the labor of creation". It was in this novel that Fedin first attempted to convey not only the internal characteristics of the biography of a creative artist — in the novel, a composer — but also attempted to penetrate into the intimate sphere of the creative process itself.

Fedin offers the reader the opportunity to be present at the moment of conception of the idea for a work of art, the "pervonačal'nyj impul's" of a melody. He reveals the psychology of the artist, his alternation between the heights of exaltation and the depths of despair, his groping searches, and his discoveries. The novel contains philosophical reflections on the nature and sources of a national art; the importance of tradition and precedents established by earlier native and foreign artists; the role of the artist in the Revolution; and, among others, the question of the extent to which the artist must sacrifice his personal life if he is to consecrate himself to the service of art.

These same questions are also treated in the dilogy where, almost from the very beginning, the reader is plunged into a setting consisting of the life and work of the actor Cvetuxin and the playwright Pastuxov and, in the second novel of the dilogy, of the actress Anna Tixonovna Parabukina.

This chapter will be devoted to the role of the theme of art in the plan of the dilogy and to an attempt to derive therefrom the theme of the dilogy as a whole.

Early in the dilogy Fedin confronts the reader with an argument between Pastuxov and Cvetuxin: Must the artist study life, or can he rely on phantasy alone, on artistic invention? This leads to the question: What is artistic invention? Is it purely the product of the writer's imagination, or is it drawn from the facts of actuality? According to one

Soviet critic, Pastuxov's reasoning is logically valid when he concludes that the artist must study life in order to understand the role of artistic inventiveness in literary creativity, but this does not help him understand current events. According to Grečnev, Pastuxov is curious about the wrong things, problems which are of no real import when Russia is on the verge of revolution.[1] Pastuxov and Cvetuxin, in the Soviet view, do not know life sufficiently, and they lack the convictions essential to successful resolution of the problems which lie ahead. They stand apart from the mainstream of life, and are thus destined to a stormy and contradictory life in coming years.

The theoretical argument which opens the first book of the dilogy is significant from a compositional standpoint. At the moment it occurs we may note the interconnection of all of the basic plot elements, the "sjužetnye linii" of *Pervye radosti*. The reader meets almost all of the main characters at this point, in effect the *noeud* of the novel, including the Izvekovs, Parabukins, and Meškovs. In the strict sense of the word, the argument over the relation of art to life directly involves only the actor and writer. Yet, in actuality, the other main characters, such as Kirill Izvekov, Liza Meškova, and Anočka Parabukina also participate, each in his own way.

Pastuxov and Cvetuxin take the position that their non-intervention in the political currents swirling about them will safeguard their creative freedom. More than once Pastuxov affirms that the artist should not mix in politics. It is only after a series of trials that both artists come to the conclusion that their difficulties are the result of their non-participation in contemporary affairs. At the end of the first book, when parting with friends, Pastuxov indicates his attitude both to the running argument about art, and toward life: "My sliškom mnogo, druz'ja, učastvuem v žizni soznaniem. Ja xoču vypit' za to, čtoby pomen'še učastvovat' v nej soznatel'no i pobol'še fizičeskoj."[2]

Cvetuxov appears to agree with this viewpoint. Just a moment prior to Pastuxov's toast, Cvetuxov, thinking about the unpleasantness of his dealings with the police, wonders aloud if their greatest sin was not one of omission, of non-participation in the revolutionary activities of which they were accused:

Мне казалось, что мы переносили это наше глупое дело по об-винению и прочее так тяжело, знаешь почему? Если бы нас привекли

---

[1] V. Ja. Grečnev, "Tema iskusstva v dilogii K. Fedina", *Voprosy sovetskoj literatury*, IX (1961), p. 396.
[2] Fedin, *Sobranie*, VI, p. 494.

не по ошибке, а поделом, за настоящее участие в деле, может, нам было бы легче, а. ... Ошибка-то была, может, в том, что мы не занимались тем, в чем нас обвиняли?[3]

Thus the argument about art plays an important role in both the structure and in the exposition of the central theme. It permits the early introduction, at one stroke, of almost all of the main characters and, at the same time, serves to clarify their attitudes toward life and art. It serves to define their position or viewpoints both in relation to one another and in relation to the central theme of the novel as a whole.

By setting forth a series of theoretical propositions in the very beginning of the novel, Fedin identifies the complex of problems which are especially bothersome to him personally, and which he intends to treat in his novel. A distinguishing feature of Fedin's novels has always been a preoccupation with the extent to which the artist should participate in contemporary affairs, and the mutual relationship between the problems of art and other social problems. At first glance, it appears that the quarrel about art consists simply of purely professional pronouncements by artists about the study of life, the nature of artistic invention, and similar questions. Then, almost imperceptibly, these discussions expand in scope, growing into very serious arguments on the reorganization of society, and the moral and ethical profile of contemporary man and the man of the future. The novel is constructed in such a fashion that all of Pastuxov's theoretical postulates are put to the test in situations in real life, not only in arguments with Izvekov, but also in clashes with the merchant Meškov, the police officer Polotencev, and the roustabout Parabukin. Fedin places people whose usual activities are little related to art in situations in which they must, in one form or other, express their views on art.

Early in *Neobyknovennoe leto*, as in the first novel of the dilogy, we find discussions and arguments about art, and again, as in *Pervye radosti*, these disputes transcend the realm of the purely esthetic, extending into the fields of politics and sociology. In the first novel, the reflections of the artists about the relation of art to life was an important device in assisting the reader to understand the central idea of the novel. In a like manner, the key to understanding the basic conflict of *Neobyknovennoe leto* is the discussion between Pastuxov and Dibič and, somewhat later, with Dorogomilov. Pastuxov strives to find a way in which he can participate in the stormy events of the Civil War. He strives to understand their meaning and to define his own position relative to the Revolution and the

[3] Fedin, *Sobranie*, VI, p. 494.

new conditions of life. Fedin painstakingly and progressively depicts, step by step, the tortuous path of the writer from his peaceful and comfortable studio, where he first found refuge long before the Revolution, to the tumult of the Civil War, from his protestations of non-participation to his eventual decision to support the Revolution.

Pastuxov is depicted as a vacillating intellectual in the beginning of *Neobyknovennoe leto*. "Ponjat' proisxodjaščee, — rassuždal Pastuxov, — mne mešaet osobennost' moego sklada ... vpečatlitel'nost' izlišne velika."[4]

The need and desire to understand what was happening became stronger with each passing day. Pastuxov felt this most of all in his capacity as a writer. The old was crumbling before his eyes, and it was difficult for him to understand the nature of the new. Only one thing was clear to him: that he could no longer write as he had in the past. Pastuxov "trudilsja prežde tak že neproizvol'no kak piščevaril. Teper' trud stal dlja nego mučitelen, potomu čto on ne znal, čto dolžen delat'. Smestilas' zemnaja kora, — mogla li uležat' na meste takaja kroxa, kak ego zanjatija?"[5]

In searching for an answer to the question of what was happening about him, Pastuxov, instead of confronting contemporary events, consulted history books, seeking analogous situations which might reveal the proper course of action for him to follow.

Of the numerous problems confronting Pastuxov in that stormy period, the most serious became that of finding his niche in contemporary society. Fedin writes that in a discussion with Dorogomilov, Pastuxov "... čustvoval, čto spor vlečet k tomu samomu glavnomu, o čem dumalos' s každym dnem bol'še i bol'še — o svoem meste v proisxodjaščem".[6]

The theoretical discussions and arguments about art, and the problem of the relationship of the artist to the Revolution, may be viewed as the main theme of the second novel of the trilogy. In other words, the problems of art which are the center of attention almost imperceptibly assume the character of profound social problems. Izvekov and Ragozin are characterized not only by their activities in the underground, or as participants in the Civil War, but also by their judgments and pronouncements on matters of culture, everyday life and mores (byt), morality, and art. To increase reader credibility, Fedin begins their cultural education long before the Revolution, when Izvekov, for example, participates in

[4] Fedin, *Sobranie*, VII, p. 37.
[5] *Ibid.*, p. 138.
[6] *Ibid.*, p. 171.

polemics with Pastuxov and Cvetuxin regarding the theatre, the "laws" of art, or Tolstoj. In a like manner, Ragozin's intellectual and cultural interests are also stressed. Thus, even during the most trying period, when he was sought by the police and threatened with penal servitude, Ragozin read voraciously, and the numerous books he read while concealed in Dorogomilov's many-tomed library left their imprint.

Fedin painstakingly develops Pastuxov, signalling changes in his outlook by a multitude of tiny details and incidents, rather than by a monumental and sudden conversion to the revolutionary cause. One of the indicators is his relation to the other characters of the dilogy. Thus, again long before the Revolution, Pastuxov carefully studied young Izvekov, and even then had begun to change his attitude toward him. In the beginning, Pastuxov's attitude was somewhat derisive and patronizing, but by the time he is leaving Saratov, at the end of *Pervye radosti*, Pastuxov, apparently with Izvekov in mind, says to Cvetuxin:

У всех у нас ... выпадают дни, когда с утра до вечера ищешь, что бы такое поделать? И то за стихи возьмешься, то к приятелю сходишь, то с какой-нибудь барынькой поваландаешься. Гладишь — пора на боковую. Иногда я боюсь, что так и состаришься. А где-нибудь неподалеку от нас кто-нибудь делает наше будущее. Сквозь дикие дебри, весь изодравшись идет к цели.[7]

The further evolution of Pastuxov's views is depicted in *Neobyknovennoe leto*. He was obliged to leave revolutionary Saratov following eviction from his home. Insulted and angry, he decided to move to Balashov. Upon being advised that Balashov was occupied by the Whites, Pastuxov replied: "V našem položenii bezrazlično — kakie. Raz menja do ètogo doveli, nam nužen dom. ..."[8]

It would be difficult to identify all of the different events and incidents which acted upon Pastuxov in converting him, over a period of a decade, to the revolutionary cause. Yet certain factors contributing to this con-conversion do stand out. Among the most salient are the interest in culture and art which Fedin attributes to his Communist heroes, Izvekov and Ragozin, and the measures taken by them in this regard, such as their concern over the fate of Dorogomilov's rich library; their interest in artistic creativity; and their patient and even respectful attitude toward Pastuxov himself. But the final blow was struck by General Mamontov, by whose orders Pastuxov is imprisoned. It is while in confinement that

---

[7] Fedin, *Sobranie*, VI, p. 494.
[8] *Ibid.*, VII, p. 354.

the final decision is made, and it is upon his release that Pastuxov informs Asja:

Мой выбор окончателен ... я сделал его там, в местном филиале Дантова ада. Решил, что если останусь в живых — первое, что сделаю, напишу Извекову, что я был олух. И Дорогомилову тоже. Чтобы знали, что я не белогвардеец.[9]

In *Pervye radosti* discussions and judgments about art are limited primarily to the artists themselves. These deliberations are confined to a rather narrow circle, and are generally held while leisurely sipping drinks, accompanying this activity with judgments of the classical masters, or the witty paradoxes pronounced by Pastuxov.

In *Neobyknovennoe leto* conversations regarding art assume a somewhat different character, becoming more general. Not only the writer Pastuxov and the actor Cvetuxin participate in these discussions, but also the party worker Izvekov, the director of finances Ragozin, and the young student of acting Anočka, daughter of the stevedore Parabukin. In the first novel of the dilogy, the young people, such as Kirill and Liza, are only involved in art as spectators. In the second, children participate actively, contributing to an exhibition of children's drawings. The tendentious function of art is stressed when soldiers going to the front comment to Anočka, now an actress, that "takie zamečatel'ny pred-stavlenija, kak *Kovarstvo i ljubov'*, ešče krepče zakalili ix volju k pobede".

In the earlier novel, *Brat'ja*, art was somewhat isolated from life, and the artist stood apart from society, his family, and love. In that novel Fedin spoke about the "tragičeskom odinočestve" of the artist, and about the "tragedijnosti" of art. Later in the dilogy, Fedin offers a different outlook, affirming the participation of art and of the artist in every aspect of life, of the power and influence of art on people, of its necessity, and of the joy of the artist himself in creating a work of art.

It is significant that in *Neobyknovennoe leto* Pastuxov again refers to the "tragedii xudožnika". But it is precisely because the tragedy is "proti-vopokazana Pastuxovu" that this may be considered as intended by Fedin to be ironic.

Despite any reluctance he may have felt about dealing with the problem of manner, as distinct from matter, in a work of art, Fedin does refer to questions of artistic method, composition, and style. In the novel *Pervye radosti*, Pastuxov, a writer, views the problem of how to create a work of art in the following terms:

[9]   Fedin, *Sobranie*, VII, p. 557.

... Надо ли действительно знать, как делается искусство? Знал ли это Бальзак? Не в том ли секрет его победы, что он вселял душу в две тысячи своих перзонажей, не отдавая себе отчета, по каким законам он их создает? Не напрасно ли биться в поисках законов искусства? Они не существуют. Они воплощены в действии. Если искусство действенно, оно закономерно. Если оно мертво для восприятия, какой закон сможет его оживит?[10]

Pastuxov expresses the view that the mode of existence of a work of art is a function not of the artfulness of its structure, but of the impression it makes, the degree to which it "infects", as L. N. Tostoj put it. Thus, while composing a play and leafing through the pages of Balzac, Pastuxov thinks that Balzac

как никто другой понимал природу искусства, заключающуюся в качестве воздействия произведения художника, а не в качестве выделки самого произведения.[11]

In developing the ideas of his characters, Fedin seems to be standing in the wings, eavesdropping on the words and thoughts of the *dramatis personae*, who appear to express the "dilogija duši" of the author himself. Indeed the "kačestvo vozdejstvija" always comprises the major concern of the artist. But does not the force of this quality, the degree of infection, depend on the quality of "vydelka"? Fedin, in treating the theme of art in its extrinsic aspects, finds it expedient to consider as well its intrinsic aspects, what Professor Roman Jakobson calls "literaturnost'", or "literariness ... i.e., that which makes of a given work a work of literature."[12]

Contrary to the idea expressed by Pastuxov regarding the absence of any laws in art, or the freedom of the artist from accountability (affirmed earlier by Puškin), a distinguishing feature of Fedin's craftsmanship is his conscious concern over the "priroda iskusstva", his preoccupation, in his later novels, with purpose. He considered the "cel', ideja, zamysel" to constitute the center of the novel. And his treatment of his themes, regardless of their complexity, is usually accomplished in a harmonious fashion. All of his works, whether novel, short story, or newspaper article, are distinguished, above all else, by their construction, by the

[10] Fedin, *Sobranie*, VI, p. 330.
[11] *Ibid.*, p. 329.
[12] Roman Jakobson, *Novejšaja russkaja poèzija* (Prague, 1921), quoted in V. Erlich, *Russian Formalism* (The Hague, 1955), p. 146. The extrinsic and intrinsic studies of literature are discussed in R. Wellek and A. Warren, *Theory of Literature* (New York, 1942), Sections III and IV.

harmonious proportions of their component parts. Fedin's skill at composition is one of his greatest strengths as a writer, and will be treated in
the next chapter.

In Fedin's novels, art serves another purpose, which is to assist in the
delineation of character by means of depicting each hero's attitude
towards art. In the dilogy there is no major character who, to some
degree, does not demonstrate his attitude towards art. In some instances
this may be no more than an expression of opinion about a particular
book, a play, or about the personality of an artist.

The theoretical polemics involving Pastuxov, Cvetuxin, and Izvekov
help the reader understand these characters as unique and separate
personalities. Tsvetuxin is a somewhat artless and simple individual, not
particularly calculating, and basically good. Pastuxov represents a more
aristocratic type, more sophisticated and worldly, but basically a man of
principle. Izvekov is characterized as a person of strong convictions,
rationalistic in the main, but sometimes overly serious and somewhat
coarse. A great deal is revealed of Liza Meškova's character by her
attitude toward the theatre and how she reacts to plays. It becomes
apparent that Liza is much more serious and has more depth than her
husband Vitjuša Šubnikov. While she is completely enraptured by the
play, *Hamlet*, her husband continually annoys her, trying to persuade her
to leave. "Oxota mučit'sja radi Gamleta. Ne my, v samom dele, dlja
Gamleta."[13] The theatrical performance enables the reader to conclude
that Liza is a tender-hearted and sensitive woman. In trying to defend
Cvetuxin's acting from Izvekov's criticism, Liza

... бросилась к Цветухину. Бледная, с протянутой вздрагивающей
рукой, она остановилась перед ним, на мгновенье словно потеряв
речь. На щеке у нее, как у ребенка, были размазаны слезы.[14]

The merchant Meškov's character also assumes greater clarity as the
result of his judgments of the theatre. All of his life he has been striving
to accumulate money so that he could occupy a higher socio-economic
position. And now, when he learns that there is to be a theatrical
performance of the play *Na dne*, he cannot suppress his agitation:

Люди изо всех сил стараются на поверхности удержаться, а театр
тянет на дно. Сочиняют невесть про что. Разные там Пастуховы.
Жизни не знают.[15]

---

[13]   Fedin, *Sobranie*, VI, p. 388.
[14]   *Ibid.*, p. 244.
[15]   *Ibid.*, p. 239.

The procurator's true nature is also revealed through his attitude towards art. At first blush it appears that this staunch upholder of law and morality is an educated and cultured individual. But when he engages in a conversation with the law clerk Oznobišin about the books he has read, it becomes clear that the procurator does not read a thing.

С тех пор, дорогой мой, как мне прописали очки, чтение дел стало для меня гораздо труднее. Надену очки — клонит ко сну, представьте себе. Сниму — ничего не вижу.[16]

A few paragraphs further his character is revealed even more fully, disclosing a hitherto unsuspected side, as he explains to Oznobišin that in the past he was fond of reading:

Я как-то, еще до очков, прочитал роман ... не могу вспомнить автора. Из новых. Но название запомнил: *Девственность*, знаете ли. Очень смело. И легко, с интересом читается. Там, видите ли, одна девушка. ...[17]

It would be difficult to name another Soviet writer who, as consistently, penetratingly, and effectively as Fedin, dealt with the theoretical, philosophical, and esthetic problems of art, as well as with the very concrete problems of artistic creativity. Fedin is notable for his persistent efforts to re-create the atmosphere surrounding the work of the artist and his "tvorčeskuju laboratoriju".

In summation, the theme of art is one of the central and persistent themes in Fedin's work. No evaluation of Fedin's importance as a writer could afford to overlook his unceasing preoccupation with the theme of art and the role of the artist, universal themes of eternal import.

[16] Fedin, *Sobranie*, VI, p. 279.
[17] *Ibid.*

IX

STRUCTURE

In his essay "O masterstve", Fedin compares the composition of a literary work to the plan of a house. After first characterizing artistic literature as the art of the word, stressing the primacy of language, its importance as the raw material of literature, Fedin attributes secondary importance to "načalo literaturnoj formy, kak kompozicija ...".

Из негодного леса (language) нельзя выстроить хорошего дома, хотя хороший дом не всегда бывает удобным: это зависит от плана (composition), а не от добротности леса. Однако что толку в удобном плане, если жилые стены не держат тепла?[1]

Perhaps the major shortcoming of this simile is that the plan for a home, although admitting minor variations, is more rigid than the compositional plan, or outline, of a literary work. Yet despite the greater flexibility of the literary outline, the skillful author must never lose sight of his overall aim and how the various segments of the work will combine to achieve it. Every episode, the entrance and exit of every character, the introduction of every new character, every variation on the theme, must all be carefully planned in advance. It is this element which creates the impression of harmony and balance in a novel, which Fedin, unlike, for example, Dostoevskij, not only understood, but took pains to actualize.

While still a young writer, Fedin was assigned by a publisher to prepare an abridged version of Victor Hugo's *Les Misérables*, for children. His task was to reduce eighty-eight printed pages to eight! Fedin recalls this incident as agonizingly difficult, yet useful, because here, for the first time, he was obliged to confront unequivocally the complex problems of language and composition. From the very beginning of his career as a writer, Fedin devoted a great deal of attention to composition. "Kompozicija — samaja trudnaja na svete vešč'", he wrote to Gor'kij after having completed the novel *Goroda i gody*. At the same time, he complained that

[1] K. Fedin. "O masterstve", 1951, in *Sobranie*, IX, p. 570.

"vsjakaja lišnjaja kostočka torčit i vypiraet korjavoj strelkoj".[2] In time the "superfluous ribs" were to become fewer and fewer.

In *Goroda i gody*, and to some extent in *Brat'ja* and in *Poxiščenie Evropy*, Fedin's plots may be categorized as adventure plots, motivated externally. This is not applicable to the dilogy, where the plot is developed in a natural, organic fashion, not by means of external impulses, but rather by the internal logic of development of the characters of the heroes, and their interrelationships. "Geroi sami složili ètot sjužet, drugogo oni složit' ne mogli", explained Fedin in one of his analyses of the dilogy.[3]

The grand design of Fedin's last three novels is actualized over a considerable period of time, and it is just this time element which contributes to the accomplishment of that design, to capture the historical essence of the entire spoch. In the third novel, which is devoted to the period of the Second World War, 1941-1945, there is a chapter devoted to Yasnaja Poljana, L. N. Tolstoj's estate.[4]

The figure of Lev Tolstoj takes on a new meaning in the trilogy. The "Theme of Tolstoj", which is encountered episodically in *Pervye radosti*, is to come to full fruition in the last novel of the trilogy, specifically, in the second part of the last novel, not yet published.

Did Fedin know, when he began the first novel of the trilogy, exactly how he would develop the "tema Tolstogo" in the last novel? Probably not, insofar as the exact details were concerned, although he must have had a general idea of his objective, formed during the pre-World War II period. But it was during and after the war years that his ideas matured to the point that he could conceive of the final outline of the third volume of the trilogy.

An author's grand design is not a firm scheme, like a draftsman's sketch, calculated with precision and checked and cross-checked, so that a building or a machine may be constructed from it. Yet, when all else is subordinated to the accomplishment of that grand design — the choice of materials, the means of representation, the composition, and the

---

[2] Brajnina (1951), p. 264.

[3] *Ibid.*

[4] As of the time of writing this study, the third novel, *Koster*, had not yet been completed. Only the first part has been completed, and was received in published book form in 1963. No detailed analysis of the third novel is attempted in this study on the basis that it would be premature, pending publication of the second half. The proposed chapter, "V Jasnoj Poljane", was published in *Literaturnaja Moskva*, 1956, pp. 7-38. Prior to publication in book form, the first part of *Koster* appeared in installments in *Novyj Mir*, No. 8-12 (1961).

scope — then, as in the case with Fedin, the book is noteworthy for its "structure", defined by Warren and Wellek as the "concept including both content and form so far as they are organized for aesthetic purposes".[5]

In the discussion of Fedin's earlier works, specifically *Goroda i gody*, reference was made to Fedin's skill in arranging scenery and players in the psychologically powerful *mise-en-scène*, evidence of his compositional skill. This skill is also evident in *Neobyknovennoe leto*, testifying to the high level of Fedin's craftsmanship. Characteristic is the scene in which Dibič and Kirill Izvekov meet in the office of the municipal party executive committee. They are seated opposite one another at a table. Kirill is reminding Dibič that they are old acquaintances. In 1916, on the German front, Lieutenant Dibič had dispatched a certain Private Lomov on a dangerous reconnaissance mission, risking death. It turns out that Lomov and Kirill Izvekov — are one and the same person!

Now the details of past events come crowding into Dibič's mind: the expectation of attack at night, the reports of the company commanders assembled in his dugout, the derogatory report of the commander of the Sixth Company about the revolutionary speeches of Private Lomov, and the order to send him on the dangerous reconnaissance mission. Dibič could hear the small-arms firing, and learned after an hour that the mission had succeeded, that an enemy soldier had been captured for further interrogation, and that Lomov had distinguished himself by his bravery.

The center of attention shifts imperceptibly, and the reader now sees Lomov on reconnaissance, follows behind him, and, as it were, is briefed by Lomov himself about his experiences. There is another subtle shift of attention, and Dibič is now seen again, this time interrogating Private Lomov alone in the dugout. The conversation assumes the character of a violent verbal duel between the two men, and Private Lomov unexpectedly gets the better of his commander. Then the action again shifts back to the office of the municipal party executive committee, as Dibič comments: "Vot kuda privela vas sud'ba."

They continue the discussion begun three years earlier, only now they have reversed their relative positions, "peremenilis' mestami".

Fedin forces the reader to eavesdrop first on one, then on the other of the disputants, shifting point of view, and moving from the present to the past and back again. The reader is made to sense the "peremeny mest" in an almost physical fashion, so palpable do Fedin's portrayals become. Finally, toward the end of the discussion, when Dibič, because of fatigue

---

[5]   Warren & Wellek, p. 129.

and hunger, loses his temper, the reader can almost feel the nervous trembling which follows these dizzying transitions from one situation to another.

This episode well illustrates Fedin's skill as regards complex composition, his keen insight into human psychology and motivation, and his precise use of language to create images.

Another episode outstanding for its construction is that in which Dibič is killed. Izvekov has authorized him leave from the detachment so that he could visit his home, which is nearby. Fedin portrays the happy, carefree Dibič on horseback, riding along through the woods along a road he has known since childhood. Then, suddenly, beginning with the phrase "Doroga perešla v tropu", the entire surroundings imperceptibly change. A mood of gloom and alarm is created, filling the reader with foreboding, with a sense of some evil about to take place.

"Неклен сплетался над ней сплошным низким сводом. ... Ветви бурно зашумели. ... Лошадь вздрогнула. ... Дибич расстегнул кобуру револьвера. ..."[6]

It appears that Dibič is lost, that he has wandered onto a path which will lead to destruction. Smirnova attaches an illuminating, because revealing the nature of soviet criticism and literary interpretation, symbolic meaning to this episode.[7] She emphasizes that Dibič has strayed from the way of the Red Army, from his idenfification with Kirill, onto a tangled path seductively leading back to the old order, to the distant past. The moral here is that it is so easy to detour from the approved course, and to follow a lonely, quiet footpath which leads to the old, the family home. One need only take the first step along this isolated path to the past, to the pre-war, pre-revolutionary period of one's youth to be doomed, rejected by life.

Fedin's first novel, *Goroda i gody* (1924), testifies to the importance which he attached to problems of structure and composition. In that novel, Fedin experimented with both composition and language, and it was not until the 1930's that his work began to demonstrate the clarity and simplicity of composition and style which was to characterize his later writings. This compositional simplicity is found in the arrangement of his materials, the logical consecutiveness of events, and the movement from episode to episode and chapter to chapter within each novel of the trilogy, and throughout its structure as a whole. Every episode, scene,

[6]   K. Fedin, *Sočinenija*, VII, p. 519.
[7]   Smirnova, pp. 54-55.

and moment is not only presented as an organic entity by itself, but is related to the others in an integrated whole. Each episode unfolds like a link in a chain of events which, in conjunction with all the other links, creates a moving picture of the flow of life itself. The internal structural union of the separate episodes suggests the logic of actual events succeeding one another on a time base, with the progressive revelation of the characters of the *dramatis personae*. Characteristic of the novels of the dilogy is the absence of any superfluous, or even transitional episodes, and it may be safely stated that all episodes advance the main action. It is as if Fedin were constantly aware of Čexov's admonition regarding the drama, to the effect that if a gun hanging on a wall is visible to the spectators during the first act, it must be fired before the end of the play.

The novel *Pervye radosti* illustrates Fedin's abhorrence of superfluous material. It is distinguished by its lack of a lengthy exposition and in the very first act the reader is immediately plunged into the milieu of the novel. The time and place in which the action is set are established at the outset, and the reader meets the main heroes. Provincial Saratov, with its crooked lanes of wooden houses, serves as a sharply contrasting setting for the carriage from which the two artists, Pastuxov and Cvetuxin, attired so incongruously, alight in front of the decrepit lodging house. Thus, in the very first chapter, the reader meets the artists and the members of the Parabukin family. The second chapter, which furnishes considerable background information regarding Pastuxov and Cvetuxin, although interrupting their visit to the doss house, brings the actor and the playwright closer to the reader and explains their strange excursion. The end of the third chapter — the flight of barefooted Anočka Parabukina from her father — is organically linked to the beginning of the following chapter — the appearance of Kirill Izvekov. By the end of the fourth chapter the reader has met all of the leading characters of the novel. Through a series of swiftly-developing episodes in the first fifteen pages of the novel, the reader is able to perceive the basic personality and character traits of the main actors: Kirill's quiet strength, steadfastness, faith in himself, and concern for the future; Pastuxov's theatrical posing; and Cvetuxin's easily aroused passions.

In the fifth chapter Meškov, in Mefodij's "fligel'" or cottage, first meets Pastuxov, Cvetuxin, and Parabukin. Fedin introduced this scene for a good reason: it is needed not only as a device for depicting these characters in bolder relief, but also for the subsequent development of the action. In the twentieth chapter, Polotencev reminds Meškov that he had met Parabukin while in the company of Pastuxov and Cvetuxin. In the

25th and 26th chapters, this meeting affords Polotencev the opportunity
of accusing Pastuxov of having passed revolutionary handbills to
Parabukin at that meeting. When interrogating Parabukin, Polotencev
tries to determine "začem priezžali v nočležku Cvetuxin s Pastuxovym,
čto oni trebovali ot Tixona i s kakoj cel'ju xodil on k nim vo fligel' Mefodija".[8] Thus these two episodes — in the doss house and in Mefodij's
cottage — become a mainspring, a motivating force, for the further
development of the action, and they unite subsequent episodes and
collisions. But the episode of the visit to the doss house fulfils yet another
function. It presents for resolution, in a natural manner, the problems
of art, and motivates the argument between Cvetuxin and Pastuxov about
the contemporary (1910) functions and roles of artistic creativity. Nor
is it forgotten significantly later, when Pastuxov and Cvetuxin meet again
and renew their discussions in 1919, in the second novel. It is clear, then,
from this brief consideration of only two of the earlier episodes of the
novel what complex and multifaceted functions are assigned to them by
the author.

The next two chapters, the 8th and 9th, introduce the reader to the
story of the early joys of the blossoming of the love of Kirill and Liza for
each other. At this point, Fedin penetrates the inner, psychological world
of adolescence. The action in the 8th and 9th chapters shifts from inside
Mefodij's cottage to the interior of the Izvekovs' apartment, and then to
the boulevards of the town, specifically, the one called "Sobač'i Lipki",
where Kirill and Liza meet and experience the emotions of first love. The
10th chapter serves as a point of concentration, as it were, for the various
plot elements, or "sjužetnye linii". Here Kirill, Vera Nikandrovna, Liza,
Anočka, Pastuxov, and Cvetuxin all meet, surrounded by the booths, side
shows, and excitement and confusion of the fair. Against the background
of the pushing, noisy crowds, Kirill and Liza carry on an intimate, deeply
significant conversation about the future, about political suppression, and
about how Liza would love to become an actress. It is also against this
background that Fedin presents Pastuxov's and Cvetuxin's jesting and
their characterization of Anočka as a "siren", which will be recalled in
1919 in *Neobyknovennoe leto*. It is in the 9th chapter that Liza first
mentions the name of Ragozin, accidentally alluding to Kirill's secret
association with him in underground revolutionary activities. In the 10th
chapter, Liza conjectures that Ragozin is actually a political worker. This
leads to the 11th chapter, in which the reader becomes acquainted with the
story of Ragozin's life and political activities, and also meets his wife

[8]   Fedin, *Sobranie*, VI, p. 348.

Ksenija' In this same chapter, Kirill visits Ragozin's cottage for the first time and begins leadings a truly double life.

In addition to the harmonious and logically consecutive arrangement of the materials, the reader is impressed by the smooth succession of scenes, each of which seems to be pitched at a different key, appropriate to the action. In the 9th chapter, Kirill and Liza hold their intimate conversations while sitting on their favorite bench or strolling along their favorite boulevard. In the 10th is the colorful description of the booths at the fair, the noise of the crowd, and the witty exchanges between Pastuxov and Cvetuxin, while the 11th chapter is devoted to the suppressed, laconic, narrative of the Ragozins' revolutionary life. Each chapter has its own unique tone, evoking from the reader a mood appropriate to the subject matter and intonation. In combination, the various tones harmonize, but with sufficient contrapuntal accompaniment afforded by the interaction of the various story lines on one another.

This tonality is maintained by the frequently used device of the succession of contrasting episodes. The 12th chapter, the First of May picnic in the hills — during which revolutionary activities were discussed — is light and airy, whereas the 13th chapter substitutes the oppressive atmosphere of the Meškov household. The 16th chapter, dealing with Kirill's and Liza's visit to the theatre, yields to the 17th and 18th chapters, with the scenes of the quarters occupied by the Ragozins and the Izvekovs, and with Kirill's arrest. This device (contrasting scenes) is especially prominent in the 22d and 23d chapters, where Šubnikov's wooing of Liza is succeeded by the scenes of Polotencev's interrogation of Kirill. This contrast serves not only to increase, and maintain at a high level, the reader's interest in the quickly developing and sharp conflicts of the action, but also affords the author the opportunity, by means of juxta-position and confrontation, to portray in greater depth the characters of the heroes. Liza's submissiveness and compliance with her father's will, and Kirill's courage and determination in the face of adversity are portrayed not only as character traits, but also because they predetermine their subsequent fortunes.

The majority of the chapters, despite their comparative brevity — they average nine to ten pages in length in *Pervye radosti* — are rich in the number and type of descriptive devices which they contain. For example, in the 31st chapter, the action is set in Meškov's doss house, then shifts to the school where Vera Nikandrovna formerly lived, and then concludes in her new quarters. But it is not only the shift of the action from one locale to another which merits comment, but the additional use of various literary devices: direct description, dialogue, internal monologue, "quoted speech" (*erlebte Rede* or *nesobstvenno prjamaja reč*"), epistolary material, and description of landscape. Remarkable is the fact that Fedin judiciously uses all of these devices in just one chapter — albeit a lengthy one — with imperceptible transitions from one device to the other. These transitions, plus the unique alternations of tone, impart to each chapter its distinctive mood and artistic effect.

The structural compactness of the dilogy is also related to the large number of characters. One would expect that the greater the number of characters, the looser the structure. But this does not necessarily follow. In order to accomplish his objective, which was to portray the "obraz vremeni" or the essential character of the time in its historical perspective and significance, as well as to introduce the social and psychological elements, Fedin found it necessary to create a multitude of characters. It was essential that the place of each character in the novel, the amount of space occupied by each, be proportionate to the overall picture of life, with its most characteristic phenomena, which Fedin intended to portray. In the novel *Pervye radosti* there are over 70 characters, and each of them occupies that space which is consistent with his importance. The resulting compactness does not necessarily represent the accomplishment of a preconceived goal which Fedin had established, but rather a distinguishing characteristic of his literary manner. When the subject matter itself impresses Fedin with its significance, he does not hesitate to broaden or deepen the scope of the narrative. Thus the novel *Neobyknovennoe leto* which, like *Pervye radosti*, has 38 chapters, has twice the volume, consisting of 737 pages as compared to 377 pages in the first volume, with an average length of 19.5 pages per chapter, as opposed to 9.9 pages in *Pervye radosti*.[9] Despite the difference in length, both *Pervye radosti* and *Neobyknovennoe leto* encompass approximately the same period of time. The sharp difference in length of the novels, then, must be sought elsewhere, in the change in character of the subject matter, and changes in concept of structure and genre. The frame of the action of the second novel is enlarged considerably, extending spatially far beyond the limits of the city of Saratov. In addition, the philosophical-publicistic digressions are of greater duration, and the whole character of the narrative changes. Its heroes are provided a much broader field of action, the collisions and confrontations involve a greater number of characters (over 100 in the second novel as compared to 70 in the first), and the image of

[9] All figures cited are based on the nine-volume collection of Fedin's works published 1959-1962.

the people, openly fighting to preserve their revolutionary gains, looms larger. It is significant in attempting to perceive Fedin's intent to note that the longest chapters are those specifically devoted to presenting historical materials. There are 27 pages in the 16th chapter, 38 pages in the 29th chapter, and 26 pages in the 38th chapter. In the 29th chapter, Fedin recounts Pastuxov's life in Kozlov, which he follows with a description of Mamontov's attack on the town.

Fedin consciously and deliberately brings to the reader's attention the shifts in point of view, indicating his preoccupation with this device, particularly as concerns battle scenes, reminiscent of Stendhal and Lev Tolstoj. Mamontov's attack on the city is first presented from the point of view of "rjadovogo kozlovskogo obyvatelja, kotoryj snačala po sluxam uznal o vnezapnom zaxvate Tambova belymi, a potom voočiju uvidel zaxvatčikov u sebja na ulicax, to raskroetsja neobyčnaja kartina".[10] After recounting the initial events related to the attack, Fedin reminds the reader that "èto glavnoe, čto uznali kozlovcy v pervoe vremja posle padenija svoego centra ...". Fedin concludes the description of events, viewed contemporaneously with their occurence, with this sentence: "Takim voočiju uvidel kozlovskij obitatel' nabeg mamontovcev na rodnoj gorod, i tol'ko iz ètogo ličnogo videnija i znanija mog togda isxodit' v svoem ponimanii sobytija ...." Finally Fedin sets the raid in the larger context of the entire civil war, prefacing his own analysis of its significance with this introduction: "Esli rassmotret' nabeg Mamontova na osnove znanij o sobytii, nakoplennyx posle togo, kak ono soveršilos', to značenie nabega v xode graždanskoj vojny progljanet jasnee." Then Fedin narrates Pastuxov's future destiny. As a member of the delegation to Mamontov, he is seized and imprisoned, and subsequently released by the Reds, motivating the change in his views and his decision to ally himself with the Bolsheviks.

The genre of the second novel assumes certain characteristics which differ from the first. The first novel of the cycle is characterized by a sense of history, with the movement of history conveyed through the medium of the progressive revelation of human destiny and individual fortunes. In the second novel, this sense of history is considerably intensified and, as concerns genre, the work assumes more of the features of a historical novel, as compared to the social and psychological elements which prevailed over the historical elements in *Pervye radosti*. It is understandable, therefore, why Fedin began the second novel with a reflection on the importance of understanding the logic of history, and

[10] Fedin, *Sobranie*, VII, p. 532 ff.

ended it with the visual image of Kirill pressing onward into the future "čtoby, otdoxnuvši, vstretit' buduščee utro".[11]

It has been seen that the composition and structure of each novel, as well as of the dilogy as a whole, is a function of the relationship of the particular and the general, the presentation of details which have broad implications, and the ability to structure the work economically. Fedin himself has acknowledged composition to be one of the most difficult tasks facing the writer.[12] One Soviet writer and critic, A. Makarenko, cited with approval by others, considers the quality of "plotnost' rasskaza", which may be rendered as the compactness, density, or solidity of the story, to be the most important indicator of a writer's compositional skill. Makarenko defines "plotnost'" as compressing the greatest "količestvo soderžanija na edinicu teksta, naprimer na stranicu ili glavu".[13] This density, which may be formulated as a ratio expressing the quantity of "content" per unit of text, such as the page or the chapter, is more than just succinctness, laconism, or economy in the use of language.[14] It also presupposes the strict selection of materials for each chapter and episode, and for the work as a whole, which is what Fedin has actually done in the dilogy. The choice of materials has evidently been subordinated to Fedin's central idea. Thus, in *Pervye radosti*, Fedin is very sparing and selective in the use of materials related to the activities of the Bolshevik underground. Bugaenko affirms that Fedin did have such materials available to him,[15] yet he did not make full use of them. It appears that Fedin may have reasoned that the more he introduced such material, the greater would be the loss of the sense of actual historical movement. An alternative hypothesis is that Fedin himself may have felt inadequate in the aesthetic transformation of purely documentary materials which he could not supplement with personal experience.

In 1955, Fedin wrote that "Istoričeskaja pravda, kotoroj ja stremilsja vo vsem sledovat', zastavila menja uvidet' v *Pervyx radostjax* otnositel'noe

---

[11] Fedin, *Sobranie*, VII, p. 744.

[12] Fedin, "O masterstve", *Sobranie*, IX, pp. 570-585.

[13] A. Makarenko, "Beseda s načinajuščimi pisateljami", *O pisatel'skom trude*, sbornik statej (Moscow, Sovetskij Pisatel', 1953), p. 110, quoted by Bugaenko, p. 141.

[14] The use of terms like "content" (or "form") presents considerable semantic problems. Discussion of some of the problems involved may be found in V. Erlich, *Russian Formalism* (The Hague, 1955). Since content implies elements of form, and vice versa, it may be preferable to adopt the reasoning of Wellek and Warren, and to use the term "materials" to describe "aesthetically indifferent" elements formerly considered part of content, and parts previously considered formal. "Structure" could be used to encompass both form and content to the extent that they are organized for aesthetic purposes. Cf. Wellek & Warren, *Theory of Literature*, p. 129.

[15] Bugaenko, *op. cit.*, p. 142.

nebol'šoe mesto gerojam revoljucii."[16] There is some literary justification
for the minimal characterization of Ragozin in the first novel, and for the
sparse description of the "delo Ragozina". Less experienced novelists
than Fedin frequently try to communicate everything they know about
their heroes, and relate everything they can, rather than everything they
should. It is not necessary that the author tell the reader everything
he knows about his characters. As E. M. Forster points out, characters
are real, convincing, when the reader feels the novelist knows everything
about the character, although he may not choose to tell us everything he
knows.[17] But Fedin makes us feel that, although Ragozin is not explained
as fully as he might be, he could be explained if Fedin chose to do so.
This is more than we can expect from real life, where there are certain
things which we will never know about each other. But we can inter-
polate, filling in the lacunae, which is what Fedin has his readers do.

Fedin himself referred to this question in criticizing the work of several
Lithuanian writers in 1954. He stated that the writer (Venuolis)

"расчертил план романа чересчур тщательно, он решил охватить
все. ... В романе не хватает того-то и того-то, профсоюзной работы
или художественной самодеятельности. Ничего, пусть, не хватает!
Пусть в книге будет именно то, на что вы, писатель, рассчитывали."[18]

In these words Fedin expresses a principle which characterized all of his
earlier writings as well. In creating a literary work, Fedin chooses that
material from life which supports his convictions, and portrays life from
a distinctive, well-defined point of view.

Fedin devotes considerable attention to plot (sjužet), which he interprets not as a literary element rooted in the raw material of life and
subordinating that material to itself, but rather as a literary element which
breaks the real bonds with the raw material of life and substitutes its own
links, according to the laws of estrangement (ostranenie).[19] Fedin, like
Gor'kij, views plot as based on real relationships, sympathy and antipathy, the actions and clashes of people, in which individual character
traits are revealed. Fedin considers that the author is not free to build
the plot, or framework of incidents upon which the narrative is constructed, merely on the basis of some outline or plan which his inventiveness may conjure up. He contends that the plot must derive from the

---

[16]   K. Fedin, "Zametka po povodu dilogii", Oktjabr', No. 8 (1955), p. 157.
[17]   E. M. Forster, Aspects of the Novel (New York, 1927), p. 97.
[18]   K. Fedin, "Soveršenstvovat' masterstvo prozaikov", Literaturnaja gazeta, 11 March
1954.
[19]   Bugaenko, p. 143.

essence of that reality which the artist is treating, from his understanding and evaluation of that reality, and from the possibilities inherent in human character. Fedin's outlook is illustrated by what he wrote about Lev Tolstoj:[20]

Он был убежден и убеждал художников слова, что надо жить жизнью своих героев, описывать в образах их внутренние ощущения, и тогда сами герои сделают то, что им нужно сделать по их характерам. Он искал и находил переплетения фабулы, развязки действия во внутренней сущности описываемых лиц, давал героям волю поступать так, как только они одни могли и должны были поступить в том пложении, в которое он их ставил или они попадали по своему же нраву, по склонностям, привычкам. Потому-то и живут на его страницах все действующие лица, что форма и содержание его произведений есть неделимое единство.[21]

Fedin's article, first published in 1935, testifies not only to his deep regard for Lev Tolstoj, but also to the similarity in their aesthetic views and the influence of Tolstoj on Fedin. Tolstoj's views on the complicated problem of the relation of plot to character were to condition Fedin's treatment of this relationship in the dilogy. Fedin stated it succinctly in this way: "Geroi s ix xarakterami slagajut sjužet, a ne sjužet delaet geroev. Vot osnova osnov pisatel'skogo masterstva."[22] According to Fedin, then, it is the *dramatis personae* who determine the plot, and characterization thereby assumes critical importance. But before examining the characterization in detail it may be well to analyze the major plot elements.

The novels of the dilogy are characterized by their complex plots (*sjužet*). This complexity is evident in the way Fedin portrays life, human characters, and the interaction of people upon one another. In both novels of the dilogy there are several different story lines, or *sjužetnye linii*. The basic story line of the work is the relationship between Peter Ragozin and Kirill Izvekov. As a youth, Kirill participates in the revolutionary struggle under the direction of Peter Ragozin. Later, in

---

[20]   Fedin, "Iskusstvo L'va Tolstogo", *Sobranie*, IX, p. 31.
[21]   It may be well at this point to define several terms. "Fabula" may be considered as representing the basic story stuff, the sum-total of events to be related in the work of fiction, or the raw material of life, prior to organization or transformation by the artist. "Sjužet" is the story as actually narrated, or the way in which the events are linked together. The raw materials of the "fabula" are shaped, organized, constructed into the "sjužet", at which time they become part of the aesthetic structure of the work. Cf. Erlich, *Russian Formalism*, p. 207 ff.
[22]   Bugaenko, p. 143.

1919, Kirill is depicted as Ragozin's friend and comrade in the military actions of the Civil War. It is through this relationship of Izvekov and Ragozin, and in the development of the action along this story line that Fedin endeavors to show how Bolshevik cadres are trained and hardened. Characteristic of this particular story line is the concealed *zavjazka*, or *noeud*, the conflict. The reader is not informed of the circumstances which bring the young student Kirill into contact with one of the leaders of the underground revolutionary movement, Ragozin. Even the growth of their relationship, the intensification of Kirill's active participation in the work of the clandestine print shop is presented very sparingly in the first novel. The First of May outing on Sokolov Mountain, Kirill's coming to Ragozin's wife with a "package", Liza's chance observation of Kirill at the Ragozins' cottage, and the reminiscences of bygone events which pass between Ragozin and Izvekov when they meet in 1919 — this is all that is presented in the novels. These isolated scenes present a series of static pictures of their early relationship which lacks the dynamic quality of their later exploits. In the second novel, Ragozin and Izvekov are sometimes brought together and sometimes separated by the circumstances of life. Thus, when they are saying good-bye one December morning in 1919 on the platform of the Saratov railroad station, and Ragozin shouts to Kirill, who is leaving for the front: "Ja skoro za toboj sledom!",[23] the reader interprets this scene as a harbinger that the two men will indeed meet again. Ragozin's words signal the last time that they meet in the second novel, but the story line involving the two men continues in the last novel of the trilogy.

The story of the love between Kirill and Liza occupies an important place in the novel *Pervye radosti*. Fedin shows the development of their youthful emotions from their first awareness of their feelings for one another until the sudden and tragic termination of the affair with the arrest of Kirill. In this story line, Fedin subtly and almost imperceptibly discloses the differences in their characters, the conflict in their outlook, and the effect of their family environments which, in combination, must inevitably lead to a parting of ways. Liza's marriage to Šubnikov is the climax, or "kul'minacionnyj punkt" of this line. Once she married Šubnikov, Liza destroyed all hopes of marrying the man she truly loved. The natural dénouement or *razvjazka* of this story line, is the scene in which Liza, who has already married Oznobišin, visits Kirill Izvekov to beg for the release of her arrested father. This scene, in which Liza is forced to humble herself, brings this particular dramatic conflict to a

[23] Fedin, *Sobranie*, VII, p. 721.

tragic end. Viewed from Fedin's philosophical and political standpoint, the unraveling of the complications of the plot in this fashion is both ideologically and artistically justified. This represents the end of what was merely a passing phase in Kirill's life, a feature of the past which was never to return.

In the second novel, there are relatively few pages devoted to this past. Nevertheless, the developing personal relationship between Kirill and Anočka Parabukina, begun in the first novel, plays an important role. Characteristic of this story line, or *sjužetnaja linija*, is the sharply-defined, *noeud*, or initial situation of conflict. Kirill, who had first met Anočka nine years earlier as a barefoot little girl of nine, now meets a fascinating young lady, one who "byla niskol'ko ne poxoža na Lizu, no imenno Lizu videl v nej Kirill".[24] In her, Kirill saw Liza as she had been at the age of eighteen; she had not changed at all, except perhaps to become even prettier. This duality of sensation is heightened by Kirill's awareness that he himself had changed, the net result being an estrangement which he found both pleasant and unpleasant. This meeting serves as the inciting moment[25] for the story line pertaining to the Kirill-Anočka relationship. The qualities with which Fedin invests Anočka are sincerity, artistic talent, wholesomeness, and deep emotional feeling, all of which attract Kirill to her. But an additional quality which Kirill finds in Anočka, which was conspicuously absent in Liza, is an ideology which is close to that of Kirill's. In one memorable scene, as Kirill and Anočka stroll through the city of Saratov at night, Kirill metaphorically compares the struggle of the Reds against the Whites to the building of an "aerodrom buduščego", and that future flights into heaven will take off from the flying fields of the future which the Communists were then building. Kirill's proposal of marriage is couched in this same imagery: "Xočeš' so mnoj vmeste aerodrom stroit'?", to which she softly answers: "Ja dumala ... my uže načali!"[26]

Another memorable scene is the one in the last chapter of *Neobyknovennoe leto* when Kirill and Anočka part at the Saratov railroad station. Again, this scene does not signal the end of the Kirill-Anočka story line, but rather a temporary suspension of their physical association, and even the culminating point, or climax, if viewed from the standpoint of the trilogy as an integrated whole. In this respect Fedin's parting

---

[24] Fedin, *Sobranie*, VII, p. 131.
[25] Cf. G. Freytag, *Technik des Dramas* (1863), in Shipley, *Dictionary of World Literature* (1960), p. 189.
[26] Fedin, *Sobranie*, VII, p. 673.

scene is pitched in a different key than those of Čexov in his short stories, or even those of Fedin's own early short stories in *Pustyr'*. In *Skučnaja istorija*, for example, with its *leitmotiv* of mutual isolation, its atmosphere of progressively increasing disillusionment, and its ending on a minor note, the reader is left in a state of depression, with nothing but hopelessness before him. This "Čexovskoe nastroenie", or Čexovian atmosphere, frequently assumes visual form in the image of the beloved face seen fleetingly through the glass window of a train receding into the distance, or of a tearful face, framed by curtains, peering despondently through a window against which torrents of rain are beating. This type of scene may be compared with the one in *Neobyknovennoe leto*:

Проводы близкого человека в неизвестность тяжелы, особенно в эту секунду ухода поезда, в секунду исчезновения последнего вагона, когда вдруг пронизывает чувство физической утраты принадлежащего тебе существа, которого миг назад можно было коснуться и которое сразу стало недосягаемо.[27]

The reader is made to feel the poignancy of this moment of parting, but it is not in the same minor key as in Čexov, where it is usually the last moment of suspense at the very end of the story. In Fedin, the reader senses the emotion of sadness is mixed with hope and optimism, and the promise of future happiness. And Anočka's strength is emphasized by awareness of her father's critical condition as he lies dying in the hospital, the knowledge of which Anočka did not share with Kirill, in order to spare him additional worry as he proceeded to the front.

Several additional story lines supplement the primary ones just discussed. These include the Pastuxov-Cvetuxin relationship and that of Polotencev-Meškov-Šubnikov-Oznobišin. The interweaving of these primary and secondary story lines (or plot elements) results in various points of conflict in the social and personal relationships of the various characters. Fedin frequently causes his characters to confront one another in contrasting or opposing situations, or after a reversal in their fortunes. In the first novel, Polotencev derisively interrogates young Izvekov in prison and, nine years later, Commissar Izvekov relentlessly interrogates Polotencev, stripping away his cover story and exposing him for what he truly is. In *Pervye radosti*, Meškov is constantly distressed by the actions of the "restless" tenants in his cottage, but, in *Neobyknovennoe leto*, he tries in every way to ingratiate himself with Ragozin, now the director of the City Finance Department, reminding Ragozin of

[27]   Fedin, *Sobranie*, VII, p. 721.

imaginary kindnesses which he, Meškov, rendered to Ragozin and his wife nine years earlier. A third reversal is exemplified by the change in situation of Pastuxov who, in 1910, lectures young Kirill Izvekov condescendingly from an imagined exalted position but, in 1919, is rebuked severely by that same Izvekov, now secretary of the Party Executive Committee.

It is through these clashes that Fedin introduces the publicistic and tendentious elements into the novels. To his communist heroes he attributes nobility of character, courage, and moral and intellectual excellence, while the Polotencevs, Šubnikovs, and Meškovs embody all of the vices of their generation and class. In this respect, Fedin perpetuates the 19th century "accusatory" tradition in Russian literature, in which lines were drawn on the basis of socio-economic class.[28] In these collisions and reversals, then, Fedin applies the principles of artistic composition and structure to support his conception of the reversals which have taken place in actual life, and the replacement of the old by the new. It is not the eternal opposition between the "fathers and sons" which interests Fedin in the dilogy, but the conflict of class.

Characteristic of the composition of the dilogy is the free development of the separate links in the plot, confrontation, and parallelism. The plot elements of Ragozin and Pastuxov, for example, never intersect directly, and Pastuxov never meets Ragozin. This is, in Fedin's thinking, a perfectly consistent peculiarity of the plot of the novel, arising from the internal logic of the characters themselves. Events and incidents related to Ragozin's life are unknown to Pastuxov. He is disturbed by a vague presentiment of their significance, but he does not have — and is incapable of having — any direct connection with them. If Fedin had decided to have these two characters confront one another, perhaps in some chance encounter, the artistic effect would have been weakened, since the reader knows that Ragozin's sphere of activity does not coincide with that of Pastuxov, and is not intelligible to him.

It is also characteristic that the *noeud* or initial situation of conflict — the beginning of Ragozin's clandestine activity after returning from exile, the organization of the underground printing press, and meeting Kirill — takes place somewhere outside of the narrative, being presented to the reader as a number of *faits accomplis*. In similar fashion, the reader learns the dénouement only from Dorogomilov's account to Pastuxov in the novel *Neobyknovennoe leto*. This artistic device helps Fedin to

[28] In the 19th century, Gončarov, Turgenev, Pisemskij, Herzen, Nekrasov, Ostrovskij, Saltykov-Ščedrin, Uspenskij, with Gor'kij carrying the tradition into the 20th century.

create the atmosphere of underground struggle, concealed from observation. It also conveys the feeling to the reader that the episode with
the printing press is only one of the many facets of Ragozin's work, that
of itself it has little importance, and that other activities, not described
in the novel, may have greater import.

By deliberately not joining various "sjužetnye linii", Fedin avails
himself of the device of hidden, or implied, contrast. In the novel
Pervye radosti, it is not accidental that, immediately following the story
of the friendly breakfast of the artists, Fedin relates the account of
Ragozin's arrest and the death of his son, or that the search of Izvekov's
home follows the scene in the theatre, or that the pages describing the
charity ball are immediately followed by the pages devoted to the details
of Ksana's death in prison. These juxtapositions add dramatic intensity
to the various situations, deeply stirring the emotions of the reader
without the need for any additional comment by the author.

In these juxtapositions, Fedin brings to mind the same technique as
practiced by I. S. Turgenev in mid-19th century. One of his narrative
techniques, particularly noticeable in *Zapiski oxotnika*, is to arouse an
emotional response in the reader merely by presenting facts in a certain
order. In the story "Burmistr", for example, the narration is constructed
in such a sequence that the mere juxtaposition reveals the contradiction
between word and deed in the personality of the spiritually and culturally
impoverished landowner. The narrator himself does not evaluate
Penočkin's conduct; he merely relates the facts. On the one hand, we
learn what a despot he really is and with what cold cruelty he treats those
dependent on him. We observe as Arkadij Pavlič "drank his tea, laughed,
scrutinized his fingernails, smoked, propped himself up with cushions,
and was altogether in an excellent humor". Then, unexpectedly, immediately following this picture, the narrator, without any embellishment
or personal commentary, relates the scene of Penočkin's cold, frightening
treatment of the waiter, guilty only of not having warmed his master's
wine!

X

CHARACTERIZATION.

THE POSITIVE HERO

As his plans for the novels of the trilogy progressed, Fedin gradually formulated his ideas of the character of his future heroes, the milieu in which they would function, and the circumstances of their life. Looking back later, he wrote: "Ja mog sočinit' ljudej, v žizni mnoju nikogda ne vidannyx, ne vstrečennyx, no kak by bezuslovno živšix".[1] In order to be credible, these characters, when confronted with specific situations, would have to act in a consistent manner. Thus Liza Meškova, for example, would lose her identity if she were to be able to oppose her father's will and follow Kirill into exile as other Russian women had done before her. It is clear that, given her basic flaw in character, Liza is destined to eternal suffering.

From the logic of character and of the circumstances of life flow the plot situations in which Fedin places Pastuxov, who appears first in Saratov, and then in Kozlov. The change in Pastuxov's views should not be interpreted as the result of a chance happening, his imprisonment by the Whites, nor as a conscious act of will on his part, asserting itself triumphantly over his character. What Fedin does is to confront his heroes with various obstacles, and then to reveal their particular character traits by the manner in which they react to these collisions. The "Ragozin Affair" is the main obstacle which Fedin creates to determine the future destiny of his heroes. Participation in this affair defines Kirill Izvekov's future character development and his path through life and it destroys any hope that Liza might have for personal happiness or a substantial change in fortune. It provides motivation for her marriage to Šubnikov rather than to Kirill, and to her subsequent involvement with Oznobišin. It also affected the destinies of both Pastuxov and Cvetuxin, involving them only slightly in the first novel, but more substantially in the events of 1919.

Fedin does more than merely place his heroes in situations of conflict corresponding to their particular character traits, allowing future events

[1] K. Fedin, "Na povodu dilogii", *Oktjabr'*, No. 8 (1955), p. 157.

to develop from the logic of their characters. He also motivates the reader to react emotionally to the response of a character to a particular challenge, accomplishing this with relatively greater subtlety, than, for example, Gor'kij. The emotional reaction of the reader is, nevertheless, deliberately, though inoffensively, evoked, and may be interpreted as reflecting Fedin's own attitude. As a Soviet critic pointed out, "sjužet-èto koncepcija dejstvitel'nosti ... v sjužete slity i ob"ektivnoe otraženie zakonomernosti real'noj žizni, i vzgljad xudožnika na dejstvitel'nost".[2]

Here is an example of one such subtle evaluation of the action taken by one of the characters when confronted with a problem situation. When Pastuxov and his family prepare to leave Saratov, the boys of the town consider their departure a defection to the Whites, a flight from deprivation and hardship, which is the way their elders, Dorogomilov and Dibič, also view it. Fedin conveys Aleša's despair that they are fleeing this way:

Вместе с мамой и папой, вместе с Ольгой Адамовной он был отверженным и бежал неизвестно куда! Его все презирали за то, что его отец был хуже бедных, за то, что сам он был ничтожнее и малодушнее Павлика с Витей.

In this manner Fedin evokes in the reader a negative reaction to Pastuxov's flight, by portraying the anguish and recriminations which Aleša must suffer.

A distinguishing feature of Fedin's artistic style in the dilogy is the objective, plastic, unusually keen and well-defined artistic portrayal of events and of the internal world of his heroes, conveying the psychological atmosphere of the epoch.

The most important device which Fedin employs for the portrayal of character in the dilogy is the one which Černyševskij, referring to the works of Lev Tolstoj, termed the portrayal of the "dialektiki duši".[3]

The composition of the dilogy is such that we see the characters — Liza, Kirill, Anočka, Pastuxov, and the others — during a relatively brief period of time. The events described in the first and second novels are of only a few months' duration. As a consequence, Fedin minimizes the possibility of portraying developing, dynamic characters like those found in most great novels whose authors depict the entire life of the

---

[2]   E. Dobin, "Zaostrenie v sjužete", *Novyj mir*, No. 3 (1955), p. 249.

[3]   N. G. Černyševskij, "Detstvo i otročestvo. Voennye rasskazi", first published in *Sovremennik*, No. 12, Dec. (1856), pp. 53-64, included in S. P. Byčkov, *L. N. Tolstoj v russkoj kritike, sbornik statej*. Izdanie vtoroe (M., GIXL, 1952), p. 93. Černyševskij also uses the expression "isobraženie vnutrennogo monologa", p. 96.

hero. Fedin concentrates on portraying the conflicts within the soul of his heroes at the most crucial moments of their lives. This technique was characteristic of Turgenev, who portrayed his characters during a brief critical period by means of juxtaposition, confrontation, and opposition, with characters being revealed not all at once, but gradually, with the reader following the details of the development up to the moment of final shock and crisis. In Turgenev, this climax, and subsequent reversal, generally comes in the form of a love intrigue in his major novels. In Fedin the stimulus is sometimes of a political and social nature, as when, in *Neobyknovennoe leto*, Pastuxov, after undergoing imprisonment at the hands of the Whites, resolves to devote his life and artistic talents to the cause of the revolution. Or it may be, as in Turgenev, of a deeply personal nature.

An example of such a critical moment in the life of one of the protagonists may be cited in the case of Liza Meškova. She had been forced to marry Šubnikov against her will, but had managed to reconcile herself to the situation. Then, unexpectedly, she receives a letter from Kirill in exile in Siberia. Fedin portrays Liza at a charity ball on the evening before receiving the letter. She has returned to her husband because of the responsibility she feels to her as yet unborn child, and tries to convince herself that she is following the proper course of action. Nevertheless she continues to experience feelings of sadness and aversion toward her husband. When Cvetuxin inquires, "Sčastlivy li vy?", she curtly replies: "Da, konečno, soveršenno sčastliva, i vy ne dolžny menja ob ètom sprašivat'."[4] But her attempt at reconciliation is short-lived. Liza could not fall asleep for a long time, but when she finally did, images and impressions kept replacing one another in her mind's eye. Awakening from fright, she feels that "uznala vo sne čto-to neobyčajno novoe i sama budto obnovilas'".[5] This sensation of newness and self-renewal, whose significance Liza herself is unable to grasp, represents a disturbed longing for the past, for the pure dreams of her youth.

The letter from Kirill which little Anočka brings her on the following morning unexpectedly reveals the meaning of her experiences of the preceding few days. The train of impressions released by the letter suddenly fuse with the disturbed visions which had accompanied her awakening that morning. In just a few pages of *Pervye radosti*, a characterization of Liza's innermost thoughts and emotions emerges with particular expressiveness: her sensitivity, her poetic nature, her purity,

---

[4] Fedin, *Sobranie*, VI, p. 483.
[5] *Ibid.*, p. 485.

and her romanticism. The construction of the nightmare scene, the letter, and the actual reference to *Evgenij Onegin* suggest a parallel between the character of Liza and that of Puškin's Tat'jana. Another character trait which emerges in this sequence is Liza's passivity, her inability to break free from patriarchal domination. At this point, Fedin's own philosophy emerges unequivocally:

Понемногу она стала овладевать своими мыслями и с мучительной горечью понимать, что, подчиняясь своему долгу сначала перед отцом, потом перед мужем, боясь нарушить этот внушенный ей с детства, непреступаемый общеизвестный долг, она пошла против того долга перед самой собою, который никому не был известен, но был несравнимо больше и важнее всего.[6]

But this is not the major point of interest. More important is that Fedin was able to capture and communicate the most significant and most critical moment in the life of one of his heroines, and to convey, in a concentrated artistic manner, the very essence of her character and her soul.

The same device is found in the hospital scene in *Neobyknovennoe leto*, in which, immediately after seeing Kirill off to the front, Anočka learns of the death of her father, Tixon Parabukin, from alcohol poisoning. On learning of the death of her father, Anočka falls into a state of profound depression, indifferent to everything happening around her, as though there were no longer any distinction between the important and the trivial. But in spite of her apathy,

... была одна черта, одна точечка, затаенная в глубине ее взгляда, в зрачках, соединявшая в себе уже почти отсутствие рассудка с жадными поисками мысли, как бывает только у человека больной души. Аночка в эти минуты равно могла поддаться бессилию и заболеть, и могла найти такую опору в самосознании, что уверилась бы в своих силах на всю жизнь.
Этой точечкой взгляда видела она острейшие миги промчавшихся суток, и ей казалось, что до нее доносится рокот колес по рельсам, и она глядит на последний вагон поезда, ускользающего вдаль, и слышит голос: 'будь немного старше себя,' и другой голос: 'еще здоровое сердце'. В бессвязности этой заключалось что-то цельное, и в то же время одно исключало другое. Как будто душа Аночки раздваивалась, и одна часть, уходя с последним вагоном поезда, оставалась надолго жить, а другая, оставаясь здесь, в больнице, уходила из жихни навсегда.[7]

[6]   Fedin, *Sobranie*, VI, p. 490.
[7]   *Ibid.*, VII, p. 727.

At this crucial moment, Anočka is confronted with the choice of suc-
cumbing to weakness and falling ill, or drawing on hidden reserves for
strength and a renewed sense of purpose. Fedin presents this "moment
of truth" as symbolizing the severing of all of Anočka's ties with the past
as she heeds the first of the two voices of conscience and commits herself
irrevocably to a future with Kirill.

How does Fedin characterize Izvekov? In a succinct, precise, physical
description of Kirill, whom Fedin presents without the benefit of any
vorgeschichte, the reader is apprised of his most important traits, his
strength and his straightforwardness.

Жесткость проступала по всем его крепком, уже по-мужски сложив-
шемся теле. Он был невысок, даже приземист, из тех людей, которых зовут квадратными: угловато торчали его резкие плечи,
круто выступали челюсти, прямые параллельные линии волос на
лбу, бровей, рта, подбородка будто вычерчены были рейсфедером,
и только взгляда, может быть, коснулась живописная кисть, тронув
его горячей темной желтизной.[8]

Kirill lives in a modest two-room apartment with his mother Vera
Nikandrovna, a teacher. His father had drowned in the Volga while
Kirill was still an infant. His family circumstances are an important
factor in Kirill's characterization, particularly his mother, an unusual,
courageous woman. Also revealing are the furnishings in Kirill's room.
Pictures of "borodatye deduški" hand on the walls, portraits of, as Kirill
calls them, "moi velikie ljudi". It is significant that although Kirill
considers Lev Nikolaevič Tolstoj one of the "great men", his picture has
been removed. "Ja s nim rasxožus'. On sčitaet, čto v čeloveke nado
nasaždat' xorošee, a ja sčitaju, čto nado borot'sja s ploxim ... Prežde
visel, teper' ja ego perevesil k mame." [9] It may be inferred, therefore, that
Kirill acknowledges his greatness as an artist while rejecting his doctrine.
This view coincides with that of Lenin, who considered Tolstoj a "great
artist ... a genius who has not only drawn incomparable pen pictures of
Russian life, but has made first-class contributions to world literature".[10]
Nevertheless, Lenin considered that Tolstoj had "obviously failed to
understand" the revolution "from which he has obviously alienated
himself".[11]

Fedin's initial portrayal of Kirill's physical appearance and confronta-

---

[8]   Fedin, *Sobranie*, VI, p. 138.
[9]   *Ibid.*, p. 212.
[10]   V. I. Lenin, *Articles on Tolstoy* (Moscow, FLPH, 1953), p. 9.
[11]   *Ibid.*, p. 7.

tion with Parabukin, as well as his relation to his mother and the description of his room, is essential to the characterization. This is particularly true since Fedin does not describe the milieu which impelled Kirill along the path of revolution, nor the internal agitation occasioned by the prevailing social evils, nor the source of his willingness to sacrifice his freedom or his love for Liza. We are rather confronted with the *fait accompli* of a static characterization.

Subsequently, all of Kirill's actions are consistent with this initial portrait. His gestures, his manner of speaking, his movements, and his way of thinking and reasoning, add depth to the characterization and permit Kirill to enter into the various conflicts of the novel in a way which is internally logical.

Kirill's first appearance in the novel is characteristic of Fedin's technique, also illustrating the romantic aura in which he envelops Kirill. Anočka, the young daughter of the roustabout Parabukin, a bright, innocent little girl, like a flower which has sprung from a crack in the asphalt, is running down the street, clutching a 50-kopeek coin presented by Pastuxov and Cvetuxin. She is pursued by her own father, disheveled and just getting over a drinking bout. Parabukin will not beat her, which Anočka knows, but merely wants the coin so he can buy a drink. But to an outside observer, this scene looks menacing, and Kirill, standing at the gate of his house, construes it as such. He signals to the girl to dash through into the yard, then resumes his place, blocking the gateway with his body.

At this juncture, a fight should result, as the burly, red-eyed, barrel-chested, infuriated father and the 19-year-old youth confront each other. But no clash ensues! The young man's attitude is so firm, and his moral superiority is so evident that the roustabout lowers his powerful arm, muttering instead of striking Kirill, "Otkuda ty takoj, satanenok!"[12] This dynamic scene immediately reveals Kirill's character, his self-confident conviction that he is on the side of justice, and his willingness to fight for it.

In opposition to Kirill Izvekov in the dilogy is another main character, the playwright Aleksandr Pastuxov. Actually they meet only two or three times, and hardly speak to each other.

Some critics have considered Pastuxov to be little more than a "potential emigre".[13] If this were so, it is doubtful whether Fedin would

---

[12]   Fedin, *Sobranie*, VI, p. 139.
[13]   V. Smirnova, "Boevoj devjatnadcatyj god", *Literaturnaja gazeta*, No. 2 (5 Jan. '49).

have devoted so much attention to him in both novels of the dilogy. It is more likely that Fedin created Pastuxov for a much more significant role, essential to the treatment of one of the major problems facing the author, that of the relation of art to life, which was discussed earlier. In order to trace the evolution of Fedin's treatment of this theme, through characterization, it may be well to refer back to Nikita Karev in the novel *Brat'ja* (1926-1928).

Nikita, like Fedin himself during that early period, in obvious sympathy with his hero, believed in remaining apart from politics. This attitude is revealed particularly clearly during the conversation with his brother Rostislav, when Nikita finds himself serving in his brother's detachment. Rostislav tells him that he "... teper', esli s nami, — dolžen idti protiv otca".

Nikita replies that he will not act "ni protiv brata, ni protiv syna, ni protiv otca ... Možeš' byt' spokoen, ja ničem ne mogu byt' polezen ni belym, ni vam". He wishes to serve Russia with his music, but does not wish to further any partisan or class viewpoint. His music is for all, not for any special interests. Equally dear to Nikita is his brother, the bolshevik Rostislav, and his father, who finds himself on the side of the Whites.

The motif of sacrifice, of the tragedy of artistic creativity, is also emphasized in *Brat'ja*. Music, for Nikita, is a hard taskmaster. It demands complete selflessness from Nikita, and even saps the will and energy of those close to him. Anna, Nikita's sweetheart in Germany, understood this, and faithfully subordinated herself. Irina was opposed to playing such a self-sacrificing role, and left Nikita for Rodion. Even Varvara Mixajlovna, who finally gains the ascendancy over Nikita with her indomitable love, parts from him. Nikita finally remains alone, but even alone he is prepared to serve his muse to the end. Fedin emphasizes his isolation by titling the last section of the novel "Utraty".

During this early period, Fedin considered that the sacrifice, loneliness, and tragedy of the artist were inescapable during a period of revolutionary upheaval when each side demanded that the artist devote his efforts to serving political ends. The true artist, according to Fedin, despite being repudiated by society, would remain aloof from both sides, standing in a position above and apart from the conflict.

Twenty years later, in the dilogy, the reader meets another artist, Aleksandr Pastuxov, assuming the same attitude but portrayed by Fedin from a completely different point of view. In *Brat'ja*, Fedin characterizes Nikita Karev with sympathy, whereas in the dilogy he coldly exposes

Pastuxov's shortcomings as his efforts to remain apart lead him into a cul-de-sac.

In *Pervye radosti*, Fedin depicts Pastuxov as a young playwright, but one who is already famous. One of his dramas is being presented in Moscow, the other in Petersburg. In the very beginning of the novel, Fedin portrays a character who is quite indifferent to what is happening in the world about him and to people, one who is completely egocentric. He remains unmoved by the squalor and the pitiable condition of the inhabitants of the lodging-house. At the sight of the unfortunate Parabukin, Pastuxov's face assumes only a "vyraženie brezglivoj skuki". Refuting Gor'kij's thesis that the fate of the "bosjak" resulted from a social and political situation which was beyond the control of the individual in Tsarist Russia, Pastuxov tells Cvetuxin:

Все эти оборванцы — ничтожные бездельники. А кто-то придумал, что они романтики. И все поверили и создали на них моду. И ты попался на удочку — вместе с другими внушаешь галахам, что они какие-то поэтичные гении. Теперь ты видал этого волосатого хама? Хам и алкоголик, больше ничего. ...[14]

Pastuxov also ridicules Zola's penchant for studying life: "Žizn' voobraženija — vot suščnost' xudožnika ili vydajuščegosja uma." Balzac and Tolstoj, according to Pastuxov, did not study life:

... реалисты Бальзак и Толстой нас обманули. Это — самые фантастичные художники из всех, какие были. Они все выдумали, все сочинили. Они совсем не занимались копированием подлинной жизни. Книги их — плоды тончайшего воображения. Именно поэтому они убеждают больше самой жизни. И я исповедую одно: мой мысленный взор есть бог искусства.[15]

In *Neobyknovennoe leto*, Pastuxov has not changed significantly. He is first seen during the Civil War at one of the railroad stations, fleeing, with his family, from the hunger and danger of life in Petersburg. Somewhat heavier, he still personifies the egocentric artist remaining aloof from his surroundings. Circumstances propel him back to Saratov, where he again comes into contact with his acquaintances of nine years previously. He hopes to be able to "sit out" the stormy period of the Civil War, finding refuge from it in his refusal to take an active part. In conversation with Dorogomilov he condescendingly explains to the old romantic that he has never belonged to any political party, nor does he plan to join one.

[14] Fedin, *Sobranie*, VI, p. 146.
[15] *Ibid.*, pp. 148-149.

That Pastuxov has the courage of his convictions, and will not yield even in the face of pressure and veiled threats is evidenced by the following exchange, which takes place in Kirill's office. Kirill has just proposed that Pastuxov write a revolutionary play for the newly organized theatre, to which Pastuxov replies that he has not yet been inspired by a suitable theme.

— А если мы вам подскажем?
— Подскажете ... замысел?
— Да.
— Вероятно, не подскажете, а ... закажете?
— Назовите так.
— Замысел художника — это его свобода.
— На вашу свободу не посягают. Но не найдется ли в ее пределах нечто такое, что понравилось бы молодому театру? Ведь ваши прежние пьесы кому-то нравились?
— Они нравились публике.
— Надо думать, вы немного зависели от того, кому нравились. Сейчас явилась другая публика.
— Вы хотите сказать: Я теперь буду зависеть от вас?
— Очевидно, если ваши новые труды понравятся новой публике.
— Устанавливая зависимость, вы меня лишаете свободы.
— Это прежде всего касается ваших бывших заказчиков, которых я лишаю свободы ставить вас в зависимость.[16]

When Kirill asserts that the Revolution has emancipated art and artists from their former dependence on the propertied classes, Pastuxov thanks him, saying "Pozvol'te mne vospol'zovat'sja osvoboždeniem."[17]

As he enjoys his emancipation, The Revolution eddies about him, passing him by. His pre-revolutionary dramas and comedies are no longer staged in the theatres, and he neither wishes, nor is able, to write new ones. "Teper' trud stal mučitelen, potomu čto on ne znal, čto dolžen delat'." And he begins to doubt himself, to wonder if indeed he is not simply "ostatkom, oblomkom, v krošku razbivšimsja karnizom koleblemogo zdanija".

The culminating point, the climax of Pastuxov's "xoždenie po mukam" comes when, imprisoned by Mamontov, Pastuxov resolves that, if ever released, he would immediately write a letter to Izvekov admitting that he had been wrong. Pastuxov resorts to a realized metaphor in recounting his conversion to Asja, his wife, as he tells her how a cricket had crawled onto him in his cell, and how he had crushed it:

[16] Fedin, *Sobranie*, VII, p. 266.
[17] *Ibid.*, p. 267.

Самым отталкивающим в этом насекомом мне показалось то, что оно — не таракан и не саранча, а какой-то межеумок. Вдобавок, в нем было что-то самодовольно важное, точно гнус считал себя неотразимым красавцем. Это невозможно видеть без содрогания! Я потом все вспомнил, и у меня по спине мурашки бегали. Бр-р-р! ... На свете нет ничего омерзительнее межеумков. И я тогда подумал, что мое положение, ко всему прочему, мерзко.[18]

Thus does Fedin demonstrate that the position of the artist apart from society is untenable, and that art must subordinate itself to political ends.

Soviet criticism emphasizes that Fedin himself has traveled the tortuous path of agonizing doubt and vacillation, and that he, like Pastuxov, finally came to the realization that the artist must serve the Revolution.[19]

Investigation of the characterization of the writer Pastuxov and the actor Cvetuxin is necessary to an understanding of Fedin's views of the problem of art and of the theme of the dilogy as a whole. Soviet criticism of the dilogy has devoted more attention to these two figures than to all of the remainder put together.[20]

Some Soviet critics have gone to great lengths in cataloguing the defects of these two characters, completely overlooking their positive features. The usual formula is to admit that Patuxov and Cvetuxin are talented, and to concede that their pronouncements are occasionally worthy of consideration, but ...! Then a stream of vituperation follows. Numerous examples of this pattern are found in Brajnina's book on Fedin.

Brajnina's analysis of the dilogy is characterized by the use of epithets, almost always employed invectively when referring to Pastuxov and Cvetuxin. "Naskol'ko blagorodno i mužestvenno vedet sebja Kirill, zaključennyj žandarmami v tjurmu, nastol'ko malodušen i žalok Pastuxov." Pastuxov, says Brajnina, is subject to fits of "isteričeskoj ozloblennosti". From "samovljublennosti on perexodit drugoj krajnosti, k samouničiženiju". Cvetuxin and Pastuxov both suffer from "èstetskaja zamknutost', soedinennaja s xolodnym ljubopytstvom". "Ne menee, čem Pastuxov, žalkim Butafornym i malen'kim-malen'kim predstavlja-etsja nam po sravneniju s Kirillom i proslavlennyj akter Cvetuxin ... Est' nekotoraja dolja pravdy v slovax ego suprugi Agnii L'vovny: 'Vse èto pritvorstvo i čuš'! prosto on staryj lovelas!'". Pastuxov also, says Brajnina, suffers from "buržuaznyj egocentrism". "Pod vsem ètim

[18]   Fedin, *Sobranie*, VII, p. 557.
[19]   Vasilij Ivanov, "Dva romana Konstantina Fedina", *Oktjabr'*, No. 2 (1949), p. 173.
[20]   V. Ja. Grečnev, "Tema iskusstva v dilogii K. Fedina", *Voprosy sovetskoj literatury*, IX (1961), p. 402.

dekadentskim bludosloviem skryvajutsja trusost' i sebjaljubie žalkogo obyvatelja, kotoromu ničego ne dorogo, propadi vse propadom ...". Brajnina calls Pastuxov a skeptic and cynic whose lack of understanding of the Revolution is not a "tragedija" but a "žalkaja tragikomedija". At the basis of his "isolation" from the Revolution "ležit cinično-merkantil'noe otnošenie k iskusstvu, kotoroe xarakterno dlja degradirujuščego buržuaznogo obščestva".[21]

Vying with Brajnina in the use of invective is C. Karasik, who wrote on the question of art and the Revolution in the dilogy: "Pošlost', pozerstvo, poverxnost' pereživanij xarakterizujut Cvetuxina v ličnoj žizni, èto neobxodimo (!) skazyvaetsja v ego igre i v ponimanii im zadač iskusstva."[22] Another Soviet critic, Safronova, frequently refers to the "intellektual'noj i duxovnoj vysote" of Kirill Izvekov, and to the "obednennom vnutrennem mire" of Pastuxov.[23]

It hardly seems necessary to offer any proof that Fedin has characterized Pastuxov as a great writer, that he concerns himself with some of the most fundamental questions of the time, and that his interests and emotions evidence a high cultural level. Grečnev is one of the rare Soviet critics who stresses these positive qualities. It is difficult to speak seriously of any "duxovnom ubožestve" in the light of Pastuxov's ideas on literature, the theatre, painting, and art generally. One cannot overlook his characteristic subtle sense of humor, his unflagging efforts at creativity, and, beyond the realm of art qua art, his serious concern over the role of the artist in contemporary events. Indeed it may almost be accepted as axiomatic that Pastuxov frequently serves as a mouthpiece whereby Fedin expresses certain of his own cherished thoughts about art and views on life in general.

Pastuxov, a truly talented dramatist, occupies a significant place in the dilogy. He is keenly aware of what is going on about him, his eyes "ljubopytnye ščuč'im ljubopytstvom", their expression is "klejkoustojčivyj, neotjaznyj". Pastuxov notices everything, and is interested in every aspect of his environment. His imagination is particularly highly developed. In *Koster* he reads the dry newspaper account of the flight of

---

[21]   B. Brajnina, *Konstantin Fedin* (Moscow, Goslitizdat, 1956), pp. 194-96, 209, 219, 224-26.

[22]   C. Karasik, "Problema iskusstva i revoljucii v dilogii K. Fedina *Pervye radosti* i *Neobyknovennoe leto*", *Učenye Zapiski L'vovskogo Universiteta Im. I. Franko*, t. XXIV, vyp. 2, p. 83, quoted in Grečnev, p. 403.

[23]   O. Safronova, "Problema iskusstva i revoljucii v romane *Perve radosti*", *Učenye Zapiski Kazanskogo Pedagogičeskogo Instituta, Kafedra Literatury*, vyp. 12 (1958), quoted in Grečnev, p. 403.

Tolstoj from Jasnaja Poljana; he sees, in his mind's eye, a vivid picture of the event, with all of the tiny, but significant details in bold relief: the black night, the white, stubby buildings of the stables, the hurried harnessing of the snorting horses who are startled by the light from the lantern, and finally the old man in his raincoat and hood, with his matted beard, white as foam, just barely visible. His imagination is equally capable of conjuring up "ljuboj nočležnyj dom". "egipetskogo faraona", "mužič'ju kljaču", or a "člena Gosudarstvennoj dumy". His ears are so sensitive that he can hear the crackling as fishermen strip the skin from a fish on the other side of the river, and he can see the silvery scales flashing in the sunlight. Pastuxov recognizes that as a result of his flights of fancy he is liable to "ugodit' mordoj v lužu", but he is not afraid of the consequences of following his inventiveness wherever it may lead, considering these flights his *raison d'être*, his profession. Of course he would prefer to be able to give free reign to his imagination, without having to concern himself about going too far and incurring official wrath. He is sufficiently astute politically to recognize that, to be perfectly safe, he would need a "bolee vysokij dar uma" than simple imagination and inventiveness, namely the gift of prophecy. "Možno sebe predstavit' putem voobraženija ljubye formy buduščego, no vybrat' kakuju-nibud' odnu, kak neizbežnuju, dostupno tol'ko predvideniju", he affirms.

At this stage of Fedin's development, the ability to foresee the shape of things to come is particularly important, because art has a sociological function and must advance positive social and political tendencies, by definition — Communist. Pastuxov has developed to the point where he fully understands that the importance and the force of art derive from its social purpose. As Pastuxov tells his friend Cvetuxin: "Ne v tom delo, čto ty — akter, ja — dramaturg, a vot on — pevčij. Važno, radi čego my poem ...".

Pastuxov's view of the proper aim of art is expressed clearly and unequivocally when, emotionally aroused at the death of Tolstoj, he declares: "Skažu tol'ko odno. On (Tolstoj) ostavil nam pravilo, ponjatnoe, kak slovo. Vot zemlja. Vot čelovek na zemle. I vot zadača: ustroit' na zemle žizn', blagodatnuju dlja čeloveka."[24] Pastuxov expresses this thought in *Pervye radosti*, in 1910, immediately following receipt of the news of Tolstoj's death. But it is not until the second half of the second novel of the trilogy that Pastuxov decides that the life which is good for man will be built by the Bolsheviks.

Despite the 1910 affirmation of the need to build a better life, Pastuxov,

[24]   Fedin, *Sobranie*, VI, p. 409.

as an artist, is unable to identify with the revolutionary movement, either before or immediately after the October revolution, and to put his art at the service of the Revolution. Fedin, writing the dilogy in the 1940's, when the Soviet regime is firmly established, is still unable to bestow upon Pastuxov the gift of prophecy which it is within his power to grant to him, ameliorating the agony of his "xoždenie po mukam". To make the pill more palatable, Fedin characterizes Pastuxov as sybaritic and egoistical; yet Pastuxov is strong enough to withstand the blandishments and promise of success which would result from discarding his principles and serving the new regime with his art.

Any attempt to determine Fedin's attitude toward the Soviet system by analyzing Pastuxov or the other characters seems foredoomed to failure. Conclusions reached would necessarily be influenced by our preconceptions, since Fedin appears to have found a viable formula, sufficiently ambiguous to be interpreted in ways which are diametrically opposed to one another. In the case of Pastuxov, for example, the Soviet critics claim that, although agreeing with Tolstoj that the greatest task of man is to create a better life on earth, Pastuxov is unable to contribute toward accomplishing that task because he lacks that love for the people which characterizes, for example, Kirill Izvekov. Pastuxov, the Soviet critic alleges, is too much in love with himself, with comfort, and with success, and he does not realize that it is the persistent search for these things which is the greatest obstacle to attaining them. In order to become a great playwright, affirms one Soviet critic,[25] Pastuxov must rid himself of his egoism. If he does, the future is his, "... vse vperedi".

In the beginning of *Neobyknovennoe leto*, nine years after our first meeting with Pastuxov, we meet him again in the noise and confusion of a railroad station, where he, his wife Asja, and his son Aleša are fleeing from starvation in Petersburg. Pastuxov and his family are on their way to a town on the Volga, closer to a source of bread. For Bregova, this situation speaks for itself, indicating how Pastuxov, now and forever, thinks only of his own personal situation, about his own convenience. This also includes his mental well-being, since he constantly seeks the opportunity "posibaritstvovat'" with a favorite book or with pen in hand. Bregova criticizes Pastuxov because he does not care what his creative work offers to others, but is only interested in what it does for him. Pastuxov derives pleasure from the very process of creating (which, as Bregova interprets it, is meaningless) and from the creature comforts, success, and acclaim which it brings. This, says Bregova, is what motivates

[25] D. Bregova, "Konstantin Fedin", *Literatura v škole*, No. 2 (1962), p. 24.

Pastuxov to write plays, to build a dača, and to discard his family for the embraces of a younger woman. His tragedy as an artist is that, when he had his opportunity to participate in the Revolution, he preferred to think of himself, to retain his personal comforts.

Of course, the exact opposite could be argued. Pastuxov, being a man of principle, is so dedicated to the proposition of pure intellect, and pure art, that he will not create merely to further social purposes, but only in accordance with inspiration. Pastuxov refuses to follow the precepts of the "civic" critics, and rejects the argument that political and social necessity should determine an artist's creativity. According to Pastuxov, the creative instinct is a thing apart from the will of the artist, manifesting itself independently. Pastuxov hails the artist's inventiveness, his imagination, citing Balzac and Tolstoj. "V voobraženii svoem, v fantazii podveržen prekrasnomu i otvratitel'nomu, ibo ja xudožnik", affirms Pastuxov. Then, raising his glass, he proposes a toast: "Za xudožnika, protiv kopirovščika. Za Tolstogo, protiv Zoli. Za boga iskusstva — voobraženie!"[26] That Pastuxov is more of an idealist than he is given credit for is evidenced by his readiness to suffer for his art, rather than to prostitute it by deliberately putting it at the disposal of the revolutionary movement in exchange for material well-being. For ten years, Pastuxov remained steadfast, refusing to create for the revolutionary theatre, deliberately rejecting the rewards which would have ensued from such cooperation. He continually resisted the entreaties and blandishments of such officials as Kirill, indicating that perhaps he does not value comfort and luxury above all else. Yet Pastuxov recognizes the possibility of other interpretations of the role of art in addition to his own. Thus, at the end of *Pervye radosti*, when Cvetuxin expresses regret "Daže ne vypili za iskusstvo", Pastuxov replies "Čto že — iskusstvo? V iskusstve nikogda vsego ne rešiš', kak v ljubvi nikogda vsego ne skažeš'. Iskusstvo bez nedorazumenija — eto vse ravno čto pir bez p'janyx."[27]

Fedin portrays Ragozin as a being apart from the throng. Except for a few brief allusions to him, his characterization does not begin until Fedin takes the reader back to 1905. During the Jewish pogrom of October 1905, Petr Ragozin is arrested by the police for belonging to a fighting squad firing at the hoodlums of the "Black Hundreds". His wife, Ksana, seeing him advancing down the street against the rowdies who were destroying everything and everyone in their path, clung to him, wailing for him to think of her and their two-year-old son, and turn back.

[26] Fedin, *Sobranie*, VI, p. 149.
[27] *Ibid.*, p. 496.

"On oborotilsja, otodral ee pal'cy ot pidžaka, s ozlobleniem tolknul ee na trotuar i ušel. Leža na zemle, ona rasslyšala ščelkan'e revol'vernoj strel'by i, utknuvšis' licom v ladoni, zaplakala".[28] Ragozin's fit of rage, then, typifies his readiness to destroy himself for a cause.

Despite his brusque exterior, Ragozin is portrayed as a tender husband and father, ready to make whatever sacrifices may be necessary to secure a better future.

Ragozin, when we first meet him in 1905, is but a proletariat, thus fulfilling one of the requirements for a positive Soviet hero. Both in Ragozin, and in Ksenija (Ksana) Afanas'evna, his wife, Fedin attempts to portray the best qualities of the Russian masses.

Ksenija continues the tradition of the courageous wife steadfastly enduring every hardship as she suffers patiently alongside of her husband. This tradition may be traced back to the wife of Avvakum, the wives of the Decembrists, the archpriest's wife in *Soborjane*, and Dostoevskij's patient, suffering wives. Fedin himself created such a character thirty years earlier in Anna Timofevna.

Ksana's heart-rending, selfless courage is nowhere exemplified more forcefully than in the painful scene, after Ragozin has been imprisoned for a year following his arrest on the day of the pogrom, when Ksana goes to bid him farewell before he is sent into Siberian exile. Their little son has died the night before, but Ksana conceals this fact from Ragozin, assuring him that the child is well. As soon as the prison train disappears from view, Ksana turns to an old man who has been Petr's comrade and appeals for help in burying the child. "Kakogo rebenočka?", asks the old man. "Synka moego pokojnogo." "Kak synka? Razve ty ne o nem sejčas a Petrom tolkovala, pocelovat' obeščalas'?" "Pridu domoj — poceluju. On u menja doma na stole ležit." At this the old man's tongue dried out and seemed to cleave to the roof of his mouth.[29]

After three years of suffering, Ksana is approached by the same old man and gladly consents to participate in underground activities. It is just a few weeks later, toward the end of that winter, that Kirill appears, in the role of a courier. And, the following autumn, Petr Ragozin returns, now no longer merely a proletariat but a card-carrying member of the Workers' Party.

A word is in order concerning Fedin's search for an ethical system. Fedin's preoccupation with psychology and with ethics is illustrated by some of the problems which Kirill wrestles with:

[28] Fedin, *Sobranie*, VI, p. 192.
[29] *Ibid.*, p. 194.

Является или совесть, абсолютным понятием, или бывают разные
совести, допустим — совесть нищих, совесть гимназистов и техников,
совесть женщин и мужчин?[30]

Fedin devotes a great deal of attention to Kirill's search for a system of
ethics. In his conversations with Liza, Kirill suggests that perhaps
conscience is pure invention, that repentance is acceptable to him because
it is functional, and that some very important purpose would justify lying.
It is apparent that Kirill is well on the way to the conviction that whatever
serves the Revolution is moral. In the meanwhile, he tries to compromise,
as when he draws a distinction between speaking an untruth or merely
keeping silent about the truth, a distinction which Liza rejects, saying:
"Po-moemu, vse ravno, molčat' o pravde ili govorit' nepravdu ...
Skaži, ty mog by skryt' ot menja pravdu? -N-nu ... esli èto radi kakoj-
nibud' očen' važnoj celi ... naverno, mog by. -A skazat' nepravdu?
-Počemu ty sprašivaeš'?"[31]   Kirill's last comment, avoiding a direct
answer, evidences his espousal of the philosophy of the end justifying the
means.

Although Fedin does not specifically so state, the reader is made to
sense that there is conflict raging within Kirill as he tries to crystallize his
ideas. Fedin portrays this internal struggle, and the maturation of Kirill's
philosophy, with a penetration and depth which bear witness to his
psychologism.

At the same time he blends these philosophical meditations with bright
pictures of the young lovers, Kirill and Liza, as they ecstatically meet not
along the big boulevard called the Lipki, with its flower gardens and
park-like square, and its crowds of young men and women promenading,
but rather in the Sobač'i Lipki, which had become a treasured emotional
landmark of their youth, and where Kirill had handed Liza his first love
letter, written before either of them had reached sixteen. Fedin draws
pen pictures of their meetings in the streets of the town and in the pastoral
setting beyond the town's limits. He reproduces their conversations on
philosophical themes, which intermittently intrude upon the disorganized
rambling dialogue of two people experiencing the first joys of love.

Fedin skillfully blends the themes of love and revolution. After
describing how Ragozin has to lead a double life, concealing his clandestine activities behind a facade consisting of the details of his everyday life,
Fedin introduces Kirill into that life.

[30]   Fedin, *Sobranie*, VI, p. 174.
[31]   *Ibid.*, p. 176.

В эту вторую жизнь скоро получил доступ Кирилл Извеков. Мечтательные ожидания, приведшие его сюда, нашли здесь перевоплощение в действительность, превратились в задачи, и самой важной из всех задач стала необходимость ото всего мира утаивать скрытую, вторую жизнь. Может быть, это была не вторая, а какая-то четвертая, даже пятая жизнь. Но она была совсем особенная, и с появлением ее Кирилл почуствовал, что другие жизни пошли от нее поодаль, точно побаиваясь ее и уступая дорогу. Труднее всего было таиться от Лизы, потому что Лиза сама была тайной, возникшей из мечты. Обе тайны обладали чем-то родственным друг другу, и Кириллу иногда казалось, что они готовы слиться в одну. Он был поражен, что Лиза напала на след его общения с Рагозиным, понемногу успокоился, увидев в этом первый шаг к будущему, когда все сольется для них в одно целое и Лиза непременно придет к тому, к чему пришел он.[32]

The motivation here is credible. It is natural that a young man like Kirill should try to merge, to fuse his personal aspirations with those of his "professional career", in this case that of a revolutionary. With the optimism and convictions of youth, Kirill is certain that Liza would come to the same conclusions as he, and would also dedicate her life to the Revolution, insuring them both a happy, purposeful future.

The figures of the bolsheviks in *Pervye radosti* and *Neobyknovennoe leto* are portrayed differently than in the earlier novels, *Goroda i gody* and *Brat'ja*. The reader immediately senses the change which has taken place in Fedin's outlook during the intervening seventeen years, 1928 to 1945. Petr Ragozin and Kirill Izvekov, the two communist heroes of the dilogy, emerge not only as positive heroes, imbued with strength of will and determination, but as intelligent and even sensitive characters with fully developed personalities, contrasting with the earlier schematic characterizations.

Fedin has devoted special attention to the characterization of Kirill Izvekov, portraying his development from a young underground worker into a seasoned bolshevik in a manner reminiscent of Gor'kij's Pavel Vlasov in the novel *Mat'*. Kirill's "first joys" result not only from his youthful love, but also from his participation in the preparatory work leading to the revolution. This is how he reacts when he is first called "comrade":

Он бросился в чащу широким шагом, распахивая перед собою спутанную, цепкую поросль, точно плывя по зеленому ромонящему морю и слыша в буйствующих переливах повторяющееся шумящее

[32] Fedin, *Sobranie*, VI, pp. 197-98.

слово: товарищ, товарищ! Это его, Кирилла Извекова, впервые назвали таким словом — товарищ, и он сам впервые назвал таким словом — товарищ — старика, из тех людей, с какими ему предстояло жить в будущем.[33]

Under the guidance of Petr Ragozin, Kirill becomes a participant in the work of the Bolshevik underground organization. This serves as his "university", not only of life, but of art. Fedin opposes Kirill's views on art to those of Pastuxov, as when, discussing Gor'kij's play, *Na dne*, Kirill tells Pastuxov: "Ne vsjakij dramaturg vidit v žizni čto skryto ... Dlja ètogo malo byt' daže poètom, dlja ètogo nado byt' ... revoljucionerom."[34] Pastuxov, laughing, changes the subject.

The Soviet critic Ivanov rebukes Fedin for what he terms a material shortcoming in his portrayal of Kirill and his mentor Ragozin in *Pervye radosti*, namely, that they are not shown in action and the reader is unable to observe the process of growth of their political awareness and their capabilities as bolshevik organizers.[35]

Izvekov's and Ragozin's practical revolutionary work is not shown in detail, remaining clouded in secrecy. They are engaged in some type of clandestine activity, but its nature is never disclosed. Fedin only hints at this activity, but in such a masterful way that the reader hardly notices the device. Ivanov also complains because Izvekov's and Ragozin's ideological and political growth take place while they are in exile, with the details again not revealed to the reader.

In *Neobyknovennoe leto*, Kirill Izvekov is again seen in Saratov, but now he is a mature, fully formed bolshevik. During the nine years which have elapsed since the end of the action in *Pervye radosti*, Kirill has manages to serve a term of exile, fight at the front, and engage in bolshevik propaganda and agitational activities. Now he is involved in work of major importance to the Soviets. The events in which Kirill now participates, as we know from Fedin's autobiography, were experienced, in part, by the author himself. Fedin drew on his personal experiences, giving them literary form in the second book of the dilogy. Thus, in his *Avtobiografija* (1957), he writes:

Вернувшись осенью этого года (1918) в Москву, я проработал некоторое время в Народном комиссариате просвещения ... я поехал в начале 1919 года на Волгу, в Сызрань. ... Я редактировал газету *Сызранский коммунар*, работал секретарем городского исполкома ...

[33]   Fedin, *Sobranie* VI, pp. 206-7.
[34]   *Ibid.*, p. 241.
[35]   Vasilij Ivanov, "Dva romana Konstantina Fedina", *Oktjabr'*, No. 2 (1949), p. 170.

революционные поволжские события 1919 года дали мне неиссякаемый материал для писательского труда. Перед тем почти пятилетие оторванный от родины и вынужденно замкнутый в себе, я очутился в мире общей борьбы за социалистическое будущее народа и быстро проходил свою начальную школу общественной жизни. ... Осенью я был мобилизован на фронт и очутился в Петрограде — в самый разгар наступления Юденича. Сначала меня направили в Отдельную башкирскую кавалерийскую дивизию, — здесь я заведовал экспедицией, снабжая печатью четыре полка дивизии, сражавшихся на фронте. Потом я был переведен в редакцию газеты 7-й армии *Воевая правда* ...[36]

Ivanov suggests that, because of Fedin's personal experiences, as well as what he was able to observe personally, it was no longer necessary to resort to mere hints in characterizing Kirill, and that the somewhat schematic portrayal in the first novel is overcome in the second.

The high point in Kirill's life comes at the end of the novel, when Fedin describes his meeting with Stalin. Kirill's worth as a Communist hero is established beyond a doubt when, during their first meeting, Stalin immediately approves of Kirill.

Он взглянул на Ворошилова. — Ну что же, дело за назначением товарища в Первую Конную. — Да я уж думаю для него о бригаде, — сказал Ворошилов. — Не маловато? По виду человек молодой, но, как мне кажется, бывалый. К тому же волжане себе цену знают. Сталин улыбнулся Кириллу и протянул руку. ... Ворошилов, оглянувшись и рассмотрев под мерклой настенной лампой лицо Кирилла, сказал: — Так ты, значит, поутру являйся ко мне! Да пораньше! ... Неожиданное, простое это 'ты', вдруг изумив, напомнило Кириллу необычайное чувство, когда в юности, на саратовских горах, впервые в жизни старик-рабочий сказал ему ласково: 'Товарищ' — и когда он побежал по горам, чтобы усмирить свое волненье. ... Кирилл вышел из дома. По прямой снежной улице, как будто поднимавшейся кверху, он двинулся в путь со своими новыми товарищами, на солдатский ночлег, чтобы, отдохнувши, встретить будущее утро.[37]

The novel ends with these symbolic words as Kirill replaces the vacillating intellectual and takes his place among the other positive heroes of Soviet literature.

[36] Fedin, *Sobranie*, I, p. 12-13.
[37] *Ibid.*, VII, pp. 743-44.

XI

FEMALE CHARACTERS

The evolution of Fedin's female characters merits study because it sheds
light on the author's artistic development and because it furnishes evidence
of the degree to which his characters, over a period of time, came to
conform to communist specifications.

Beginning with his early stories, such as *Anna Timofevna*, we observe
variants of a type of woman who subordinates her own interests to that
of her husband and her children, making whatever sacrifices she must for
the sake of her love. Anna Timofevna is this type, as are Rita and Mari
Urbach of *Goroda i gody*. Anna Timofevna is gifted, beautiful, and
capable of great feeling, but she is destined to devote her life to back-
breaking toil and humiliation. Her contribution to life is the generous,
self-sacrificing love, tragically directed toward the ugly and the deformed.
Mari Urbach is also capable of great sacrifice and selflessness. Out of
love for Starcov, Mari Urbach attaches herself to another Russian soldier
who is making his way from Germany to Russia so that she may accompany him, thus re-joining Starcov, unmindful of the tragic reception
which awaits her.

Another variant of this type is the secondary, minor character in the
novel *Goroda i gody*, the actress Klavdija Vasil'evna, wife of the aviator
Ščepov, who, while under arrest, a hostage for her husband, bitterly
thinks about the fact

"... что она одинока, никому не нужна, что Щепову надоел ее
молящий голос и запачканные карандашом глаза ... что ... вот она
мерзнет два дня в затхлой темноте, и человеку, который для нее —
как для собаки — хозяин, не пришло на ум порадовать ее пачкой
папирос и коробкой спичек. ..."

A similar type is the merchant's daughter Varvara Ščerstobitova in
Brat'ja. She is well-endowed, yet pitiful; she is prepared to be ruthless in
demanding what she considers to be her just portion from life, yet she is
overpowered and subdued by her all-powerful love for the musician

Karev, for whom she is prepared to sacrifice her parents, her youth, her husband, and her child.

Cast of the same mold are Irina Kareva, who subordinates her own life to that of her beloved husband, and the main female characters of *Sanatorij Arktur*, the dying Inga and the woman doctor, Gofman.

Klavdija van Rossum, in *Poxiščenie Evropy*, is also a variant of the dependent female, devoting her life to her beloved. But she, unlike the others, is not a victim of love, for one can hardly grace her relationship with her husband, or with Rogov, with the name of love. It is probably for this reason that Fedin does not attempt to evoke sympathy toward her, as he does with his other heroines.

The beauty Asja Pastuxova completes the gallery of what Smirnova calls the "bourgeois" type of woman in Fedin's novels.[1] But Asja is characterized differently from her predecessors. Fedin portrays as negative characteristics, in a satirical vein, her femininity, her aristocratic bearing, her cultural pretensions, and her overwhelming beauty, all of which apparently exist only as a refuge for her husband from the harsh realities of the world.

Such an attitude is not necessarily attributable to Fedin's maturing political and social consciousness, as Soviet criticism would have us believe.[2] Rather it may be due to a number of factors, alone or in combination, including the maturity which comes with age (Fedin had reached his fifties), the effect of the war on his outlook, and actual changes which had doubtlessly taken place in women who had lost sons, fathers, husbands, and lovers in two world wars, a major revolution, a civil war, and an extended period of suppression, imprisonment, and exile for dissidents. Finally, Fedin must have been influenced by Soviet emphasis on equality for women in all areas of endeavor, stressing their role of builders of the revolution side by side with the men, and not limiting them to domestic tasks as wives and mothers.

Liza Meškova is portrayed in *Pervye radosti* as a simple and charming girl, attractive, youthful, sincere, fresh, and pure. But later, in describing her development and future destiny, Fedin shows her dependence on her father in the old patriarchal tradition, then on her fiance, on her husband, and eventually on her son. When she is with Kirill, Liza, enraptured, finds support in his love, and appears his equal. Sometimes she even seems older and wiser, as do many women whose maternal instincts are aroused by love. But the first blow of adversity, which takes Kirill away

---

[1] Smirnova, *op. cit.*, pp. 43-44.
[2] *Ibid.*, p. 43.

from her, deprives her of her courage and ability to withstand her father's urging that she marry a man of his choice, fulfilling her "vnušennogo ej s detstva, neprestupaemogo obščeizvestnogo dolga". She marries a man she does not love and then, when she wishes to leave him, cannot do so because a newer and higher responsibility — toward her child — demands that she return to her husband.

But although Liza is portrayed as a dependent and suffering woman, such as are encountered in Fedin's earlier novels, in the dilogy a new element is noted in Fedin's attitude toward such a woman. Her suffering is not, as it were, exalted, and she is not characterized as a sacrificial victim. Rather she is portrayed as lacking a true sense of responsibility, as being weak and without the fortitude, and even the love, to withstand parental pressure and remain true to Kirill throughout whatever privations life might have in store.

She is punished not only by the loss of Kirill's love, but by being deprived of happiness, tranquility, and, worst of all, by having to marry the petty, dull, base — and also illfated — Oznobižin, one of those who had in the past tried to separate Liza from Kirill.

Fedin's new attitude toward his heroines is best illustrated in his characterization of Anočka, whose destiny is completely different from that of the others. She represents the new, positive Soviet heroine, the fulfillment of the dream which Liza entertained in her youth.

It is for adequate reason that Liza is so envious of Anočka in the first performance of the play *Kovarstvo i ljubvi*, in which Anočka plays Luiza Miller. "Otkuda že èta devočka vzjala sily otvažit'sja na takoj boj i vyigrat' ego?", Liza asks herself and, griefstricken, thinks that she herself could have had the part, rather than Liza. "No aktrisoj sdelalas' ne sovsem skladnaja i — pravo že — ne očen' krasivaja Anočka. A Liza tak, naverno, i umret obyknovennoj ženščinoj provincii, v grustnoj nezametnosti ...".

There is one detail in the relationship between Kirill and Anočka which is felt as a new and important feature. Earlier, in the last chapter of the novel *Brat'ja*, Varvara Ščerstobitova says to Nikita:

Вот тебе само собой понятно, что твоя жизнь и твои дела должны быть для меня самым главным, что ты у меня — начало и конец. ... Тебе тяжело, а я должна это знать. Тебе плохо — я обязана сочувствовать ... в тебе выросло это несносное сознание, что самый близкий тебе человек — только твое подспорье, твое житейское удобство, не больше, что он, естественно, обязан тебе служить. ... Должен же ты хоть раз подумать, что для меня оскорбительна эта моя ... второстепенность в твоей жизни. ... В сущности, тебе безразлично, какой человек живет с тобой рядом. Важно только, чтоб жил, чтобы эта вторая жизнь облегчала твою первую, главную. ... Как это сказать? — чтобы тебя здесь заряжали, а там ты стрелял бы. ...[3]

This, of course, is more than the mere "isk k muzyke", as Nikita Karev thinks. It is a woman's protest against that "služebnoj roli" for which love has destined her.

Under the influence of love, Anočka becomes impatient and demanding. She refuses to content herself with the knowledge that she and Kirill can see each other only sporadically, that he "propadaet na dva mesjaca". She tortures herself with the thoughts that Kirill has not been able to forget Liza, his first love, or that he "bol'še vsego ljubit vlast'". She tests him, as it were, by asking: "Vse delo, stalo byt', v tom, čtoby podčinit'sja?" And when he quietly replies: "Doverit'sja", he senses that his relations with her "otkryly v nem osobuju mjagkuju storonu duši, kotoruju on redko v sebe slyšal". And he brings her an example of that "doverija", disclosing to her what is, for him, the most important thing in life at that particular moment: "Èto ja govorju tol'ko Vam. Ponimaete? Pal Caritsyn."

But, despite this overwhelming proof of Kirill's love, Anočka continues to doubt, to feel injured, and to be angry at the fact that she must part with Kirill. Finally, in a decisive moment, at night after her first play, happy and proud because of her first success, as well as because of Kirill's love, she asks: "Kogda že konec ètomu beskonečnomu 'nado'?"

This question recalls to mind the dialogue in Avvakum's *Žitie*, when the archpriest and his family have been trudging across the ice on their way back to Western Russia after extended Siberian exile. The archpriest's wife, exhausted, trips and falls, and others in the party, equally weary, trip over her prostrate body. "How long, Archpriest, are these sufferings to last?"

"Markovna, till our death", replies Avvakum. Then the wife courageously comments: "So be it, Petrovič; let's be getting on."[4]

Kirill Izvekov's reply is not nearly as laconic, though it does serve to characterize him as a staunch and resolute paragon of the new Soviet man: "Ty ne vidiš' konca moemu 'nado', potomu, čto èto 'nado' ne tvoe. Esli ono stanet i tvoim i moim, tebe ne tak važno budet — skoro li nastupit emu konec." As he says this, Kirill smiles, since "konec nastupit vse-taki nemnožko skoree — ved' odnim zemlekopom budet bol'še".

---

[3] Fedin, *Sobranie*, III, pp. 411-412.
[4] N. K. Gudzij, *History of Early Russian Literature*, p. 392.

And, like Avvakum's wife, Anočka understands and accepts this answer as a guide to the pattern of her future life.

This conversation, which is so important in defining future relations between Kirill and Anočka, is, at the same time, a reply to the conversation between Varvara and Nikita Karev which was cited above from the novel *Brat'ja*. It also serves as a reply to all of the other expressed or implied protests which may be made by other Fedin heroines.

The firmness and loftiness of Kirill's beliefs, and his courage in defending his convictions, may be attributed to the upbringing he received from his mother. Yet his consciousness of justice and equity, and his dedication to "dobro", to not only seeking but actively fighting for what is "good", must be attributed to an external influence. Vera Nikandrova was able to sense that Kirill had compartmentalized his personal life, and was excluding her from certain of his thoughts and activities. Yet she was proud that she had raised her son on the basis of mutual respect, as well as of mutual love, and she was proud that she respected her son. "V rannem detstve ona vnušala emu samostojatel'nost', nezametno podskazyvaja, čto volja syna, po prirode, ne možet protivorečit' materi, čto želanija roditelej i detej estestvenno sovpadajut".[5] Vera Nikandrova was convinced that this philosophy would yield excellent results. And indeed Kirill always acted as he considered was right, and therefore felt no need to hide anything.

Vera Nikandrovna understood that as Kirill matured, there would be changes, but she never expected that lack of frankness, that secretiveness which she now encountered. It was when a doctor diagnosed Kirill's acute eye inflammation as lead-poisoning (due to his activities in the underground print shop, and not at the technical school as he led the doctor to believe) that Vera Nikandrovna suddenly realized that Kirill was lying, and that a veil of secrecy had intruded to disturb their hitherto frank and trusting relationship. Fedin resorts to an image taken from nature for his simile expressing the change:

"Сердечность отношений между матерью и сыном, конечно, не исчезла, не могла исчезнуть, но едва заметным пятном обозначилась новая пора в нерушимой близости, как обознается конец лета первым желтым листом, еще скрытым от вздора яркой зеленью."[6]

Vera Nikandrova remains alone after Kirill is imprisoned and exiled, she loses her job and home, but retains the strength to surmount her grief.

---

[5]   Fedin, *Sobranie*, VI, pp. 166-167.
[6]   *Ibid.*, p. 168.

In her pride, courage, and moral strength, she is a mother worthy of Kirill.

These qualities are not evident at once, but develop in her over a period of time, as she experiences some of the tragedy of life, such as the death of her husband and, years later, the arrest and exile of her son. This strength is portrayed with particular beauty and emotional force the night the old man brings her a letter written by a "comrade" of Kirill's in exile. The old man removes the letter from his boot, where it was hidden for safekeeping, and Vera Nikandrovna reads that her son has dedicated himself "na bol'šuju žizn'" and will never regret it because "zamaxnulsja po silam".[7] Vera Nikandrovna immediately writes an answer, entreating the anonymous friend — whom she knows to be Ragozin — to help her son through the dangers that lie ahead. At the same time she dedicates herself to this "larger life": "Ja že obeščaju vam, čto on ne uslyšit ot menja ni slova goreči i ne uznaet ni ob odnoj moej sleze ... pust' ja budu emu posoxom, a ne sumoj s kamnjami na ètoj doroge. Pomožem emu delat' bol'šuju žizn' ..."[8]

In the scene immediately following, Fedin blends the visual image of the town coming to life, industrious and full of promise, with Vera Nikandrovna's mood of optimism and quiet determination. Fedin blends these motifs by resorting to the simile of tinted puffs of smoke with steam intertwined in milky strands like ribbons in braided hair:

Вера Никандровна не легла спать ... рассвет прочертил ровненькие линеечки в щелях ставен. Она вышла на улицу ... белесые тучи свисали на землю, и со станции тяжело поднимались к ним густые, медлительные дыми. Они будто состязались в разноцветности окрасок, — сизо-синие, золотисто-рыжие на путях, огненно-багровые, вишнево-черные над цехами депо, они, как косы — лентами, были перевиты молочными струями пара, перегонявшими их по пути к небу, где все соединялось в сплошную навись гари.[9]

Vera continues to stand there and watch the smoke struggling, threatening to overcome the whole world. The smell of coal, oil, paints, and lubricants, mixes with the sound of iron clanking and grating as the morning light surges in and Vera Nikandrovna opens the shutters. Thus does Fedin revert to synaesthesia, the blending of visual, auditory, and other sensations which, corresponding to each other, symbolize the strength and joy of the future.

---

[7] Fedin, *Sobranie*, VI, p. 427.
[8] *Ibid.*, p. 428.
[9] *Ibid.*, VI, p. 431.

In the relationship between Kirill and his mother may be seen the influence of Gor'kij's *Mat'* (pub. 1907).

In this novel, Gor'kij attempted to portray the revolutionary, the New Hero of his time. Gor'kij based the novel on the 1902 strike and political demonstrations in the industrial town of Sormovo, and patterned his hero and his mother after actual participants. Paul, a young worker, joins the revolutionaries, carries the red banner in a mass demonstration, and is jailed.

Nilovna, his mother, a simple-minded, illiterate (unlike Vera Nikandrovna, Kirill's mother) woman of forty, is worried about her son and is afraid of his association with the Reds. Yet when she gets to know his companions better and realizes their integrity and spirit of sacrifice, she feels that they are the salt of the earth, the seekers after truth, the true disciples of Christ, and little by little she comes to side with them.

She begins by rendering them small services, helps them more and more, and finally becomes converted to their faith because she senses "the truth that is bound to triumph".

XII

LANGUAGE

Characteristic of Fedin's development as a writer over a period of four decades has been his constant search for better means of expression. In his earlier works, Fedin deliberately wrote in an intricate and mannered style, influenced by contemporary ornamentalism, and stressing a rhythmic prose. Gradually this poetic language was replaced by a language which was characterized by simplicity, clarity, and precision of thought. In his efforts to perfect his language, Fedin followed Gor'kij's dictum: "Podlinnaja krasota jazyka, dejstvujuščaja kak sila, sozdaetsja točnost'ju, jasnost'ju, zvučnost'ju slov, kotorye oformljajut kartiny, xaraktary, idei knig."[1]

This explains why, for the second book of *Poxiščenie Evropy*, Fedin chose the following epigraph, a quotation from Stendhal: "U menja est' tol'ko odno sredstvo pomešat' svoemu voobraženiju razygryvat' so mnoj šutki: èto idti prjamo na predmet."[2] By this epigraph Fedin seems to be announcing his intention to use direct, succinct language, free of adornment.

A year or two later, Fedin again expressed his preference for direct, purposeful language, used for communication and not merely to demonstrate the writer's ability to turn a phrase. In 1936, Fedin wrote:

Слишком бедный запас чувств, всятых у жизни, слишком призрачные познания — и вот начинается восполнение недостающего надуманным описаниями природы, которые не служат никакой цели, мнимо подлинными диалогами, вроде: — Ну, как? — Да ничего. А ты как? — Я тоже ничего. — Та...а...к.[3]

In 1951, Fedin, referring to literary craftsmanship, began his discussion by stressing the primacy of language:

Разговор о мастерстве писателя следует начинать с языка. Язык

---

[1] M. Gor'kij, "O literature", *O socialističeskom realizme* (Moscow, Sovetskij Pisatel', 1937), p. 344.
[2] Fedin, *Sobranie*, IV, p. 236.
[3] *Literaturnyj Leningrad*, No. 17 (1936), p. 162.

всегда останется основным материалом произведения. Художе-
ственная литература — это искусство слова. Даже столь важное
начало литературной формы, как композиция, отступает перед
решающим значением языка писателя.[4]

In the chapters devoted to Fedin's earlier works, it was seen that, after
a period of experimentation with the highly colored prose style of
ornamentalism, Fedin was attracted by the grace and succinctness of
Čexovian laconism. By the late 1920's, Fedin had come to believe, with
St. Augustine, that "any ornamentation exceeding the bounds of
responsibility to the content of the work is sophistry".[5] Beginning about
1928, and continuing until 1934, Fedin published several articles expressing his views regarding the language appropriate to literature. Fedin
criticized those who would create a "new" language, those who concentrated on "creating" new words, and those who made excessive use of
dialectisms.[6] Representative passages from these articles follow:

Новшеств сторониться, конечно, не следует, но хорошо бы почаще
срамить грамотеев, выдающих косноязычие за новаторство.
    Выступить против искажения старого языка — значит выступить
в защиту существующего, растущего, живого языка.[7]
    В работе своей я не преследую целей словотворчества. ... Борьба за
новое слово для меня заключается в постоянном обновлении фразы
путем бесчисленных сочетаний тем самых 'обыкновенных', 'не-
красивых' слов, которые усвоены нашей живой речью и литера-
турой.[8]
    В нашей критике последнее время все чаще отмечается засоренность
художественных произведений областными словами и оборотами.
Требования от писателя чистоты русского языка справедливы.
Здесь только надо избегать педантизма.[9]

These extracts from Fedin's articles illustrate the major tendencies and
characteristics of Fedin's use of language which, coinciding with the views
of A. N. Tolstoj (d. 1945) and A. A. Fadeev (d. 1956), have influenced
other contemporary Soviet novelists.
    Fedin has devoted himself to the study of all the many facets of the use
of language in literature, including lexical inventory, the semantic content

[4] Fedin, "O masterstve", *Sobranie*, IX, p. 570.
[5] Shipley, p. 295.
[6] This criticism may be found in the following articles: "Fel'eton o jazyke i kritike",
Zvezda, No. 9 (1929); "Jazyk literatury", *Literaturnaja učeba*, No. 3-4 (1933); *Kak my
pišem, sbornik statej* (Leningrad, 1930).
[7] *Zvezda*, No. 9 (1929), pp. 141, 148.
[8] *Kak my pišem*, p. 170.
[9] *Literaturnaja učeba*, No. 3-4 (1933), p. 113.

of individual words, syntax, and phonology, the latter including euphony, rhythm, and meter. He has also consciously studied the use of various stylistic devices, including image, metaphor, symbol, and myth. In his theoretical writings, Fedin presents his theories on the use of the word, and combinations of words, in the speech of his characters, in the author's own speech, and in various narrative techniques, such as dialogue, description, and portrait, and also in the various functions of language: imparting facts, making various philosophical judgments, in lyrical digressions, in depicting psychological characteristics, and in describing nature and landscape.

Fedin contends that mastery of the word, of linguistic skill, is not an end in itself, but is rather the most important means to "peredat' bol'šuju pravdu žizni. ... Slovo-samocel', v konce koncov, bessmyslenno, kak bessmyslenno vsjakoe orudie, esli ono ne prinosit pol'zy".[10] From this concept, Fedin derives what he considers to be the most important activity of the writer in his use of words, which is to select, from all possible synonyms, that word which is capable "s naibol'šej točnost'ju opredelit' mysl'".[11] But in addition to this requirement of maximum precision, the individual word in an artistic work is also a means of literary representation (comparable to paint, as a means of visual representation), and therefore the word "dolžno byt' muzykal'no-vyrazitel'no"[12] and it must harmonize with the rhythmic construction of the phrase.

Proceding from individual words to their arrangement in the sentence, the paragraph, and longer periods up to the linguistic fabric of the work as whole, Fedin considers that the writer must avoid verbosity, super-fluous words, and deliberate complexity. The author must cultivate "samye dorogie kačestva, neobxodimye xudožestvennoj proze; kratkuju formu, točnost' vyraženija, jasnost' mysli".[13]

It was noted earlier that Fedin's style is characterized by certain features found in the language of Lev Tolstoj and Anton Čexov. Brajnina, in an article in 1954, commented as follows:

В своей работе над поэтическим языком, Федин стремится сочетать на новой основе традиции толстовского подробного психологи- ческого анализа с традициями чеховского лаконизма. Эта трудоем- кая и плодотворная работа дала блестящие результаты.[14]

---

[10]   K. Fedin, "O masterstve", *Sobranie*, IX, p. 581.
[11]   *Kak my pišem*, p. 170.
[12]   *Ibid.*
[13]   Fedin, *Sočinenija v šesti tomax*, VI, p. 558, cited Bugaenko, p. 150.
[14]   B. Brajnina, "Iskusstvo slova", *Oktjabr'*, No. 1 (1954), p. 164.

Fedin's basic lexical stock is drawn from the contemporary literary language. This applies both to the speech of his characters, and to that of the narrator himself. In an effort to identify the distinguishing characteristics of Fedin's choice of words, the critic Poljak wrote: "U K. Fedina ... povestvovanie svjazano so specifikoj knižnogo jazyka s prisuščimi emu osobennostjami-otvlečennost'ju slovosočetanij, slovesnyx obrazov, kotorye nosjat často obobščennyj xarakter."[15] Fedin may be opposed to A. N. Tolstoj who, according to the same critic, bases his language "na osnove živogo, razgovorno-bytovogo narodnogo jazyka, široko ispol'zujuščego prostorečnye slova, ustnye, a inoj raz skazovye intonacii".[16] Poljak's statement is misleading. From it, one might conclude that the basis of Fedin's lexicon is the conscious and deliberate reliance on abstract word combinations and syntactical arrangements, and a deliberate avoidance of colloquial speech. Neither Fedin's theoretical pronouncements nor his actual literary practice support this thesis. Fedin, both in his early works and in his contemporary writings, has consistently used various levels of the live, dynamic, everyday speech, blending it with literary speech in an unobtrusive fashion. Examination of the text of the novels of the dilogy reveals the use of such sub-standard words and expressions (prostorečie) as: gul'nut', poluzgal vvolju, samooogljadka vesennego dnja, sučil nogami, nosaki, mal'čugany v tjat'-kinyx dolgopolyx šineljax, postavil na popa. Specific colloquialisms are exemplified by such words and expressions as: fliger', makovaja rosinka, vzjat' xotja by vašu neprijatnost', bol'šoj sdelalsja peretomit, razbubnilsja, podumaeš', trebovajut ot načal'stva posadki, bog, nynče otmenennyj, tot v šljape, entot pod zontom, za pošenom za kartoxoj, za svekolkoj. These are just a few of the examples evidencing Fedin's use of collo-quialisms and *argot*. They are by no means bookish or part of the lexical stock of the Russian literary language, but are characteristic of the speech of the Saratov region.[17] They are used in various descriptions by the author of the everyday life of the Volga stevedores, as well as in their dialogue, serving the literary function of providing local color and verisimilitude at appropriate places in the novels.

Fedin is one of those writers who is keenly aware of and sensitive to the various levels of spoken speech, and who thoughtfully and sparingly draw upon this rich linguistic source of supply for the material for his works.

---

[15] L. Poljak, "Pervoèlement literatury", *Literaturnaja gazeta*, 15 Sept. 1955.
[16] *Ibid.*
[17] Bugaenko, p. 152.

Absent from the dilogy is the ostentatious use of words and expressions drawn from the colloquial stock, dialecticisms, jargon, or argot introduced solely for ornament, to call attention to itself. But Fedin does not hesitate to use such expressions, not only in the dialogue of the characters, but also to express the thoughts and emotions of the narrator in those circumstances when they have a direct bearing on the dialogue, or when they enhance description by augmenting local color.

Yet the use of colloquial speech is just one of the several stylistic devices which Fedin uses. In the same chapter, and even on the same page, Fedin may mix words and expressions of a completely different lexical origin and intonation. In the 19th chapter of *Pervye radosti*, for example, Fedin does this as he transports the reader from scene to scene. First the reader observes Cvetuxin, thinking idle thoughts and dreaming impractical, naive dreams as he strolls along the wharf to a rendezvous with Pastuxov. Then Fedin portrays the two, actor and playwright, on the bright deck of the steamer, where they enjoy a leisurely, gourmet luncheon of crayfish and sterlet, and engage in idle conversation touching, like dilettantes, superficially, art, philosophy, and culture in general. Then the scene shifts to the ground beneath the piles supporting a huge warehouse, where the stevedores kneel in a circle around a big pot which contains their hot stew, and each man ladles out his own portion, watched by the others to insure he does not take more than his share of meat. Then the scene shifts to the gang of stevedores as they tug on an anchor line while chanting a rhythmic Volva riverman's song to lighten the task. Then the scene again shifts, as Anočka visits the two artists on the deck of the steamer, then Parabukin suffers an injury as he bosses the gang of stevedores, then Cvetuxin tries to help and is significantly cautioned: "ne mešajsja, barin", and finally, the last scene of the chapter, in which Pastuxov, up above, is smoking nervously after having heard from Anočka that Kirill was arrested, and Cvetuxin, down below, being rebuffed for a second time as Anočka refuses a proferred handkerchief with which she might wipe her injured father's face.

All of this action is compressed into just twelve pages of the 19th chapter. In it, Fedin makes use of a variety of narrative devices, shifting from a description of nature and the setting from the point of view of the omniscient author in the third person, to the use of what is variously called "quoted speech",[18] "free indirect discourse",[19] "erlebte Rede",[20]

---

[18]   D. Čiževskij, *Evgenij Onegin* (Cambridge, Harvard University Press, 1953), p. xxiv.
[19]   E. Auerbach, *Mimesis* (Princeton, Princeton University Press, 1953), *passim*.
[20]   W. Kayser, *Das Sprachliche Kunstwerk*, 2d ed. (Berne, A. Francke, 1951), p. 145.

and, in Russian, "nesobstvenno prjamaja reč'". This technique in this chapter assumes the form both as interior monologue[21] and as stream of consciousness,[22] the second differing from the first in the extent of the flow of ideas and emotions as response follows stimulus in what appears to be a completely random order, with no apparent relevance to one another. In the same chapter, Fedin describes the dialogue of Cvetuxin and Pastuxov, the contrast in the lunches of the two groups of men, and the back breaking work of the stevedores in contrast to the indolence of the artists. As Fedin shifts the content and the various artistic devices, he also varies the lexicon, using it for characterization and conveying his own attitude toward events. Examples of colloquialisms are: èdoki, vydjužil, mordoj v lužu, taskaj so vsem, djužij upor. Examples of the peculiar jargon of the Volga stevedores are vereteno, zapleč'e, čalka, krjuč'ja. Bookish aphorisms are represented by: ljubov' i radost' xodjat po pjatam za slavoj; èto byl ne brak, a sudebnoe razbiratel'stvo. Expressions in the literary language, suggesting a high level of pathos, are: čudesnoj volnoj pobežala nad beregom dvuxgolosaja, radujuščaja i utešajuščaja dušu bolgarja pesnja, nexitrye slova kotoroj prepirajutsja i podzadorivajut, a napev edinit i vedet ljudej, vedet v nogu ljudej iz goda v god, iz veka v vek. These expressions, by virtue of their syntax, the multiplication of epithets, the use of characteristic participial phrases, and even the use of individual words are reminiscent of some of Gogol'. Here one also finds sentences which Fedin has constructed on the basis of sound patterns: *Tu*po *tu*kali *po* v*z*vozam *po*terjavšie *z*vonkost' *po*dkovy. (tu-tu-po-zv-po-zv-po). The recurrence of the initial sounds in this sentence is so great as to eliminate the possibility of it being anything but conscious alliteration.

The breadth and variety of lexical devices is even greater in the novel *Neobyknovennoe leto*. To a greater degree than the first novel, it includes historical chapters and a greater publicistic element, requiring the use of military, political, and historical terminology. Thus, in the 29th chapter of the novel, Fedin introduces a number of military terms: ukreplennyj rajon, korpus, komendant, garnizon, bronevoj otrjad, brigada s artilleriej, perestrelka, raz"ezd, operacija, čvakuacija, mobilizacija, eskadron, rejd, demonstrativnoe dviženie, and taktika. In context, these military terms do not present any problem to the reader, forcing him to consult a

---

[21] E. Dujardin, *Le monologue intérieur* (Paris, 1931).
[22] L. E. Bowling, "What Is the Stream of Consciousness Technique?", *PMLA*, LXV (1950), pp. 337-45.

military dictionary and thus interfering with the flow of the narrative. On the contrary, they intensify the real, historical, documentary effect, essential to the narration of military events.

In addition to the variety of linguistic devices, their subordination to the subject matter, and the absence of any deliberate effort on the part of the author to call attention to the language for its own sake, Fedin exhibits particular sensitivity to the relationship between the semantic content of a word and its phonology. This is particularly evident in the entertaining "linguistic" discussion between Patuxov and Cvetuxin about the pronunciation of the words "studen'" and "stjuden'", and Pastuxov's reaction to the word "volnitel'no". These scenes are reminiscent of Leskov (d. 1895), particularly *Levša* which, in Leskov's delightful *skaz* manner, is replete with hilarious neologisms invented by the author himself, or by words mutilated in pronunciation and use by the hero of the tale.

Fedin himself has referred to his desire to rejuvenate the sentence by means of unique combinations of the most ordinary words. This "obnovlenie frazy", these new combinations, appear in various forms in Fedin's works. Thus, for example, he uses epithets like *ustalaja* prelest', *omertvevšee* nerjašestvo, *legkie* i *pyšnye* odejanija Pastuxova, *prožorlivoe* ljubopytstvo, *zastraščennaja* devočka, *samozabvennoe* kručenie, *uvesistye* šagi, *mirotvornaja* ten', *kengirovoe* složenie, *puglivyj* reverans v golose, *ser'eznye* efiry. Similes are represented by the following phrases: pered nej, kak na perevernutoj stranice, otkrylas' ulica; golova nabita plotno, kak mešok; uskol'zal ot vnimanija, kak voda iz dyrjavogo čelna; on ostanovilsja pered dverjami, kak pered kreščenskoj prorub'ju; deržalas' rovno i prjamo, kak ottočennyj melok; èto tak že protivo-estestvenno, kak golovnaja bol' dlja djatla. Metaphors are exemplified by the following: golosa snujut čelnokami; rasterjanno breli v nebe kučnye oblaka; sinjaja poskon' štanov trepyxalas' flagami signal'ščika; kudri perelivalis' na solnce sputannym klokom, vygorevšego sena. Some of these metaphors are less effective and do not result in a more palpable image, as, for example, "golosa, *snujščie* čelnokami", or "voda, kotoraja *uskol'zaet*". Other combinations make no pretense at being particularly noteworthy artistic constructions or innovations.

In fact, it is not difficult to find in the dilogy such cliches as: lysiny bulyžnika, strekotan'e jazykov, ploščad' ryčit, bezljudnaja ulica, smolja-nye usy. The dilogy also contains word combinations associated with the work of other writers. Thus the phrase "deržalas' rovno i prjamo, kak ottočennyj melok" is reminiscent of Čexov's "deržalas' rovno i prjamo, kak ikona".[23] Some of Fedin's syntactic units are characterized by a large number of subordinate clauses: "On tol'ko soznaval, čto esli skažet, čto pravy belye, to èto budet oboznačat', čto pravy francuzy, napavšie na nego v Kenigštejne, a on voznenavidel ix za to, čto oni nenavistno govorili o Rossii". This type of complex sentence is also characteristic of Lev Tolstoj.

Not all of Fedin's word combinations are uniformly fresh, new, and "infectious"; they run the gamut from those which are somewhat hackneyed and trite, having lost their novelty through repeated prior use, to those which are truly remarkable artistic refinements, so unique and effective that they can only be repeated if enclosed in quotations marks. The basis for this sweeping generalization may be better understood by examining a few specific examples, typifying the freshness of some of his combinations and representing, as Bugaenko calls them, "malen'kie otkrytija".[24] These may be categorized as: Unusual combinations of modifier and thing modified, such as mirotvornaja ten', ustalaja prelest'; unusual comparisons of objects from different classes, such as golovnaja bol' i djatel; subtle transfer of qualities from one object to another, such as trepyxanie sinix štanov gruzčika — trepyxanie sinix flagov signal'ščika. Fedin also uses everyday words in such unusual combinations that they assume new shades of meaning, previously concealed behing their conventional meaning. This type of foregrounding is illustrated in the following sentence; "Žara kak budto obkusyval i pogošlala zvuki, ne davaja im slit'sja v šum." The unusual nature of the metaphor, the heat gnawing at sounds, evokes an emotional response as well as conveying almost a visual image of heat which is so overpowering as to stifle sound. In the phrase, "utrennyj serebristo-opalovyj čas", the epithet silvery-opal is not only an unusual combination, but an effort to intensify the visual image of early morning and to evoke a definite mood in the reader.

In his efforts to attain maximum visual and emotional specificity, Fedin resorted to another device, the multiplication of epithets, as in these examples: tjagučij, xrustal'nyj zvon špor; svetjaščijsja, široko raskrytyj vzor Anočki; gorjačij, nepodvyžnyj, tomitel'nyj znoj; grivastoe, smutnoe, uvalažennoe lico Parabukina; vpervye otkrytoe, nevidannoe i neverojatnoe; iznurennymi, vytaraščennymi ot natugi glazami, žadnym, dergajuščimsja licom v temnoj borode; otčajanno-vlastnym krikom; sijajuščij, tixij, sčastlivyj Xvalynsk; molčalivoj, lučistoj ulybkoj; sčekočuščij, volglyj, smolistyj zapax derevjannoj barži. This proliferation of epithets

---

[23]   Bugaenko, p. 154.
[24]   *Ibid.*, p. 155.

enables Fedin to economize in his descriptions, since greater concreteness is attained through supplementary epithets rather than through lengthier syntactic constructions.

Fedin's aversion to lengthy, involute syntax is apparent throughout the dilogy except, as noted earlier, where he makes occasional use of complex sentences with a number of subordinate clauses. In the 29th chapter of *Pervye radosti*, Fedin, by means of a series of brief, abrupt, sentences, conveys Pastuxov's reaction to the news of the death of Lev Tolstoj:

Он вытер мокрый холодный лоб. ... Он торопился по улицам неизвестно — куда. Спустившизь по всвозу, он повернул назад, в гору, и тотчас опять направился вниз, почти до самой воды. Тьма пеленала Волгу. Бледные сигналы баканов, казалось, умирали от бессилия. Огни пристаней были жидки. Шум волны упивался своим всесильным господством. Сеяло тонким, как крупчатка, дождем.[25]

These short, unconnected, sentences, besides conveying the atmosphere of that autumn night, help the reader penetrate into the subconscious of the disturbed playwright and share his bewildered grief. The predominance of parataxis helps establish the tone of impulsive urgency and drama.[26] Complex, drawn-out constructions would have been inappropriate in this scene, in which Fedin describes the place and time of the action, creates the atmosphere in which the scene is enveloped, and then proceeds to the revelation of the mood of the artist. This mood, consisting of a disorderly mixture of confused emotions, is best conveyed by means of a more complex construction, which is what Fedin proceeds to do in the next paragraph:

Он чувствовал свое совершенное одиночество, но уже не в тех тончайших оттенках, которые доставляли грустную усладу, а в безжалостном, грубом тоне все заливающей собою беспросветной тьмы. Он уже был убежден, что уход человека, нежданно овладевшего самым хребтом его сознания, был не просто уходом, он был уходом-смертью. И как обычно в этом мире действительно важные события непоправимы, так и это собитие было до очевидности непоправимо.[27]

A feature noted by the Soviet critic Smirnova is the "narodnyj", meaning the national, Russian character of the speech, rather than its folk character.[28] This is expressed by both syntax and lexicon.

[25] Fedin, *Sobranie*, VI, pp. 395, 396.
[26] Cf. E. Auerbach, *Mimesis*, on the anatomy of hypotaxis and parataxis.
[27] Fedin, *Sobranie*, VI, p. 396.
[28] Smirnova, p. 57.

In the very beginning of *Neobyknovennoe leto* the former lieutenant in the Tsarist army, Dibič, returning from internment in Germany, is seen traveling through the Soviet Union. "Rossija-rodina", for which he pined, and which he now eagerly observes from a boxcar, flows by "v lenivoj smene" of typical scenes of the Russian countryside: ploughed fields, villages, peasants, and little boys draped in army greatcoats.

The feeling of nature and the land is conveyed by numerous, earthy, folk words and expressions, carrying a warm emotional charge, consistent with the mood and impressions of the returnee. Dibič is seated in the doorway of the boxcar, his legs "svesiv na volju". Fedin speaks of the "polotna s telegrafnymi polinjalymi stolbuškami", the winter corn "okačennaja solncem".

"Леса и закустившиеся пни бырубок отсвечивали рябью масля-нистых, едва пошедших в рост листочков. ... На выгонах ... стояли врассыпную ... буренушки и пестравки, и мальчуганы в тятькиных ... шинелях ... заплетали кнуты, сидя на припеке .... .Изредка семенила по взмету обок с прыгающей бороной баба. ..."[29]

All of these expressions seem to have been chosen to convey how small, poor, and shabby everything had become in comparison with his pre-war recollections, yet it all had become dearer to him.

Smirnova has compiled a list of words appearing in the beginning of *Neobyknovennoe leto* which characterize Dibič himself, as he struggles to understand the new situation in which he finds himself at the railroad station: povyskočiv, skučivalsja, nemudrennaja sned', torg, poljubovnoe obmerivanie i obsčityvanie, zatirali, nemoščny, nerazberixa, vzjat' v tolk, tolkučka, raspixal, za pasuxu, mosolki, uvalen'oxrannik, protiskivalsja, tolčeju, svoe dobro. These terms serve as guideposts, indicating the fundamental nature of the period and of the characters.

Another example of their use for character delineation is found in Pastuxov's speech. Pastuxov is a member of the intelligentsia, a writer, one who knows the value of words and is sharp-witted. He is fond of including in his speech carefully-chosen, even affected, extracts from the French classics; expressions from Holy Writ; words peculiar to the ver-nacular, such as "sponadobilos'". At times they are used almost as quotations, and the reader feels that Pastuxov is showing off with them. Pastuxov knows exactly when, and with whom, to introduce the desired expression. "Vy xotite mne *prisobačit'* èti proklamacii?", he casually asks Lt. Colonel Polotencev when summoned to police headquarters. At the

[29]   Fedin, *Sobranie*, VII, pp. 9, 10.

railroad station at Rteščevo he demands of the responsible official:
"Otprav'te menja *k čertovoj babuške, pixnite* nas kuda-nibud' v tambur."

Yet, when sophistication is called for, the elements of the vernacular, creating an impression of "prostonarodnost'", vanish from Pastuxov's speech, and we hear only the literary bookish language characteristic of the beginning of the century.

Fedin's use of overall tone, manner of speech, and choice of words as devices for characterization is reminiscent of I. S. Turgenev.

In *Fathers and Sons*, Bazarov, as one would expect, uses simple, generally accepted words and turns of speech. He shuns foreign words and those expressions characteristic of the philosophical abstractions, aesthetics, and "romantic" feelings of the upper class intelligentsia of the 1840's. Bazarov occasionally uses Latin words, which he learned in the classical middle schools and when studying medicine (bene, pater familias) but, overall, he strives for maximum clarity and precision of speech. Wherever appropriate, he uses popular speech, even substandard speech (prostorečie), folk sayings, and proverbs.

Pavel Petrovič Kirsanov speaks quite differently, using French expressions. He does this for two reasons. On the one hand, he has been taught French since childhood, so that he is able to think and to express all concepts in French, especially when he is at a loss for the proper Russian word. A second reason for using French is to communicate with his brother or nephew when he does not wish the servants to know what he is saying.

Like Bazarov, Pavel Petrovič also employs popular speech, but for completely different purposes. For Bazarov, popular speech and folk sayings have become an organic part of his own speech, and he uses them simply and naturally, as he would any other words. But for Pavel Petrovič the use of folk expressions is an affectation, a mannerism. Turgenev attaches to this peculiarity of Pavel Petrovič a social-psychological motivation: "Ja *èf*tim xoču dokazat' ...." When Pavel Petrovič grew angry, he deliberately inserted the *f* in èto. This may be attributed to his identification with the nobility of the Alexandrine period, some of whom deliberately flaunted rules of grammar.

In an essay written in 1954, Fedin cited Turgenev as a 19th Century classical model for contemporary writers.[30]

Just as Pastuxov's speech is characterized by premeditation, a certain artificiality and affectation, and egotism, thus serving for character delineation, so is that of Cvetuxin, an actor, used to stress his preoccupation with

---

[30] K. Fedin, "Slovo k litovskim prozaikam", *Pisatel', iskusstvo, vremja*, p. 395.

appearances, pose, affectation, and mannerisms. Here, by way of example, is a fragment of a conversation:

— Чем отличается плохой актер от хорошего? ...
— Плохой актер завидует успеху, хороший — таланту.

The aphorism is clever and pertinent. But who is its author? Cvetuxin? No, he is an actor himself, and such self-criticism would be inconsistent with his character. Anočka? No, she is too young and inexperienced, has not been in the theatre long enough to dare express such an attitude toward what, to her, is still sacred. Dorogomilov? No, he is childlike in his lack of skepticism, is ecstatic over the theatre and actors, and could never entertain the thought that actors could be differentiated not on the basis of talent, or even popularity, but on types of envy.

In this aphorism, probably used before and held for appropriate situations, calculated to produce the impression of worldly experience on the part of the speaker, there is an element of cynicism which is characteristic of almost everything which Pastuxov says and does. Of all those present during this conversation, Pastuxov is the only one capable of such an utterance. And he doesn't make this observation innocently, but with the intent of irritating Cvetuxin, so enthused by his work with the young aspiring actors and in love with Anočka. At the same time, he wishes to impress Anočka, who does not appear to be imbued with sufficient veneration for the famous playwright Pastuxov.

Each of Fedin's heroes, like those of Turgenev, is distinguished by his own lexicon, by his preferred choice of words and phrases. The language of the old Meškov is a mixture of polysemantic and ambiguous "learned" terms from religious literature, Old Church Slavonic, combined with coarse expressions from the vernacular: "pregrešenija", "zemnoe bytie", "prepony", "gospod' miloval", "mirnaja končina". Indiscriminately juxtaposed with these are the following: "slovčil", "miraž-fiksaž", "ne pozvolju flanirovat'", "notarial'nyj uxažor".

The thought to be expressed appears to be the leading principle in determining Fedin's choice of language. In his later works it is only occasionally that he permits himself the luxury of "word-braiding", as in the following example, in which he is unable to abstain from the ecstasy of the gourmand in describing the books in Dorogomilov's library:

Книги пахли книгами: этот аромат несравным ни с чем. Особенно книги восемнадцатого века, из тех, которые понемногу перекочевывали из усадеб в город, с обветшалыми дворяными или с поповичами, изменившими сельским церковным слободкам отцов —

желтые или пепельно-голубые, с едва улавливаемой на свет водяной сеткой страницы "Нового Плутарха", "Словаря суеверий", "смеющегося Демокрита". Но и позднейших лет книги, прошедшие базарным "развалом", через руки содержателей ларьков и букинистов, несли в своих разворотах букет неповторимой кислятники и заболони, напоминая и винный бочонок, и обчищенный прут лозняка — первородный запах легко принимающей влагу древесины, которую, со временем, все больше добавляют в бумагу. Старинная тряпичная бумага немного похожа на выветриваемый бельевой комод или донесшийся издали дух белошвейной мастерской. Но все это только приблизительные уподобления, потому что книга пахнет книгой, как вино — вином, уголь — углем, — она завоевала место в ряду с основными стихиями природы, это не сочетание, но самостоятельный элемент.[31]

In this passage one may sense the connoisseur and lover of books, such as the writer Pastuxov and, doubtlessly, Fedin himself. Yet Fedin is able to make use of this same book motif in another manner, as part of the characterization of Kirill Izvekov. Kirill is depicted eagerly rummaging through the books taken from Dorogomilov's library, and being sorted for rag manufacture. Kirill has always dreamed of a library of his own. As he picks up four exquisite volumes of Shakespeare he thinks that they would be nice for Anočka. On second thought, however, he concludes that she could borrow them from him. Becoming greedy, he sets aside a pile of books, mentally earmarking some for his mother, some for Ragozin. His orgy of acquisition is suddenly interrupted when he hears the sound of a Bolshevik march coming through the window, reminding him of his immediate responsibilities.[32] Thus does Fedin portray the various attitudes toward things, events, and people, on one hand by the characters themselves, and on the other by the author, depending on the specific scene, the character of the hero, and his function in the book.

Fedin's prose lends itself to comparison with a work of music. This feeling of "musicalness" in Fedin's novels results from the rhythmic structure of the entire work, the alternation of chapters, and the unique tone of each individual work, peculiar to that particular work. The rhythmic design of *Goroda i gody* is different from that of *Brat'ja* and *Sanatorij Arktur*, and the rhythm of *Pervye radosti* or of *Neobykenovennoe leto* is unlike that of the preceding novels.

In Fedin's earlier works could be noted a certain predilection for the "skaz", as well as for the devices of ornamentalism, highly colored prose

---

[31] Fedin, *Sobranie*, VII, p. 163.
[32] *Ibid.*, VII, pp. 636-40.

which was more concerned with the use of language than with the content. In the novels, however — and this becomes increasingly apparent with each successive work — the rhythm of the prose corresponds more closely to the course of the action, and the progress of the thought, and the tonality of a particular segment of any work becomes a function of its content, of the leading idea.

Typical are the beginnings of many chapters of *Neobyknovennoe leto*. They are structured in a manner to set the tone for the entire chapter which follows. The epic-like beginning of the novel, in which Fedin deliberates on the logic of history, imparts the basic tone to the entire novel.

It is in the second novel of the trilogy that Fedin achieves the highest degree of simplicity, naturalness, and realism, or to word it differently, that he is most free from any deliberate and obvious artfulness. And this achievement is all the more noteworthy because of the greater complexity of the "counterpoint" or interweaving of different tonalities, the intricacy of the composition, or the abundance of detail. This perfection of craftsmanship must be credited to Fedin's maturation as a writer, despite the protestations of the Soviet critics that it must be attributed to Fedin's political maturation, this being defined as increasing identification with government and party politics.

Fedin adds another element to his imagery, nature, in first acquainting the reader with Anočka Parabukina, setting her against the spring landscape:

Природа часто переживает важные перемены и очень много-значительно отмечает их странным выжидательным состоянием, которое разливается на все окружающее и волнует человека. ... Девочка пропиталась этой минутной самоглядкой весеннего дня.[33]

Kirill's strength and determination are depicted with Puškinian precision in the scene in which Kirill confronts Parabukin: "... v podžarom, suxom ego ustoe vidno bylo, čto ego nelegko sdvinut' s mesta".[34] Vera Nikandrovna, Kirill's mother, instantly recognizes her son's courage and transition to manhood "v èto bezžalostnoe mgnovenie", when Kirill is arrested.[35] Meškov's fawning nature is portrayed in the metaphoric phrase "reverans v golose" when, terrified at Kirill's arrest, he tries to court favor with the policeman.[36] Additional examples, cited by

[33] Fedin, *Sobranie*, VI, p. 126.
[34] *Ibid.*, VI, pp. 138-39.
[35] *Ibid.*, p. 254.
[36] *Ibid.*, p. 263.

Brajnina, are found when Kirill looks at Anočka "slovno otyskivaja ee sočuvstvie"; Anočka's cheerful "legkoe lico"; and the lines of Kirill's face as he gazes at his beloved "budto v nakaljajuščem luče sveta smjagčilis'".

These represent just a small fraction of the many examples which could be cited of Fedin's facility in the novel combination of ordinary words into striking images. It is important to note that Fedin does not manipulate lexical inventory and syntax for their own sake. They are always, as in the above examples, subordinated to what Fedin considers the more important goal of revealing the internal, psychological world of his characters.

It is for this same purpose that Fedin introduces separate words and expressions drawn not from the literary language, but rather from territorial dialects, archaisms, and the vernacular. This device assists to characterize the speaker by imparting a particular intonation which may denote irony, vulgarity, humor, naivete, shrewdness, or scorn, or may signal his profession or social and intellectual level. Thus the modernized young merchant, Šubnikov, upon meeting Liza for the first time, ecstatically exclaims: "Soveršenno ničego podobnogo!" Meškov, in conversation with the policeman, uses the dialectal word "strekulist", hoping thereby to emphasize his scorn for the younger generation who, in his opinion, are trying to destroy the old way of life. The old-fashioned actor, Mefodij, invites guests into his "fligel'", and the infuriated Ragozin, wishing to add more force to the word "besporjadok", juxtaposes the dialectical work "kavardak".

Fedin ordinarily confines the use of the vernacular and of dialectisms to the dialogue of his heroes, for the purpose of characterization. He occasionally resorts to the use of archaisms, however, in his own third person descriptions. They are most frequently used to emphasize some particularly great or solemn moment. Thus, for example, in describing Kirill's emotional reaction during the review of the First Cavalry Army, Fedin writes: "Edva vse èto vzgljad Kirilla vyxvatil iz belokipennoj klubjaščejsja tuči, kak uže èskadron umel'knul daleko vpered." The word "belokipennyj" no longer appears in contemporary dictionaries.

The archaism serves a different purpose in the speech of Pastuxov when, in reply to Kirill's suggestion that he write a revolutionary play, the playwright says, in an ironic and haughty tone, that "ešče ne osenilo podxodjaščej temoj".

It has been noted that a distinguishing feature of the composition and structure of Fedin's later novels is the succinctness of the presentation, the compactness with which the subject matter is organized. In this respect Fedin follows the traditions of that line of development of the classical Russian novel which leads from Puškin, through Lermontov, Turgenev, and Lev Tolstoj, rather than the line leading from Gogol', through Dostoevskij and Remizov. These qualities are valued highly in contemporary Soviet literature. I. Kozlov, in his article on compactness in prose,[37] praises those novelists who can advance the central idea of their work by moving from one situation to another over the shortest distance, a straight line. In addition to attributing this quality to Fedin's dilogy, Kozlov also singles out for praise A. Fadeev's *Razgrom*, A. Serafimovič's *Železnyj potok*, Pavlenko's *Sčast'e*, and E. Kazakevič's *Zvezda*. In these novels, says Kozlov, "... dviženie zamysla ot odnogo sjužetnogo uzla k drugomu dano ... kak vpolne celesoobraznoe, a èto i est' dviženie po kratčajšemu rasstojaniju".[38] Fadeev goes so far as to consider prolixness sinful, as when he refers to "... grex rastjanutosti povestvovanija, izlišestva v podrobnostjax ...".[39]

The problem of the manner in which Fedin accomplishes this "dviženie po kratčajšemu rasstojaniju" and how he achieves economy and compactness of composition is directly related to the problem of succinctness and economy in the use of language. Fedin's succinctness, or artistic laconism, does not imply an effort on his part to dispense with details. On the contrary, Fedin does use details, but they are so selected and organized as to be representative of something larger, a concept or a trait of character which may be generalized or, in the Marxist glossary, may be considered "typical". In *Neobyknovennoe leto*, there is a scene in the 10th chapter in which Fedin introduces the episodic figure of a young lady "v očen' korotkoj uzkoj jubke", with shoes laced to the knees, bearing down hard on the loud pedal of a piano, squeezing out "A Maiden's Prayer", an old melody symbolizing provincial life in bygone days "v vekax ostanetsja pamjatnikom mečtatel'nosti staroj provincii".[40] This detail, the brief encounter with this young representative of a new generation playing the music of the old, in a theatrical, artificial setting, triggers a stream of thought which courses through Pastuxov's mind, and which is presented by Fedin by means of "nesobstvenno prjamaja reč'" or "quoted speech". In this scene, Pastuxov wonders if he himself is not a remnant of bygone times, a forgotten fragment of history, an anachronism from the preceding century.

[37] I. Kozlov, "O sžatosti v proze", *Novyj mir*, No. 6 (1955).
[38] *Ibid.*, p. 264.
[39] A. Fadeev, "Zametki o literature", *Sobranie sočinenij v pjati tomax* (Moscow, GIXL, 1961), V, p. 18.
[40] Fedin, *Sobranie*, VII, pp. 140-41.

В облике смешной любительницы музыки он, однако, увидел что-то новорожденное и настолько самонадеянное, что не она показалась ему курьезом, а он сам — со своими поисками прошлого века. Прошлый век! — это слово ошеломило его, примененное к недавнему времени, о котором он привык думать, как об идущем, а оно уже невозвратно ушло. Не был ли он сам прошлым веком? Остатком, обломком, в крошку разбившимся карнизом колеблемого здания? Застывшим в воздухе отрывком давнишнего напева, какой-нибудь жалкой ноткой провинциальной 'Молитвы девы'? — Какая чушь! — отмахнулся он.[41]

This passage is typical of Fedin's use of the device of interior or internal monologue, which conveys to the reader the direct impression of Pastuxov's thoughts and emotions, transmitted by the narrator, rather than by Pastuxov himself, but preserving Pastuxov's own lexicon, syntax, and intonation. Thus Fedin employs an episodic figure, a tiny detail which interrupts the normal time sequence but which provides the key to understanding Pastuxov's emotional state and uncertainty regarding his role in contemporary events.

[41] *Ibid.*, pp. 142-43.

XIII

STYLISTIC DEVICES

There are a number of narrative devices available to the author composing a novel. He can tell his story through letters, diaries, or journals, or he can develop the story from anecdotes. He can include short stories within the novel, can tell the story from the first person or from the omniscient third person or, if he wishes, he can vary his mode of narration and point of view.

The central problem of narrative, however, concerns the relation of the author to the narrative.[1] Here, two basic possibilities emerge. The first is what might be called the dramatic, or play method, in which the actors and the reader are in direct contact with each other, and the author or narrator has vanished completely. The second method is that of the epic bard or story teller, which includes the narrator's own comments, giving the narrative — in contradistinction to the dialogue — its own style, mood, and tone.

Fedin, as has been observed in the discussion of the structure of the dilogy, is somewhat eclectic, choosing to vary his mode of narration and point of view, and resorting to either the dramatic or the epic techniques, selecting the one he considers most effective. Sometimes Fedin chooses to narrate as an observer would who is viewing the action from the sidelines. On other occasions, he becomes an active participant in events, and his attitude is conveyed either in the tone in which he narrates the events themselves, the way he juxtaposes or arranges the material, light hints and allusions, outright declarations, and even pedagogic affirmations. Typical of the allusion, with deliberately contrived ambiguity, is the scene when Cvetuxin, having been approached by Liza with a request that he help Kirill, offers her ice cream! Fedin, as omniscient narrator, sounds a note of foreboding in the scene in which Pastuxov and Cvetuxin, in the ominous darkness which is descending on the town, discuss the fact of their suspected implication in revolutionary underground activities along with Ragozin and Kirill. "... vdrug iz temnoty, ob"javšej gorod, vyrvalsja

[1] R. Wellek and A. Warren, *Theory of Literature* (New York, 1956), p. 212.

jasnyj pugajuščij vykrik izvozčika: — Beregis' ej!"[2] This warning
portends suffering for Pastuxov who, proud and wilful like the chief
character in a Greek tragedy, is blind to his destiny until the very moment
of ultimate disillusionment, his imprisonment by Mamontov. All of the
elements essential to irony are present: the ironic will which, in the
Marxian framework, is the irresistable forward movement of history
(replacing the Greek gods), and which prepares the dramatically sudden
disillusionment of a deluded character; the victim (Pastuxov); and the
spectator for whom the reversal, or *peripeteia*, betrays an unmistakable
mocking intent on the part of the powers that be and, in the dilogy, on
the part of the author. Fedin also betrays his emotional attitudes towards
his characters in the form of chleuasm, the jeer or mock, as when he
characterizes the police officer Poltencev as a zealous official "revniv k
delam služby", who demonstrates his zeal by imprisoning the pregnant
Ksenija Afanas'evna Ragozina in an effort to extract from her the secret
of her husband's location. Polotencev "revno" subjects her to privation
and hunger, resulting in her death in the hospital as Polotencev proceeds
to a formal dinner party after one last unsuccessful interrogation immediately prior to her death.

In the dilogy, Fedin resorts to the classical device used by Tolstoj,
termed "nesobstvenno-prjamaja reč'", or "quoted speech". Quoted
speech is transformed into the internal monologue or internal dialogue
of the character. Fedin, like Tolstoj, employs this device for characterization, for revealing the innermost thoughts and emotions of the
characters.

Quoted speech is a complex, subtle, and most effective device for
characterization, or more properly, self-characterization. It permits
personal characteristics to emerge with particular vividness, and also
affords the author vast possibilities for expressing his own evaluation
and attitude toward the character.

It is conducted in the name of the author, but the content, lexicon,
rhythm, intonation, and syntax correspond to the individual peculiarities
of a particular character.

Fedin frequently employs this device to reveal the "dialect of the soul"
of one or another of the characters, the internal conflict that may be
raging at a critical moment of a person's life. This type of "psychological
eavesdropping" is illustrated in the sene in *Neobyknovennoe leto*, when
Kirill learns that Ipat Ipat'ev, one of his best soldiers, has disappeared
during the wolf hunt. It is then that Kirill

[2] Fedin, *Sobranie*, VI, p. 344.

будто впервые понял, что один отвечает за всю охоту и за все, что бы ни случилось с Ипатом. Он был тем сознанием, которое взяло на себя ответственность за каждого человека — от Дибича до последнего деревенского мальчугана, ради забавы увязавшегося с облавщиками в лес.[3]

Fedin employs internal monologue to reveal Kirill's attitude toward the actor Cvetuxin when he, recognizing that he has fallen in love with Anočka, imagines Cvetuxin to be a rival:

Прежде всего он решил, что у него нет никакой неприязни к Цветухину, как к человеку. Наоборот, Цветухин делал в сущности как раз то, что Кирилл мог бы ожидать от актера в революционное время. Правда, Кириллу было неясно, что надо было делать в искусстве, но искусство должно было быть с революцией, по эту сторону баррикад. Цветухин разделял такой взгляд и, значит, был, естественным союзником. Отсюда следовало, что Кирилл прав, давая обещание поддержать Цветухина.

Но, поддерживая его, он поощрял одержимость Аночки театром. Разве это плохо? Наоборот — Превосходно! Молодое увлечение, молодая страсть. ... Ах, да! Не может же Кирилл Извеков из каких-то личных соображений поступать против принципально правильного дела! Это умаляло бы нравственное сознание, весь умственный строй Извекова. Да и что за соображение в конце концов? Откуда Кирилл взял, что они — личные, эти соображения? Разве у него родилось какое-нибудь особое чувство к Аночке? Да если бы и родилось, если бы нахлынуло, как ветер, как буря, как тайфун. ... Чорт возьми! ... Все равно Кирилл никогда бы не мог свалить в одну кучу совершенно разные вещи — общественное дело и личное чувство. Слава богу, ему не занимать выдержки!"[4]

There is little, if any, difference between this type of self-analysis and that of Tolstoj's characters. Fedin uses quoted speech not only for self-analysis but also to portray the internal agitation which accompanies a moment of great emotional stress, as in the scene in which Anočka, immediately following the death of her mother, Ol'ga Ivanovna Parabukina, thinks about her mother's last day alive, the hopes she had for her recovery as from previous illnesses, and her own refusal to accept her mother's last gasps as final.[5]

Fedin uses quoted speech with equal force to reveal the character and internal, emotional states of children, not only of adults. In the following excerpt, Fedin enters the internal world of young Aleša, his first joys and

---

[3] Fedin, *Sobranie*, VII, p. 498.
[4] *Ibid.*, pp. 313-314.
[5] *Ibid.*, pp. 201-202.

his first grief. In this excerpt, Fedin also characterizes Arsenij Romanovič Dorogomilov and, to a lesser extent, his own father and foster mother:

Несчастья Алеши идут скорее всего от Ольги Адамовны. Она только и делает, что наговаривает на Арсения Романовича: он испортит нашего бедного Алешу! Это все от зависти, конечно, потому что — где ей до Арсения Романовича! С ним никто не может равняться. Если бы не мама, то Алеша мог бы твердо сказать, что ему больше всех на свете дорог Арсений Романович. И если бы Алешу спросили, кем он хочет быть, он ответил бы: — Арсением Романовичем.

Он хотел бы им быть на всю, на всю жизнь, хоть с горечью понимает, что этого ни за что не достигнешь. Разве когда-нибудь будешь столько про все знать, сколько знает Арсений Романович? Откуда взять такой дом с садом и вещи, какими набит целый коридор? а верстак? А спасательный круг? Да разве за Алешей будут ходить толпой мальчики? И разве поступишь когда-нибудь на службу, на которой служит Арсений Романович? Вот папа — так совсем не ходит на службу. А, наверно, хотелось бы! А шляпа Арсения Романовича? А борода? Где уж там Алеше отрастить такую бороду.[6]

Fedin also uses other devices with telling effect to characterize his heroes, explaining their behavior and revealing their true nature. Among these are the dialogue and the use of speech peculiarities, or "rečevaja xarakteristika". In the following extract may be noted the flexibility of syntax, as well as the recourse to Old Church Slavonic borrowings, which help characterize Meškov's domestic despotism and his hypocritical readiness to use religious referents to further his own personal ambitions. This monologue is part of Meškov's campaign to force his daughter Liza to marry Šubnikov against her will:

Спасти может одно послушание, ничего больше. Как я тебя растил? В беспрекословии. Кабы ты с отцом пререкалась, ничего бы в жизни, кроме несчастья, не увидела. А что такое послушание? Как понимает послушание церковь? Один святой отец, желая испытать послушника, повелел ему посадить в землю, на высокой горе, кол и ежедневно поливать тот кол, принося воду из-под горы. И послушник исполнял приказание, не прекословя и так смиренно, что даже на ум ему не пришло, что он совершает бессмысленное дело, поливая простой кол. И по смирению его была ему награда: через пять лет поливания кол пустил корень и дал ростки. ... Разумеется, то был истинно монашеский послух, и я от тебя такого не требую. Но дочернего непрекословия отцу я ожидать вправе, и ты мне в нем не отказывала, за что я тебя ценю.[7]

[6] Fedin, *Sobranie*, VII, p. 338.
[7] *Ibid.*, VI, p. 306.

In Parabukin's speech, Fedin captures the exact intonation and tone of
a proud man poignantly mocking himself and his feigned superiority,
intensifying the sympathy aroused in the reader by his destitute condition.
"Ne tuda adresuetes'", he tells Pastuxov and Cvetuxin when they visit
the doss house.

Мы — не бедный класс. Мы, так сказать, временно впавшие ...
впавшие в нужду. Дочь моя, по наущению матери, повторяет, что
ее отец — крючик ... Извините. По сословию — никогда. По
сословию я человек служилый. И живу, как все служилые люди, —
семьей, в своем помещении, со своим входом. Вот возьму — воз-
душный звоночек проведу и медную карточку приделаю к занавеске,
как на парадном, чтобы все понимали.[8]

Fedin's dialogues sometimes suggest the meter and rhyme of poetry, as
in this exchange, in which he conveys all of the charm and wistfulness
of love:

Кирилл улыбался Аночке неуверенно и будто с удивлением. Она
сказала:
    — Лиза ужасно изменилась ...
    — Очень изменилась.
    — Правда ее жалко?
    — Очень жалко.
Он ждал каких-то иных вопросов и стоял против нее, не двигаясь.
Она взглянула из-под опущенных низко бровей.
    — Я, как приехал, решил сейчас же пойти к вам, — сказал он,
словно ощупью отыскивая ее сочувствие.
Она все испытывала его взглядом. Он подошел к ней близко.
    — Вы, правда, не знали что я приехал?
Она неожиданно схватила его пальцы, прижала их с женской
жадностью к своей груди и, слыша, как они, поддаваясь ласке,
теряли свою жесткую силу, сказала тихо:
    — Отлично знала, что приехал! Потому и прибежала. ...[9]

Here the author's interpolations seem to accompany the music of the
conversation, reinforcing and directing this music. Sometimes the
author's descriptions of the setting, and the emotional state of the heroes,
emerge into the foreground, and the dialogue becomes the accompaniment to the author's description. Here is a characteristic scene, in which
the soldier Strashnov carries the wounded Ragozin back from the field
of battle:

---

[8]   Fedin, *Sobranie*, VI, pp. 133-134.
[9]   *Ibid.*, VII, p. 610.

Среди криков, долетавших до него, Рагозин услышал сильнее всего:

— Комиссар! ... Комиссар! ...

Он еще больше повернул голову, чтобы посмотреть — кто его так прижал сапогом к земле.

Он увидел прямо перед своим лицом будто знакомое, но неузнаваемое лицо скуластого человека с раздутыми ноздрями и тяжелым, подавляющим все черты подбородком. Человек этот, оскаливаясь, кричал ему на ухо:

— Куда тебя? Куда?

Рагозин не понял, что нужно этому человеку, но тут же вспомнил, что это — Страшнов, и почему-то обрадовался, и хотел ему крикнуть в ответ, но не мог, а только прокряхтел кое-как:

— Я сам, — и стал подыматься.

Никогда не испытанной силы боль в ключице и плече принудила его не двигаться.

— Что сам? Несогласный! Сам ... — сердито гудел Страшнов, поворачивая его и подсовывая свои руки ему под спину и под колени.[10]

By combining dialogue and description, Fedin intensifies the dramatic quality of this scene, and gives it even greater lyrical coloring. By this act, Fedin characterizes Strašnov as a simple and modest patriot.

Fedin's dialogues frequently assume the abbreviated, elliptical form of actual speech, assuming the intonation of the spoken, as contrasted to the literary, language.

— Как тебя зовут?

— Меня Аночкой.

— Кто у тебя отец, Аночка?

— Крючик на пристани. А вы — господа?[11]

The laconic "A vy — gospoda?" is the psychological key to understanding the whole scene, in which Pastuxov and Cvetuxin appear among the destitute lodgers of the doss house.

This brief dialogue exemplifies Fedin's mastery of "Čexovian laconism", the ability of the author, in a most succinct and pungent form, to reveal the essence of the events or the human emotions which he is describing. Here is another brief dialogue illustrating the same technique. This exchange is between a Red Army soldier and Pastuxov when the Reds, having chased the White general Mamontov out of Kozlov, set about releasing all prisoners from the jails.

[10]   Fedin, *Sobranie*, VI, p. 581.

[11]   *Ibid.*, p. 128.

— Вы кем, гражданин, будете?
(Как ни был выпачкан и смят на Пастухове костюм — вид его бросался в глаза). Он ответил:
— Театральный работник.
— А! Театр! — весело посмотрели на него из-за стола, и дали ему какой-то квиток, и сказали:
— Ну, выходите.[12]

In the exclamation "A! Teatr! and the adverb "veselo" are packed a maximum of emotional content, expressing not only the soldier's apparent appreciation of the theatre, but also the probability that Pastuxov will finally collaborate, applying his talents to the creation of a revolutionary theatre.

Reference has already been made to the way Fedin characterizes Kirill by a description of his physical appearance. The portraits of Anočka, Ragozin, Pastuxov, Cvetuxin, Meškov, Polotencev, and other heroes in the dilogy serve similarly to apprise the reader of their characters and personalities. This, for example, is the way Pastuxov looks to the reader meeting him for the first time:

... легко нес на себе светлое, цветом похожее на горох, широкое ворсистое пальто, песочную шляпу с сиреневатой лентой, и лицо его, чуть рыхлое, но молодое, холеное, довольное, было словно подкрашено пастелью и тоже легко и пышно, как пальто и шляпа.[13]

From this brief, impressionistic description of Pastuxov's appearance the reader may infer the playwright's outstanding personality traits.

Not only external appearance of the characters, but landscape as well is introduced by Fedin for a specific psychological effect. Thus the scene in which the actor and playwright visit the doss house is set against the bright, cheerful background of a day in early spring, a week after Easter:

Комната освещалась обильно, промытые к празднику окна открывали огромный расмаш неба в яркобелых облачках и ту стеклянную дорогу, что лежала поперек Волги, от берега к берегу.[14]

Fedin uses the expanse of sky, the abundance of light, and the glassy path spanning the Volga to expose all the more mercilessly the squalor and hopeless poverty of the doss house and its inhabitants.

The description of any incident, even the apparently most insignificant or casual word or gesture of any of the characters, is always intended to

---

[12]   Fedin, *Sobranie*, VII, pp. 550-551.
[13]   *Ibid.*, VI, p. 127.
[14]   *Ibid.*, pp. 131-132.

serve a larger purpose, frequently being used as another device for characterization. Here, for example, is a description of Šubnikov during his first visit to the Meškovs when, in a condition of internal agitation and confusion, he knocks over the lamp, breaking the globular glass shade:

Виктор Семенович прижал ладони ко лбу. Почти вырвалось у него какое-то слово, вроде — оплачу или отлечу, — но нечленораздельно застряло в горле, и он только шаркнул ножкой и картонно кланялся по очереди Меркурию Авдеевичу и Валерии Ивановне, не смея повернуть голову к Лизе.[15]

In the brief "oplaču", Fedin portrays Šubnikov's obtuseness and his belief, as a well-to-do heir to a fortune, that money can buy or repair anything.

Fedin boldly combines abstract words with words expressing concrete action to achieve artistic specificity and palpable concreteness. Analytical descriptions such as the following thereby assume a psychologically precise and subtle coloration:

"Он оживал от запахов, точно *приказаясь* к радостному *смыслу существования*"; "*вспыхнувшее* женское *всепонимание*", "*неподвижность покоилась* в небе, неподвижность на земле".

These figures of speech assist Fedin in attaining precision of description and concreteness in portraying the most complex and subtle experiences of his characters. In the sentence "Nepodvižnost' pokoilas' na nebe, nepodvižnost' na zemle", the word "nepodvižnost'" is ordinarily used in combination with nouns in the genitive case, such as "nepodvižnost' lica, nepodvižnost' vodnoj poverxnosti". Without such a noun, it assumes a broader, generalized meaning, while simultaneously concretely representing a state of being. In combination with the verb "pokoilas'", suggesting personification, the word "nepodvižnost'" assumes a shade of meaning having a poetic flavor, characteristic, for example, of such words as "tišina" or "mrak".

Fedin also employs epithets for palpability and exactness of description. In the dilogy he uses a large number of complex double and triple epithets:

Листва серебристо-молочная, дымно-серые полосы тумана, что-то заманчиво-жизненное, затаенно-многозначительный взор, насильственно-важная улыбка.

This feature of Fedin's prose style is also reminiscent of that of Turgenev.
Typical of the dilogy is the use of modifiers, either adjectives or

[15] Fedin, *Sobranie*, VI, p. 304.

participles, to emphasize the contradictory nature of certain phenomena. This device offers another means of expressing the "dialekta duši"; "ulybka, kotoraja mogla pokazat'sja i očarovatel'noj, i vyzyvajuščej", "gordaja, xotja nemnogo grustnaja uslada", "komandujuščij i odnovremenno isstuplennyj vopl'".

The concrete and detailed portrayal of the internal world of the characters, and of their surroundings, is only one of the stylistic characteristics of *Pervye radosti* and *Neobyknovennoe leto* as historical and psychological novels. Another distinguishing feature of the style of the dilogy is the use of artistic laconism in imparting a universal character to events. In following the characters through a variety of events over a two-year period of their lives, the reader never loses the feeling that he is present at some of the most significant moments in history.

In the novel *Pervye radosti*, Fedin avoids making any direct evaluation of the historical significance of the times in his own name. The historical atmosphere, or "dyxanie istorii" in the first novel is created only by means of a vigorous and sharply defined portrayal of the moods and thoughts of the protagonists, representing certain well-defined segments of the Russian population. This will be discussed more fully in the chapter on Fedin's historicism.

Fedin's continual interweaving of the "dialect of the soul" of the heroes with the great events and critical moments in the history of Russia imparts special depth and intensity to the analysis of the mental world of the heroes. Here Fedin does not limit himself only to showing how great events are reflected in the internal world of the characters. In the persons of Kirill Izvekov and Anočka Parabukina, Fedin is particularly concerned with defining the attributes of the "new" Soviet man and woman, the positive hero being forged on the anvil of revolution and civil war. The precedents established by Lev Tolstoj and Maxim Gor'kij were to influence Fedin. Tolstoj conducted artistic investigations of the process of moral self-purification of the hero under the action of the facts of objective reality (Pierre Bezuxov and Andrej Volkonskij, in *War and Peace*). Gor'kij emphasized the formation of the revolutionary, the new "hero of his time" (Petr Vlasov and his mother Nilovna, in *Mat'*; Kutuzov, in *Klim Samgin*). Fedin carries the process to its ultimate conclusion, portraying in Izvekov the ideal Soviet man.

In *Pervye radosti* there is the following lyrical digression:

В горах, если столкнуть с высоты камень, он сорвет в своем полете другой, третий, они повлекут за собой десятки, которые обвалят сотни, — и вот целая лавина каменьев, глыб и комьев земли рушится в пропасть с нарастающим устремлением, и гул раскатывается по горам, и пыль, как дым, застилает склоны, и перекатами бродит по ущельям грозное эхо. Страшен обвал в горах, и раз начался он, поздно жалеть, что сброшен первый камень.

Так одно решение, вдруг принятое, облекает человека десятками, сотнями неизбежностей, и они вяжут людей, цепляясь друг за друга, и действительные неизбежности перевиваются вокруг мнимых, и часто мнимые властвуют сильнее действительных, как эхо кажется грознее породившего его звука.[16]

In a sense this lyrical reflection by the author offers a clue toward understanding his approach to life. It appeared to be pure accident, a random happening, when Kirill, in the very beginning of the novel, offered sanctuary to Anočka Parabukina, who came into his home and became acquainted with his mother. But this first, seemingly casual, encounter evoked an echo which reverberated throughout the entire dilogy.

Fedin sees in the fate of his heroes either actual inevitabilities or seeming inevitabilities. Sometimes the two appear to be intertwined in some wondrous fashion, resulting in the motley, but real and stormy, stream of life. But it would be erroneous to conclude that Fedin confines himself to comparing the flow of life to a mountain landslide. He does show how the capricious combination of circumstances leads to a revelation of the essential nature of life. The entire structure of the dilogy consists of numerous plot elements which combine to transform their apparently random nature into an inevitable result. There is yet another important feature of the dilogy which warrants comment. To those characters who lack will and the impulse to act, Fedin opposes others, who actively participate in shaping the future. Whereas this characteristic may be attributed to the demands of Socialist Realism, it may — with equal validity — be traced back to the confrontation of characters and oppositions found in the novels of such nineteenth century Russian writers as Gončarov and Turgenev.

A. NATURE

Fedin's descriptions of nature are frequently impressionistic in that scenes are depicted with broad simplicity and little elaboration of detail, transformed by the character of the observer. Fedin often depicts landscapes by focussing on their general shapes or forms:

---

[16]   Fedin, *Sobranie*, VI, p. 375.

Вдруг из-за церкви появился на воде небольшой уголок, и уголок этот стал вырастать, будто выдвигаться из церкви, как крышечка из пенала. Затем уголок превратился в квадратик, и на этом квадратике появился второй квадратик, и они оба продолжали выдвигаться из церкви, и нижный вез на себе верхний, и потом сразу на верхнем выехал третий, совсем так же, как второй на первом, и все они начали вытягиваться в полосы и вдруг ярко забелели на солнце, и Алеша отчетливо разглядел на каждой полосе маленькие окошечки, и окошечек стало выдвигаться из-за церкви все больше и больше, и Алеша понял, что это идет пароход.[17]

The landscape here is viewed, and transformed, through and by the eyes of Aleša Pastuxov, a boy for whom all objects which he encounters for the first time take on a play-like or game-like character. In this instance, the real world is viewed as a series of geometric shapes, suggesting building-blocks in motion, dramatically forming different images until they assume their true identity. This is another example of "ostranenie", in which familiar objects are "made strange" because encountered for the first time.

But even when landscape is presented from the point of view of the narrator himself, of the author, it is not simply a photographic type of portrayal retrieved from his stock of memories. Each time it is created anew as a unique and necessary environment in which particular characters or events are set.

Sometimes, in Fedin's works, this natural setting is so compressed that it assumes a symbolic significance. In the dilogy there are two "storms", one in *Pervye radosti* and the other in *Neobyknovennoe leto*. In the first, the presentiment of approaching political and social storms is mixed with the feeling of the approaching "torrents of spring" which would unleash the hidden power of love in the youthful heroes, and in nature itself. In the second instance, the storm likewise anticipates a powerful shock — the meeting between Dibič and Izvekov, giving a new direction to Dibič's future life. This storm, however, Fedin portrays as having a purifying effect, and Kirill emphasizes its symbolic significance by referring to the "banja".

Fedin's descriptions of landscape, like the descriptions of the thoughts and emotions of his heroes, are precise and well-defined. Fedin himself frequently has said that he derived particular pleasure from depicting Saratov, its streets and surroundings, as they actually existed.[18] But the lively, concrete pictures of nature not only force the reader to penetrate

---

[17] Fedin, *Sobranie*, VII, p. 44.
[18] R. V. Komina, "Dilogija K. Fedina *Pervye radosti* i *Neobyknovennoe leto*", *Literatura v škole*, Vol. 17, No. 5 (Sept.-Oct. 1956), p. 26.

deep into the psychology and mood of each of the heroes, but also serve imperceptibly to convey what might be called the historical mood. Thus in the lyrical digression about the properties of early spring, in the very beginning of the first novel, Fedin manages to suggest what he calls the "obraz vremeni", or the living embodiement of the time, which he desired to include in the story on an equal footing with the other characters, or even to give it precedence over them.

Постоянное мое стремление найти образ времени и включить время в повествование на равных и даже предпочтительных правах с героями повести — это стремление выступает в моем нынешнем замысле настойчивее, чем раньше. Другими словами, я смотрю на свою трилогию как на произведение историческое.[19]

Fedin describes spring in the following terms, stressing the state of expectancy:

Природа часто переживает важные перемены и очень много-значительно отмечает их странным выжидательным состоянием, которое разливается на окружающее и волнует человека. Весна, когда она совершит перелом, задерживается на какое-то время, приостанавливается, чтобы почувствовать свою победу. Поторже-ствовав, она идет дальше.[20]

In this passage, Fedin intertwines three motifs: spring, history, and the youth of nine-year old Anočka. The element which all share is the optimistic looking ahead, the feeling of being on the threshold of a bright future, the renovation of nature, of social and political organization, and of the individual.

The use of scenes from nature is also related to Fedin's conciseness. To write concisely does not mean to eliminate details. The author is always faced with the problem of which details are necessary to convey the particular image or idea to the reader. Fedin, especially in the dilogy, combined the parts and the whole, the general and the particular, in a way reminiscent of Tolstoj's combination of "generalizacija" and "meločnost'". This is a problem not only of language, but of composition. The individual episodes and scenes, and the smallest details, are organized so as to contribute to the whole, to advancing the development of the central idea. The dilogy is devoid of the highly-colored prose, valued for the manner of narration rather than the content, which characterizes Fedin's earlier work, such as *Goroda i goda*. Kozlov, a contemporary critic,

[19] Fedin, *Sobranie*, I, p. 19.
[20] *Ibid.*, VI, p. 126.

makes the point that such ornamentalism might be found in Fedin's notebooks, but not in the finished novels.[21]

To cite just one example, in chapter 37 of *Neobyknovennoe leto*, Fedin succinctly but clearly depicts a winter snowstorm, recalling the classical blizzards of Puškin and Lev Tolstoj. At first it appears only as a detail of the winter landscape, a more or less ordinary change in the weather. Then, almost instantaneously, the blizzard becomes an important part of the plot. The automobile in which Kirill is riding to Anočka's house, following the meeting to enlist volunteers for the cavalry troops, breaks down while still far from the city. Kirill decides to make his way through the dark and the snowstorm on foot, and he arrives at Anočka's quarters more than two hours later than they had agreed upon for the rendezvous. As Anočka waits, she becomes more and more agitated, and doubts begin to arise in her mind as to whether she is worthy of Kirill, and that the "raznica meždu bol'šimi delami Kirilla i malen'kimi — Anočki nikogda ne isčeznet".[22] This feeling that everything that Kirill did was noble and heroic, and everything which she did was commonplace and trivial kept growing in Anočka's imagination, being transformed into a veritable storm of doubts regarding the possibility of finding future happiness with Kirill. In the meanwhile, "skvoz' žgučee metanie v'jugi Kirill videl teplyj svet malen'koj komnaty v kotoruju emu xotelos' skoree vojiti".[23] The blizzard, increasing in intensity, gradually becomes a necessary accompaniment to the entire narrative. The snowstorm is no longer a mere visual detail of the scene being created by the artist, but becomes an essential, indeed the major distinguishing component. Thus the part imperceptibly fuses with the whole.

B. PORTRAITURE AND THE USE OF COLOR

Characteristic of Fedin's style in the dilogy is his constant preoccupation with creating a unique portrait of each of his characters, conveying both their external and internal features. These portraits frequently reveal the ordinarily concealed complex psychological conflicts within the individual, and the nature of his thoughts and emotions.

For the most part, the portrait is not conveyed by descriptions on the part of the author, but rather by means of the actions and impressions

---

[21] I. Kozlov, "O sžatosti v proze", *Novyj mir*, No. 6 (1955), p. 268.
[22] Fedin, *Sobranie*, VII, pp. 707-8.
[23] *Ibid.*, VII, p. 706.

of the characters themselves. In such cases the details of the portraiture serve to reveal the essence of the acts and experiences of the particular hero, and also of the character through whose eyes the author, at a given moment, may be observing him.

A particularly expressive description of this type is found in the scene in which Liza and Kirill meet for the first time after a period of nine years, when Liza comes to beg for the release of her father, Merkurij Avdeevič Meškov, arrested by the revolutionary authorities. Liza, emotionally upset at her father's arrest, views Kirill as three different persons, and by means of the alternation of her impressions, Fedin conveys the essence of this dramatic confrontation. In the "dialect of the soul" which rages internally as Liza debates with herself whether to appeal to Izvekov, she sees Kirill as her first love. She quickly dispels this image, rationalizing that the Izvekov whom she loved no longer existed. Kirill next appears to her as the Secretary of the City Soviet, the Comrade Izvekov whose name she had read in the newspaper, and to whom she can appeal as a functionary, not as a youth twho once loved her.

The meeting is painful for both of them, as the past is resurrected, rebuking Liza for not having awaited Kirill's return from exile, and rebuking her father for having refused to help Kirill when he was in trouble. Liza is unable to understand Kirill's argument that he could not promise to help since he did know the nature of the charge against Meškov. When Anočka bursts in unexpectedly, and extracts from Kirill a promise to help, Liza suddenly sees a third Kirill, a synthesis of the other two.

В первый раз за эти короткие отчаянные минуты она увидела в Кирилле не человека двух раздельных существ (как ей все казалось), а слитного в одно целое, такого памятного, юного Кирилла и нового, чем-то ей недоступного Извекова. Она увидела в то же время глаза Аночки, в которых светилось не только великодушное сострадание к ней, не только детски наивный страх, но и счастливое, чуть дикое торжество.[24]

Fedin does not confine himself to this type of analytic portraiture to express the complex and often conflicting elements of his characters' personalities as an integrated whole. He also employs the device of capturing brief, fleeting characteristics and separate details which enter into construction of the portrait as a whole, rendering it more dynamic. In the last example, such a detail would be represented by the expression in Anočka's eyes. Tixon Parabukin's smile, as he begged the artists for

[24]   Fedin, *Sobranie*, VII, p. 609.

the price of a glass of vodka, was "prositel'noj, no v to že vremja nasmešlivoj". Liza's smile, when she herself was burdened by confused thoughts about the baby she was expecting, is described as "zadumčivaja, i v to že vremja bezdumnaja, sčastlivo-pustaja". Pastuxov's expression, when observing Merkurij Avdeevič Meškov for the first time, is portrayed this way:

... рот и щеки приподнимала любезная гипсовая улыбка, а глаза совершенно не были связаны ни со спокойствием лица, ни с обязательностью улыбки, — любопытные щучьим любопытством, жадно-холодные глаза.[25]

Here Fedin does not try to capture the fleeting expression, as in the previous examples, but rather tries to portray a lasting feature of Pastuxov's personality and character by means of a description of his face as it might appear in repose, seen from Meškov's point of view, reflecting his own personality as well as that of Pastuxov.

There is always a danger that an author, in trying to analyze particular psychological elements, and to reveal the essential psychological basis and meaning of the experiences and the moods of his characters, will find that direct characterization, by means of the gestures and speech of the protagonists themselves, conflicts with, or contradicts, indirect characterization, such as intrusive comments by, and in the name of, the omniscient author. This is not the case in Fedin's later work, where description and analysis are always integrated, succinctly and consistently, as in the characterization, "Zadumčivaja i v to že vremja bezdumnaja, sčastlivo-pustaja ulybka".

The combination of the description of external features, with analysis of the internal, psychological world of his heroes, is found not only in the portrait itself, but in the characterization attributable to the omniscient author. These appear in the form of comments or remarks which accompany the dialogue and, at the same time, provide additional details of external characterization. These interpolations by the author are relatively infrequent, but they do serve to help the reader determine the real import of a given fragment of speech. They include interpolations like the following:

"сказал равнодушно", "сказал, сдерживая раздражение", "оживая от усталого безразличия, воскликнул", "произнес увещевательно, как старший", "сказал полегче, но попрежнему задорно", "сказал по виду обиженно, однако со странным облегчением".

---

[25]   Fedin, *Sobranie*, VI, p. 156.

This device, serving as it does the function of direct revelation by the narrator, commits him to participation in the fate of his heroes, and serves as a type of critical commentary, usually expressing his ironic attitude toward one or another of the characters. Turgenev also uses the device. In "Burmistr", for example, one of the tales in *Zapiski ohotnika*, Turgenev portrays Penočkin's contradictory nature by means of such direct revelation.

Turgenev introduces this device in the very first lines of the general characterization of Penočkin. After having described Penočkin's spacious estate, the house built after the design of a French architect, the capital dinners he serves, and how cordially he receives guests, the narrator immediately adds: "... and, with all that, one goes to see him reluctantly". This aside at once compels the reader to be on guard, and arouses mistrust of Penočkin, despite his formal education and apparent culture.

In order that no doubts might remain in the reader's mind, the narrator introduces specific details in the description of Penočkin's appearance at the very moment when he is playing the role of father to his subjects. "When this *so-called* (again an insertion by the narrator) painful necessity arises, he eschews all sharp or violent gestures, and prefers not to raise his voice, but with a straight blow in the culprit's face, says *calmly* (again narrator's irony), 'I believe I asked you to do something, my friend?'"

In the preceding examples from *Neobyknovennoe leto*, it was noted that Fedin modified the verb "skazal" with an adverb or participial phrase which set the meaning of what was said in its true light. Fedin also expresses the action of speaking by means of a large number of synonymous variants, all having a slightly different shade of meaning, helping the reader to evaluate what is actually said. Among them are the following:

"воскликнул", "проговорил", "пробасил", "надбавил голоса", "скороговоркой вытолкнул", "буркнул", "полуспросила", "выжимали из себя словечки", "начал лепетать", "признался", "отбарабанил", "выпалил", and "прикрикнул".

Fedin also uses verbs in no way related to "skazal" or "otvetil" as descriptive and functional synonyms carrying additional meaning:

"Ну, Саша, разве так можно? С Ольгой Адамовной еще родимчик случится! — с обаятельным сочувствием к старой даме *улыбнулась* жена". "Мы проверим! — *воодушевился* солдат. — Проверим, чего он вздумал искать в Балашове!"

Among the devices which Fedin employs for portraying the external appearance of his characters, light and color predominate. Even before reaching the age of sixteen, Fedin was attracted to the paintings of Russian and Western artists which he could view in the art gallery of the Radiščev Museum in Saratov, where he lived from 1892 to 1908.

Здесь (в Саратове) складывались начальные понятия о прекрасном — из картинной галереи Радищевского музея, где было много отличных русских мастеров и западных художников — барбизонцев, собранных известным Боголюбовым; из школьных спектаклей в которых участвовал и я; из драматических и оперных театров; из уроков на скрипке, которые мучили меня и одно время совсем охладили к музыке.[26]

At one period in his life, at the age of fifteen, Fedin was "infected" with a desire to paint in oils.

К пятнадцати годам дом показался мне невыносимым гнетом, я стал очень худо учиться и в декабре 1907 года бежал в Москву, заложив в ломбарде свою скрипку. Один мой школьный товарищ, учившийся живописи и когда-то заразивший меня тягой к малеванию маслом, приютил меня в своем подвале, на Кисловке, и мы вместе мечтали, что я тоже буду художником, а пока я служил ему натурой, стоя посередине мрачной комнаты в позе Бонапарта.[27]

The portraits of the characters of the dilogy reflect Fedin's sensitivity to form and color. In the following example, the description of the physical appearance of Cvetuxin and Pastuxov suggests all of the expressiveness, the visual imagery of a painting done by a graphic artist:

На первом была надета черная накидка, застегнутая на золотую цепочку, которую держали в пастях две львиные головы, мягкая черная шляпа с отливом вороного пера, и сам он казался тоже черным — смуглый, с подстриженными смоляными усами. Второй легко нес на себе светлое, цветом похожее на горох, широкое ворсистое пальто, песочную шляпу с сиреневатой лентой, и лицо его, чуть рыхлое, но молодое, холеное, довольное, было словно подкрашено пастелью и тоже легко и пышно, как пальто и шляпа.[28]

In this brief excerpt, there are twelve references to light or to color. Fedin is particularly fond of depicting the color of clothing, such as Cvetuxin's black cape, fastened by a gilt chain. The word "gilt" itself, in Russian "zolotaja", includes the element of color. Pastuxov is not only wearing

---

[26] Fedin, *Sobranie*, I, p. 7.
[27] *Ibid.*, pp. 9-10.
[28] *Ibid.*, VI, p. 127.

a light-colored overcoat, but one which is of the color of sand. Even the face of each character is described in such a fashion that it begins to appear three-dimensional as on a painter's canvas. Fedin's sensitivity to the visual world of the artist is also made apparent from his use of the professional artistic lexicon, so that Patuxov's face looks as though tinted with pastels, giving the impression of lightness and showiness. When describing eyes, Fedin almost always makes some reference to their color:

всгляд медлительный, не по возрасту вдумчивый — синий взгляд Аночки. Правда, глаза ее мелькнули и сразу подменились другими — мягкими, будто испуганными, зеленовато-голубыми глазами Лизы Мешковой, и с этим мгновенным ощущением зрителя, как глаз Лизы, Цветухин вышел на сцену.[29]

Fedin, with the sharpened perception of the painter, conveys to the reader his heightened awareness of the effect of light and shadow on human being and inanimate object alike, and weaves the descriptive power of light and shadow into the narrative itself, exploiting it for literary ends.

Перед Лизой стоял не тот Цветухин, который только что улыбался ей. Солнце охватывало его льющимся в окно свечением, стан его силуэтно-черным, неподвижным, с откинутой рукой на эфесе шпаги, острием воткнутой в пол.[30]

A little later, when Liza is in the street again, after the darkness of the theatre, she becomes aware of the "singing sunlight of the day", and the sun itself

как будто светит только затем, чтобы перед ее взором, не исчезая, сияло окно с неподвижным черным силуэтом и чтобы она очер-ченней видела руку, так музыкально положенную на бронзовый эфес шпаги.[31]

Fedin's control over light, shadow, and color in this fashion evokes both joy, with the reader sharing Liza's delight, and wonder, that mere words can create so powerful a verbal image. And it is this very imagery which becomes an important narrative element, and one of the means used to portray the psychological development of Fedin's characters.

[29] Fedin, *Sobranie*, VI, p. 239.
[30] *Ibid.*, p. 221.
[31] *Ibid.*, p. 223.

XIV

HISTORICISM

Fedin's historicism, his ability to blend historical facts and materials into the plot of his novels, suggests a comparison with M. Šoloxov (*Tixij Don*) and A. Tolstoj (*Xoždenie po mukam*). However certain differences are immediately apparent. Unlike the genre of the historical epic represented by these two multi-volume works, Fedin's dilogy is constructed like a novel, a narrative dealing with the separate and individual fates of a handful of characters, artistically compressed into a definite plot framework. In *Tixij Don* and *Xoždenie po mukam*, the portrayal of historic events like the revolution and the civil war form the very basis of the plot, and must be given a broader treatment than in *Neobyknovennoe leto*, where only individual episodes are depicted, introduced mainly in conjunction with the portrayal of secondary plot elements and characters like Ipat, Karnauxov, Strašnov, and Dibič.

The plot of the two novels of the dilogy is unique in that Fedin concentrates not so much on the fate of broad classes of the population, but rather on the drama of the birth and development of the "new" Soviet man, and new social relationships. To do this, Fedin blends into the plot, in considerable detail, the portrayal of the fate of such varied characters as Ragozin, Pastuxov, Parabukin, Dorogomilov, Izvekov, and Anočka. All but Kirill and Ragozin met each other by chance, and their destinies are interrelated for only a relatively brief duration of time. Dibič dies tragically, the old romanticist Dorogomilov passes away, Ol'ga Ivanovna Parabukina does not live to see her daughter, Anočka's talents reach fruition, and Tixon Parabukin does not outlive his wife for long. It is likely that, looking back, the two dissimilar trips which Pastuxov made to Saratov, in 1910 and 1919, will appear as separate, unrelated incidents in his life. Even Kirill and Liza move through life along different paths. Although they had met in the first novel, and despite the indelible impressions left by their youthful encounter, they meet as strangers, with little in common, in the second novel.

Nevertheless there is a basic purpose, an underlying thought motivating the interweaving of all of the secondary and primary plot elements.

One of the distinguishing features of the plot of the dilogy, imparting purpose and meaning to ordinary events, is that all incidents and characters are correlated to the story of the birth of what is presented as a new type of artistic talent, and the awakening in all of the protagonists of a new, poetic consciousness of life. Awareness of this fact is essential to appreciation of the principles of the grouping of the characters and the principles underlying the portrayal of the individual characters.

Fedin introduces references to Lev Tolstoj for the purpose of intensifying the sense of rupture in people's consciousness during the period immediately preceding the revolution. Tolstoj is not included as one of the *dramatis personae*. But the brief account of his flight from Jasnaja Poljana, and his subsequent death, are so vividly portrayed that the reader, like the characters in the novel, feels his presence as palpably as though he were one of the actors.

Tolstoj died in 1910. This event, like the commanding figure of the sage of Jasnaja Poljana himself, plays an exceptionally important role in the novel. Fedin avails himself of Tolstoj to develop and intensify the theme of Kirill's revolutionary participation. Here Fedin follows the lead of Lenin who wrote that Tolstoj's death signaled the end of an era:

> Tolstoy has passed away, and pre-revolutionary Russia, whose weakness and impotence are expressed in the philosophy and depicted in the works of the artistic genius, has retreated into the past. But the heritage he has left us contains something which has not retreated into the past, which belongs to the future.[1]

References to Tolstoj keep recurring in the novel whenever the most important themes are introduced, such as art, literature, the old culture, and the new revolutionary outlook. At this stage of Fedin's work, these problems are discussed from various points of view, but are not resolved.

The preparations for a new revolutionary uprising is symbolized in *Pervye radosti* in the story of the underground printing press and in the double life led by Ragozin, Kirill, and Ksana. When the press is discovered, Kirill is sent into distant exile, and Ragozin's wife, Ksana, dies in prison. But the chief organizer of the operation, Ragozin himself, is not found by the Oxrana and continues his clandestine activities. The end of the first novel, *Pervye radosti*, constitutes, then, the *noeud* or initial situation of conflict of the second.

The second novel, *Neobyknovennoe leto*, is devoted to the critical

---

[1]   V. I. Lenin, "L. N. Tolstoy", *Articles on Tolstoy* (Moscow, FLPH, 1953).

period of the Civil War, 1919, when the revolutionary forces had to fight
for their continued existence. In *Neobyknovennoe leto*, the framework of
the narrative expands considerably. The underground forces personified
by Ragozin, Matvej, Ksana, and Kirill now manifest themselves openly
as the prime movers of the story. Fedin presents Petr Ragozin and Kirill
Izvekov in a variety of situations, as party organizers and activists, as
military leaders, as philosophers, as politicians, and as *cognoscenti* of
the arts.

In *Neobyknovennoe leto*, Fedin, with an even higher degree of craftsmanship than in *Pervye radosti*, demonstrates his deep historical sense.
In his first novel, *Goroda i gody*, Fedin demonstrated his ability to re-
create a historical atmosphere and to introduce, as an integral part of the
narrative, required documentary material in the form of vivid, unforgettable, historical details. In the earlier novels, however, history is sensed
only as a generalized background for the narrative. The first World War
and the revolutions in Germany and in Russia in the novel *Goroda i gody*
are depicted in scenes and episodes invented by Fedin. Those episodes
which were, in fact, based on actual documented happenings, did not
interest Fedin for their historical implications.

This is not the case in *Neobyknovennoe leto*, where the scenes of the
defense of Saratov are of value specifically for historical content. Fedin
portrays the action at Saratov as one of the main links in the defensive
chain of actions throughout the entire Volga region, actions which were,
to a large measure, decisive in determining the outcome of the Civil War.
It is precisely through such an approach that Fedin is able to relate these
historical events to the developing characterizations of his heroes. The
portrayal of actual events in this fashion imparts to the plot that sharpness of relief and sense of timeliness which, in the historical and social
novel, are so effective in the revelation of human character.

Neobyknovennoe leto is a completely independent and finished novel;
yet, at the same time, it is related to the first part of the dilogy. In it,
Fedin further develops the story, among others, of the Meškovs, Šubnikovs, and Parabukins. Liza, struggling not only for her own future, but
also for that of her son, finally leaves Šubnikov. By so doing, she frees
herself from the patriarchal authority of both her father and her husband.
Anočka overcomes the obstacle of her humble birth, and as her artistic
talents increase, her destiny becomes increasingly intertwined with that
of Kirill Izvekov. As for Cvetuxin, he adapts easily to the new order,
finding new avenues for self-fulfillment in the revolutionary theatre.

It is Pastuxov, however, who undergoes the most profound transformation of all. In *Neobyknovennoe leto*, the essence of the conflict between Izvekov and Pastuxov manifests itself as a dispute about the philosophy of history, a dispute which is to be resolved by life itself, specifically by Pastuxov's personal experience, brought to a climax by the catalyst of his imprisonment by Mamontov. In 1910, intellectuals like Pastuxov could vacillate, could entertain a certain skepticism that a political upheaval would result in a structuring of society which would be superior to the old. By 1919, however, historical actuality had transformed the situation from an academic to a real problem, threatening the Pastuxovs' very survival.

The first novel of the dilogy begins with Pastuxov's arrival in Saratov. The second novel begins the same way, but this time it is not a carefree excursion, but a flight from the hunger of Petersburg. During this flight, Pastuxov keeps coming into conflict with characters representing the strength of the revolution and the bolshevik theory of history. Among these characters are the former peasant but current soldier of the red army Ipat, the officer Dibič, and the old intellectual Dorogomilov. Also, as it develops, Pastuxov meets a number of former acquaintances, among them the actor Cvetuxin.

In his effort to make the trilogy a series of historical novels, Fedin imparts documentary character to it by integrating actual historical events and personages. As we have seen, these include the reactions of the characters to Lev Tolstoj's flight from Jasnaja Poljana and his subsequent death, the scene of Kirill Izvekov's participation in the parade at Novyj Oskol, the battle episodes of the Volga flotilla, and the other actual historical facts of the years 1910 and 1919.

In addition to integrating such events into the narrative structure, Fedin, in *Neobyknovennoe leto*, introduces historical-publicistic digressions. These interpolations are not fused organically with the artistically-structured narrative, and the device strikes a discordant note because it is so foreign to the style of the remainder of the novel.

Fedin uses another device for expressing his own ideas directly, and with greater artistic success. This is the rather infrequent lyrical-philosophic digression. It is not equivalent to a direct social or historical evaluation. In it, Fedin merely directs the reader's attention to the essence of certain phenomena which he treats artistically. In individual digressions, Fedin touches upon problems of morality, art, and philosophy. But he does not attempt to explore or resolve these problems in the digressions, reserving that for artistic treatment in the intrigue of the novel itself and in the experiences of the protagonists.

The novel *Neobyknovennoe leto* begins with such a digression.

Исторические события сопровождаются не только всеобщим воз-
буждением, подъемом или упадком человеческого духа, но непременно из ряда выходящими страданиями и лишениями, которых
не может отвратить человек. Для того, кто сознает, что происходя-
щие события составляют движение истории, или кто сам является
одним из сознательных двигателей истории, страдания не перестают
существовать, как не перестает ощущаться боль оттого, что
известно, какой болезнью она порождена. Но такой человек пере-
носит страдания не так, как тот, кто не задумывается об историч-
ности событий, а знает только, что сегодня живется легче или
тяжелее, луще или хуже, чем жилось вчера или будет житься завтра.
Для первого логика истории осмысливает страдания, второму они
кажутся созданными единственно затем, чтобы страдать, как жизнь
кажетзя данной лишь затем, чтобы жить.[2]

This exposition, stylistically similar to Tolstoj's numerous historical and
philosophical digressions in *Vojna i mir*, plunges the reader directly into
the historical atmosphere of the novel. It prepares the mind of the reader,
helping to reproduce the frame of reference which Fedin considers
essential to a proper appreciation of what follows in the novel. This
device establishes the reader's receptivity, so that the author may convey
his own intuitive experience, "infecting" the reader with his own feelings.
What Fedin does in this exposition is to polarize his cast of over thirty
characters into two main groups, with some mobility between them.
First there are the positive heroes, those who recognize that the events
taking place are part of the general movement of history. These favored
individuals, the "new" men, understanding the logic of history, are able
to appreciate the meaning of any suffering they may have to undergo, and
derive sustenance from that appreciation. The second group does not
appreciate the historical significance of events, and their suffering, therefore, is devoid of meaning. The way is now prepared for the further
development of the plot, and the different paths to be followed by Kirill,
Ragozin, Dibič, Pastuxov, Dorogomilov, the Meškovs, the Parabukins,
and the other characters of *Neobyknovennoe leto*. The device, then,
corresponds to the prevailing style of the dilogy, characterized by concreteness of description, and also by a minimum of direct intrusion by the
author, who prefers to present his ideas through the actions and experiences of his heroes.

Fedin published *Neobyknovennoe leto* in 1948. In it, he eulogizes

---

[2]   Fedin, *Sobranie*, VII, p. 7.

Stalin as both a military and a political leader. Much of this eulogy has been deleted from the 1961 edition of *Neobyknovennoe leto* published as part of Fedin's Collected Works in 1961. Thus, for example, the following passage has been removed:

By this time the Southern front had come to associate Stalin's name with the sweeping drive launched against Denikin. This name was spoken not only at staff headquarters, but throughout the army. There were cavalrymen who remembered their first meeting with Stalin in the Salsk steppe as far back as the summer of 1918. A little more than a year had passed since Stalin smashed Krasnov's Cossacks at Tsaritsyn, and there were a great many commanders and commissars in the South who could tell the Red Army men about the revolution's early battles for the Volga. Now the name "Stalin" had spread to all armies and all fronts. After Stalin's telegram reporting victory at Voronezh, his name resounded on every front, acquiring for the entire Red Army a new purport as the hallmark of military genius. The final words of this telegram were imprinted in Soviet Russia's memory: "The halo of invincibility created around the names of Generals Mamontov and Škuro has been trampled in the dust through the valour of the Red heroes of Comrade Budyonny's Mounted Corps."

Most Communists, Izvekov included, were aware that Stalin's role in the struggle waged on the civil war fronts by no means exhausted his activities since the October Revolution. Yet in spite of himself, Kirill came more and more frequently to regard Stalin as a military man. While thinking of the July events in Petrograd, he recalled that it was Stalin who had suppressed the counter-revolutionary uprising of the Krasnaja Gorka and Seraya Loshad forts in Kronstadt. And when he thought of the Soviet cavalry, it came to him that it was Stalin who had signed the order of the day on the formation of the First Mounted Army. While Stalin still remained for Kirill a great Party leader, he had already become for him, as for all Red Army men, a great Soviet military leader.

For this reason, the vision of the carpeted sleigh that he had glimpsed through the crowd kept returning to Kirill's mind. And it was understandable, however strange, that one indivisible impression should have arisen out of the two distinct impressions of the cavalry streaming over the steppes, and the man in the army greatcoat skimming swiftly over the snow in that light Russian sleigh.[3]

The political implication of the death of Stalin in 1953, and his subsequent denigration by Xruščev beginning with his so-called "secret" speech at the Twentieth Party Congress in 1956, are reflected in the third novel of the

---

[3] This passage has been copied verbatim from the English-language translation, *No Ordinary Summer* (Moscow, Foreign Languages Publishing House, 1950), Book II, pp. 717-719. It is conspicuous by its absence from chapter 38, p. 737 of the 1961 Russian-language edition, Vol. VI of the Collected Works. The reader who is interested in the deletions and additions to the work of one of Fedin's contemporaries is referred to David H. Stewart, "The Textual Evolution of *The Silent Don*", *American Slavonic and East European Review*, XVIII, No. 2 (April 1959), pp. 226-237.

trilogy, *Koster*. Even Kirill has to do penance for his support of Stalin and the "cult of the personality". In 1937, Kirill was summoned to appear before the Party Control Commission, accused of lack of vigilance and forgetfulness of his duty as a Communist, evidenced by his having given a favorable recommendation to a man who later defected while abroad on an official mission for the Soviet government. Kirill does not consider himself guilty, since suspicion and lack of faith in others are foreign to him. He is also offended deeply by the tone of the official of the Control Commission, as well as by his veiled hints, leading Kirill to suspect that the affair was not as simple as it appeared.

Ты не думаешь, кто-то меня хочет замешать в Ленинградские дела. ... Не знаю, со старой оппозицией, может быть?[4]

Kirill asks Ragozin. Ragozin's reply is very important to Kirill. Ragozin has been a friend for thirty years, and was his mentor when Kirill first began to participate in the underground activities of the revolutionary movement prior to the overthrow of the Tsar. Furthermore, Ragozin personifies the ideal Communist. But he replies, frowning, "Sovest', čto l', ne čista?" Kirill hears nothing but reproaches from Ragozin, and leaves crestfallen, feeling that his old friend had abandoned him in a bitter moment. Soon afterward the Party examined his case and Kirill was required to relinquish his post and accept a lesser assignment in Tula.

Fedin arouses the sympathy of the reader toward Izvekov, who seems to be suffering for an offense which he did not commit. Yet his characterization assumes greater credibility thereby. Kirill again reacts just as the reader would have predicted when, upon receiving the news of war, Izvekov accepts personal responsibility for its outcome, subordinating his personal welfare.

---

[4]   Fedin, *Sobranie*, VIII, pp. 262-63.

XV

KOSTER

Koster (*The Bonfire*), is not yet complete, although the first part has been published. It first appeared in the Soviet publication *Novyj mir*, Nos. 8-12 (1961), but separate chapters and extracts had been published prior to that date in various newspapers and journals.[1] The first part of *Koster* has been published as the eighth of the nine-volume collection of his works.

Koster continues the epic canvas which Fedin began twenty years ago. At that time, Fedin turned to the past of his characters before taking them through the ordeal of the second World War. In the first book of the trilogy, readers found more than the discussions on art, the theme of the intellectual and the revolution, and the search for a positive hero, all problems which had been treated in his earlier novels, particularly *Goroda i gody* and *Brat'ja*. In *Pervye radosti*, Fedin went further, portraying the formation of the "new" Communist man.

In 1948, the second novel in the series, *Neobyknovennoe leto*, was published, telling the story of the same characters nine years later, in 1919. The October Revolution has taken place, and Izvekov is now the secretary of the Saratov executive committee. He later leaves to fight on the red side in the Civil War. Ragozin, in charge of the finance department of the town soviet, participates in the Civil War as a commisar of a division in a naval flotilla. Anočka also realizes her dream. She becomes an actress in the revolutionary theatre directed by Pastuxov, dividing her time between performances for the troops, and her husband, Kirill, whom she has in the meantime married. The greatest change is wrought in Pastuxov who, during imprisonment by the whites, re-examines his philosophy of art and its purpose. He comes to side with the bolsheviks, offering to write a play on the theme of "liberation" for the new theatre, beginning a new stage in his work.

In *Koster*, the same characters are shown 22 years later, in the grim summer of 1941. It may be summarized as follows:

The news of the outbreak of war reaches Aleksej Pastuxov, son of the

[1]   Fedin, *Sobranie*, VIII, p. 461.

playwright, a young engineer at the Ižorsk works, while he is on holiday in the Crimea. The same day — Sunday, June 22, 1941 — he leaves for home. In Moscow, begging his travelling-companions, Begičev and Sočin, who work with him in the same factory, to do all they can to get places on a Leningrad train that night, he goes to see his father whom he had not met since he was a student.

Five years previously, Aleksandr Pastuxov, again a well-known playwright, left his family and went off with another woman. A year later, Aleksej yielded to his mother's plea and paid a visit to his father. Aleksej's mother still cherished the secret hope of a reconciliation. The dull indifference with which he was met offended him so deeply that he did not even write to his father when he obtained his diploma and became an engineer. Now he breaks the promise he made to himself and decides to go to Aleksandr Pastuxov to ask him to help his mother when he, Aleksej, joins the army. The news of the outbreak of war drives away his old antipathy. He does not find his father at home and, after a short talk with Julija Pavlovna, his father's second wife, who is preparing for her husband's birthday party, he goes away, leaving a note.

Aleksandr Pastuxov returns home later that afternoon when the guests are arriving. Although it is a company of old friends and everything seems the same as usual, the party falls flat. Only after the departure of the guests does Julija Pavlovna tell her husband about Aleksej's visit and the note he left. She tells him that she forgot about it during the bustle of the party.

On Sunday morning, Kirill Izvekov, now a deputy chairman of the Tula executive committee in charge of municipal affairs, sees his daughter Nadja off to Moscow where she is going to apply for admission to the university. Returning home, he starts thinking about his family life: about his daughter leaving school, his wife's engagement in Brest (she is now a famous actress, Anna Ulina), and about his brother-in-law Pavel Parabukin, who had been brought up in the Izvekov family and who had married the previous day. The smooth flow of his thoughts is interrupted by a telephone call from Pavel who tells him that the Germans have invaded the Soviet Union. As he hurries to the regional Party committee where an emergency meeting is to be held, his thoughts rush disjointedly over his recent past.

The reader had parted with Aleksandr Vasil'evič Pastuxov in *Neobyknovennoe leto*, in 1919, when he, after experiencing agonizing doubts and vacillation, resolved to ally himself with the bolsheviks and to write a play for the revolutionary theatre, to be called *Liberation*. In *Koster*,

Pastuxov reappears more than 20 years later (1941), truly a changed man. He is no longer the vain upstart whose first attempts at dramaturgy were acclaimed in the capital. He has been transformed by his experience during the Civil War and subsequent events into a mature writer. He has, of course, finally come to believe in and support the Soviet regime, and "serves" it with his art.

Pastuxov has parted with much of his earlier life, and has acquired much. He has left his wife, the beauty Asja, for a much younger woman, one who, it appears to him, is more modern and more in harmony with contemporary events. He has also acquired a substantial position in Soviet public life, having attained fame and the material accoutrements such as wealth, an automobile, and a dača. The war disrupts his comfortable existence and, distraught and disturbed, he is evacuated in the direction of Jasnaja Poljana. Pastuxov appears to the reader on his way to pay homage to the remains of Tolstoj, something he had never found time to do before. Draped over his shoulders is a "golubovato-stal'noe legkoe pal'to ... redčajšego cveta", which Pastuxov feels ashamed to wear in the presence of Tolstoj. This is the second instance in which Fedin employed the overcoat in a symbolic sense. In the first, it represented the young playwright's vanity and fastidiousness. When Pastuxov was released from Mamontov's prison, he left the coat behind, symbolizing his discarding of his old prejudices and ideas, and his identification with the new order. The use of this subtle artistic detail in *Koster* reveals that the new Pastuxov still retains traits of the old, the ostentatious coat representing Pastuxov's continued vanity and striving to differentiate himself from the mass, and the need for still further "purification".

One of the themes in *Koster* is the testing of the moral worth of the characters during the most crucial moments of life, and their reaction to death or the possibility of death. Fedin is indebted to Tolstoj for this theme, and for his artistic treatment of the meaning of life:

По-моему, одним из основных приемов, которым Толстой пользуется в своей лепке образа, является испытание нравственной ценности героя и решающей черты жизни и смерти. Прием этот вытекает из главной темы Толстого, художника и философа, и неразрывен с нею — из темы о смысле, о содержании жизни.[2]

In the same essay, "Iskusstvo L'va Tolstogo", Fedin refers to *Vojna i mir*, *Tri smerti*, and *Xozjain i rabotnik* as three works clearly demonstrating

---

[2] Fedin, *Sobranie*, IX, p. 29.

Tolstoj's repeated use of the same device. It is as if he were to say to his characters:

Show us your attitude toward death! Does death come to you naturally, do you fight it off, do you dread it, do you welcome it, do you try to hasten its arrival? Show us your attitude and demeanor in the face of death and we will know your worth as a man, we will be able to understand such as you.

Fedin wrote that

Сложнейший сюжет давал Толстому неограниченную возможность проверять любой характер на страшной грани между жизнью и смертью.[3]

But in his critical writing Fedin went one step further, generalizing from the individual to the nation, applying the same logic to the nation in time of national emergency:

Тут уже подвергался проверке характер целой нации, и как удивительно, с какой мощью написан этот характер, изваян этот великан истории-русский народ![4]

Fedin appears to be resorting to this same device, as he portrays the nation in the throes of war. Many of Fedin's heroes have to prove themselves in battle. They either perish in its flames, or emerge with renewed strength. Andrej Starcov, beset by doubts and misgivings about the morality of the revolution, perished. It is improbable that Pastuxov, having traveled so far along the road to reconciliation, will perish.

In his first novel, *Goroda i gody*, Fedin expressed the conflict by means of a double opposition. On the one hand, Andrej Starcov, desiring to identify with the revolution but unable to do so, is opposed by representatives of the old world, the former aristocrat Sergej L'vovič Ščepov and the German Count von Schoenau. On the other, he is opposed by the figure of the German revolutionary Kurt Wahn and the Karataev-like figure of the soldier Fedor Lependin.

There is an analogous double opposition in the novel *Brat'ja*, and in Fedin's subsequent novels. It seems that Fedin has elected to portray the development of the new Soviet positive hero not by means of one, but rather of two characters. One of them represents the man of intellect, the other the revolutionary activist, the man of action. By the end of the second novel of the trilogy, Fedin had not yet synthesized the two into a

[3]   Fedin, *Sobranie*, IX, p. 30.
[4]   *Ibid.*

single positive hero. In *Koster*, the system of contrasting and supplementing characters continues to prevail. But now this system assumes even greater depth and complexity, reflecting Fedin's greater maturity and artistry.

In *Koster*, Fedin boldly and penetratingly reveals the conflicts raging in the soul of each of his heroes, including that group which were heretofore portrayed with monolithic consistency. Now each group of characters, without losing its identity as a group, is shown to consist of diverse individuals, and each individual is shown to possess internal contradictions and inconsistencies. In the dilogy, the world of Izvekov and Ragozin unequivocally rejected the world of Šubnikov and Polotencev. Characters like Pastuxov, Cvetuxin, and Liza, being somewhat more complex than some of the others, sought their place in the sun by varying degrees of identification with one or another of the two groups. In the third novel, after more than 20 years have gone by, each of the characters has defined his position either for or against the Soviets. It may be more accurate to say that those who have been categorized as "enemies of the revolution" have disappeared somewhere beyond the narrative framework, with the exception of one or two minor episodic figures who appear for the first time as a consequence of the German invasion.

The inconsistencies in Pastuxov's character are exemplified by his initial reaction in the first days of the war, when he considered that the war was used as a convenient pretext for the director of the theatre to refuse to stage his play. This attitude immediately brings him into conflict with all those who recognize the war for the serious and tragic trial which it is, rather than merely as a transitory inconvenience.

The conflict between Pastuxov and Kirill Izvekov, which reached its climax in *Neobyknovennoe leto*, continues in *Koster*. Although they had not openly clashed since Pastuxov's reversal in the earlier novel, the sharp differences dividing them ideologically is shown in the chapters describing how each of them reacts to the sudden onset of war. Pastuxov "fights" for his play, and, as though nothing is happening, celebrates his birthday with a party. His second wife, Julija Pavlovna, is portrayed as an affected, rather shallow, and egoistical young woman, and his friends, the guests at the birthday celebration, are depicted as a host of parasites. By way of contrast, Kirill Izvekov, at the same moment that Pastuxov is entertaining his guests, is attending an emergency session of the regional Party Committee. As he participates in the conference dealing with the fate of the nation at war, Izvekov also finds himself thinking as well about personal matters, but in his case he is concerned over the fate of his wife, the renowned actress Anočka Ulina, at that moment in the city of Brest which is besieged by the Germans. Only gradually does Pastuxov come to realize the immensity of the tragedy of war, and only through its effect on him, personally, is he able to rouse himself from his lethargy and break out of the confining circle of his own selfish interests. It is ironic that the event which makes him aware of the enormity of the war, and all that it implies, is the news (which his calculating wife had "forgotten" to impart to him before the birthday party) that his son had come to see him on his way to a military assignment, and had left a message for him. Again by way of contrast, Fedin portrays Kirill as he waits for the secretary of the regional committee to have a free moment, so that Kirill might discuss with him the fate of his wife in beleaguered Brest.

The circle of positive heroes, the "new" Soviet men and women, has widened considerable in *Koster*. Now active as adults are the children of the heroes of the dilogy, such as, for example, Aleša Pastuxov, who has far outstripped his parents in his political growth as an unquestioning young Communist.

The figures of Communists who, in the dilogy, personified the leitmotif of revolution, are now reinforced by a large group of characters referred to as representing the countryside, "derevnja". "-Na derevne stoim. Nado — ona deretsja. Nado — zamirjaetsja ... Da vsegda pašet", shrewdly observes Pastuxov's chauffeur, Matvej Il'ič, who formerly lived in a little village himself. Pampered by Pastuxov and by Julija Pavlovna, who value him because he adds elegance to their driving, Matvej is by no means an "ideal" hero. But in Fedin's portrayal, Matvej emerges as a simple man, deeply rooted in the mass, who from the first moment of the war, feels a deep resentment toward his employers and the way of life which they represent.

In 1956, Fedin published a chapter which was to be included in the final novel of the trilogy, calling it "V Jasnoj Poljane".[5] From reading it, the references to Tolstoj in the trilogy, and the various articles in the volume devoted to Fedin's critical articles and memoirs, *Pisatel'*, *iskusstvo, vremja*,[6] the reader begins to understand the importance of Lev Tolstoj to Konstantin Fedin.

Лев Толстой — мировая школа литературного искусства. Это — русская литературная школа, вызвавшая небывало широкое течение художественной мысли на земном шаре. Это — школа, в которой

---

[5]   *Literaturnaja Moskva* (Moscow, Goslitizdat, 1956), p. 7-28.
[6]   Fedin, *Sobranie*, IX, *passim*.

наша советская литература черпает познание искусства и вдохновение к своим новым трудам о новом человеке.[7]

Fedin is till working on the second book of *Koster*, in which the chapter "V Jasnoj Poljane" will appear. In the second book the Tolstojan theme assumes greater importance than in any of Fedin's previous works. As Fedin wrote to one of his correspondents:

... Тема выплыла на важнейшее место в *Костре*. Во-первых, потому, что Лев Толстой воскрес во всем мире к новой жизни в Отечественную войну; Ясна подверглась поруганию фашистами и была блистательно возвышена и озарена освобождением священного очага Льва Толстого; роман *Война и мир* стал вдохновителем советских армий, очищавших землю родины от врага, и в романе этом иноземцы отыскивали объяснения 'чуда' нашей победы. Во-вторых, потому, что мои герои 1910 года продолжали жить в 1941 году и несли с собой развитие чувств и мыслей, однажды всколыхнувших их душу, то есть замыкали *Костром* сюжет *Первых радостей*.[8]

In this letter, Fedin assigns first priority to Tolstoj's political effect, the stimulation of patriotism as a result of reading *Vojna i mir*. Fedin does essentially the same thing in "V Jasnoj Poljane", which deals with Pastuxov's first wanderings during the evacuation of 1941. Now, 31 years after Tolstoj's death, Pastuxov comes to him, as to a live source, to seek an insight into the essential meaning of the invasion, and to define his own role in repelling it.

In this chapter, Fedin expresses a number of ideas. It is at Jasnaja Poljana that Pastuxov comes to understand "kuda my vse idem". He also comes to recognize the role of literature in the war.

As Pastuxov walks through the woods toward Tolstoj's estate, filled with trepidation about the future, his own psychological state prepares him for something unusual. Thoughts about past invasions and critical periods whirl through his mind, preparing the way for artistic invention. Fedin introduces nature as a participant in events, as Pastuxov seems to hear the birds calling to each other in alarm as they follow his invasion of the woods and advise one another of his movements. All of nature, it appears to Pastuxov, is awaiting the enemy, each element prepared to defend itself in its own way. In this agitated state Pastuxov weaves a fairy tale in his imagination, a tale about an old wise man to whom one may come with questions or problems needing resolution. It suddenly

[7] Fedin, *Sobranie*, IX, p. 33.
[8] *Ibid.*, VIII, p. 462.

becomes clear to Pastuxov that the old man is Lev Tolstoj, whom Pastuxov had consulted more than once in the past.

Pastuxov permits his imagination to range far and wide, and he fancies that he meets the live Tolstoj on the road to the estate:

Он увидел его с откинутой ветром на одно плечоо бльшой бородой. Зажженный солнцем голубой зоркий глаз глядит на дорогу из-под космато оттопыренной белой брови. Дугой раз затенен широким мягким полем шляпы, прижатым ко лбу со стороны ветра. Он сидит накренвшись набок. Он — в двухместной коляске, но едет один. Левое печо его приподнято — это с того бока, куда он накренился и где зорко горит глаз. Руки сильно выброшены вперед: он держит натенутые вожжи.[9]

Despite the fact that the image of Tolstoj exists only in Pastuxov's imagination, Fedin delineates his physical features as vividly as though he had appeared to Pastuxov in the flesh. Furthermore, Pastuxov is prepared to be guided by any sign he might receive from the venerable sage.

Even more convincing is the second "vision" of Tolstoj, when Pastuxov finds himself alone in the now empty "komnate pod svodami", following his unexpected encounter and reconciliation with his son under the "derevom bednyx" and after witnessing the evacuation of the household. As Pastuxov, with his whole being, reaches out to Tolstoj for guidance in that critical period, he again sees

Низко опустившуюся над столом бородатую голову с огромным ухом и льбом в жилах, веточками сбегавших к темным, насупленным бровям. ...[10]

Tolstoj, having again materialized in the imagination of the artist, was writing. And the artist — Pastuxov, with all of his weaknesses and doubts — unable to withstand the tremendous power of the being he had resurrected, fled like a schoolboy. Tolstoj, unlike the countess in Puškin's *Pikovaja dama*, had given no sign. Pastuxov knew what he had to do as the result of the entire experience, including the meeting with his son. He had to dedicate himself to helping win the war, supporting the cause of the "good people".

... чем дальше позади оставался усадебный дом, тем прозрачнее становились его чувства, соединяясь с душистой прохладной осенью в ее многоцветно-металлических красках. Он думал как много на свете хороших людей и что, наверно, только хорошие люди будут

---

[9] "V Jasnoj Poljane", p. 11.
[10] *Ibid.*, p. 32.

решать судьбу событий. Что как ни страшны эти события, хорошие люди их не страшатся, а ведь очень вероятно, что самое главное в жизни — ничего не страшиться.[11]

Thus does the intellectual at last find the courage and the strength to ally himself with the Kirill Izvekovs and the Ragozins, the men of action, and thus does all vacillation disappear.

To dispel all doubt that Fedin considered that Pastuxov's identification with the future of his country is the highest possible purpose, he opposes Pastuxov's final optimism to his thoughts immediate preceding. Earlier, by eavesdropping on Pastuxov's internal monologue, the reader is able to observe the logic of his thinking. If he had come to Tolstoj in 1909 or 1910, reflects Pastuxov, in the year of his early successes, when his plays were being acclaimed in the capital, he would have asked Tolstoj about such "glupostjax" as the meaning of life, knowing beforehand the reply, echoing Tixon of the Optin Monastery, of Zosima, would be that "the kingdom of God is within you". Continuing in the same ironic vein, Fedin attributes to Pastuxov the thought that Tolstoj would be somewhat skeptical regarding a celebrated playwright like Pastuxov coming to see him to save his soul. In all probability, thinks Pastuxov, Tolstoj would have interpreted his visit in 1910 correctly, namely that Pastuxov had come out of vanity, merely to be able to assert that he had visited Jasnaja Poljana and had met with Tolstoj. But now, in 1941, Pastuxov is characterized as having matured to such an extent that these earlier vanities no longer existed, and Pastuxov could now "serve the people".

[11] "V Jasnoj Poljane", p. 37.

CONCLUSION

Fedin wrote his first short story in the year when Tolstoj died, more than half a century ago. This was a period when Russian intellectuals were faced with agonizing problems on the nature and essence of humanism, and the very future of civilization as they knew it. Ahead lay an era of struggle, and the individual had to declare himself. For Fedin, this was a period of excrutiating soul-searching.

During this period, Fedin retained his artistic integrity, neither bowing to the demands of the revolution, nor blindly opposing it. He thoughtfully treated the theme of the tragedy of the individual in an epoch of revolution, posing a variety of questions and problems, without presuming to know their final solution. In a number of digressions in his first novel, Fedin presents his own views of war and pacifism, of the relation of art and culture to the revolution, of Western European mores and politics, and of the iron discipline of Communism. These views assume artistic form in the dialogues and actions of the *dramatis personae*, and the early novels are not so much novels of character as they are vehicles for the expression of conflicting points of view.

Unlike the pattern followed in his later novels, Fedin, in 1924, subordinates both characters and plot to the enveloping background of cities and years portrayed during a period of social upheaval. The *sjužetnye linii* of *Goroda i gody* are numerous, but all lead to the main hero, the vacillating intellectual who, although possibly expressing Fedin's personal convictions, yet is condemned and meets a tragic end.

The influence of Tolstoj is apparent during this early period not only in the literary devices used for psychological analysis, but also in Starcov's abhorrence of violence. The influence of Čexov is noted in the artistic laconism, and of Dostoevskij in the sense of guilt, suffering, and compassion evident in Fedin's early short stories and novels. Turgenev's influence was also noted, evidenced by Starcov's kinship to the Superfluous Man, as was that of Gončarov, the opposition between Starcov and Wahn reminding the reader of that between Oblomov and Stolz.

Fedin's early works impress the reader with their sincerity, good faith, and profound humanism, portrayed with dignity, and serving as a link with the Golden Age of Russian narrative literature.

The 1930's were a particularly significant period in Fedin's literary development, as indeed they were for most other Soviet litterateurs. For Fedin they were years of intense ideological and artistic development. This was the period of the first five-year plans, the adoption of a new constitution and, of perhaps greatest significance, the announcement of certain guiding principles at the First All-Union Congress of Soviet Writers held in 1934.

During the twenties, Fedin was able to stand apart from contemporary events, and to treat universal themes and motifs in his writings. But during the thirties he began to write numerous publicistic articles in which he affirms that "the great problems of current events have become the problems of our literature". In the twenties, Fedin had asserted the right of the artist to write about whatever he pleased, rather than to be obligated to treat contemporary themes. But a decade later he had reversed his stand. Fedin's views that literature must be tendentious are evidenced in the novel *Poxiščenie Evropy* and in numerous other minor works written in the thirties.

It was during this same period that Fedin conceived the idea of writing the trilogy, its main purpose being to present a "kartina nravov" and "obraz istorii". The study of the pre-natal history of the trilogy is particularly significant. Although limited in scope to the evidence acquired by Berezkina, the study of Fedin's method of work serves to deepen our understanding of the creative process at work in the evolution of a Soviet writer, and is of inestimable assistance in enabling the investigator to identify part of the basis for his creative achievements and shortcomings.

It was assumed at the outset that Fedin's works have literary value, so that this investigation, rather than attempting to prove their value, could concentrate on identifying, describing, and analyzing Fedin's literary craftsmanship. It was recognized, nevertheless, that it might be necessary to include evaluation as part of the critical process, and this has indeed been done.

The high level of Fedin's literary craftsmanship has been demonstrated in the examination of his style, the peculiarities of his linguistic expression. Fedin has made use of a variety of linguistic devices, has exploited the possibilities inherent in the Russian lexical inventory, and has stressed precision and the achievement of freshness and renewal of the canonical language through unique word combinations. He has also demonstrated his craftsmanship through manipulation of syntax to serve his artistic purpose, selecting those constructions which best convey the thoughts and emotions which Fedin wishes to transmit to the reader. In analyzing Fedin's portrayal of life by means of novelistic fiction, emphasis has been placed on the various stylistic devices characteristic of the author. As was seen, these devices are inextricably intertwined with the subject matter itself and with the ideological content of the works. Fedin's creative works may be characterized by the same words with which he described the artistic principles of Lev Tolstoj:

Приемы толстовского письма, первостепенные и дополнительные, органично вытекают из его основной темы, диктуются смыслом изображаемого, служат уяснению содержания. В них нет никакой искусственности, они не придуманы заранее, не существуют оторванно от произведения. Это не только доказано чудесной по естественности, по живой ясности прозой Толстого, но мы знаем это из прямых высказываний писателя об искусстве, о форме, о слове.[1]

It may be said of Fedin that, after passing through an early period in which he experimented with ornamentalism, he rejected the pursuit of a style in which the manner of narration would be more important than the subject matter. Fedin recognized that the dichotomy between "form" and "content" is more apparent than real, and he strived to attain an organic fusion of the two into an inseparable whole. In this attempt to mold what he considers epic subject matter into an aesthetic structure lies Fedin's importance as a contemporary Soviet novelist.

A major problem, which remains unresolved, is the extent to which Fedin has adjusted to the requirements of Socialist Realism because of external pressure, as opposed to genuine conviction. It is doubtful that this problem is susceptible to resolution on the basis of the external evidence afforded by Fedin's creative writings, since it involves penetrating the innermost recesses of Fedin's mind. Nevertheless, as this investigation has established, Fedin's novels have, over the years, increasingly conformed to the tenets of Socialist Realism, regardless of motivation.[2]

[1] Fedin, "Iskusstvo L'va Tolstogo", *Sobranie*, IX, p. 31.
[2] The Union of Soviet Writers, whose governing board is headed by Fedin in his capacity as First Secretary, according to *Soviet Literature*, No. 4 (1952), p. 126, has defined Socialist Realism as the "basic method of Soviet artistic literature and literary criticism, demanding of the writers a truthful, historically concrete portrayal of reality in its revolutionary development, whereby truthfulness and historical concreteness must be combined with the task of the ideological reforming and education of the

His novels have lost some of their primitive freshness, and the anguished outcries of Andrej Starcov and Nikita Karev are no longer heard. All meaningful internal conflict has vanished in the trilogy, with complete victory for the "New Soviet Man", occasionally subject to doubts, but inevitably destined to succeed in whatever he may undertake. In part, Fedin's conforming may be attributed to the mellowing influence of time, with a period of almost four decades separating his earlier novels from the later. With the passage of time, Fedin's reactions to his subject, his treatment of the themes of art and the role of the artist, and his portrayal of the intellectual seeking a niche in society lose some of their youthful fervor.

Although the influence of time cannot be ignored, neither can ideological pressure. Although not a measurable quantity in any individual case, certain facts do demand recognition. Over the period of Fedin's creative life, despite several thaws, the Soviet system has been characterized by minimal tolerance of literary expressions of doubt. Ideological pressure has been brought to bear on exponents of unpopular literary views, on the so-called Decadents, Ornamentalists, and Formalists. The regime has opposed Freudian preoccupation with hysteria and other psychopathic phenomena, the psychology of the subconscious, and the theories that abnormal mental reactions are due to repression of desires consciously rejected but subconsciously persistent. These views explain the partial rejection of Dostoevskij, and possibly the disappearance of this type of probing in Fedin's later literary work. The result is the uniform aspect of many Soviet novels.

This investigation has also demonstrated the futility of any attempt to determine Fedin's attitude towards the Soviet system by analyzing his characters. Any conclusions reached would necessarily be influenced by our preconceptions, since Fedin appears to have found a viable formula, sufficiently ambiguous to be interpreted so as to yield diametrically opposed conclusions. This is not the case in his theoretical writings, in which his position is unequivocal. Thus he begins the article "Čto že takoe sovremennost'?" by affirming, before all else, his complete identification with the aims of the Soviet Union. It would be difficult to find an American author of Fedin's stature, say, Steinbeck, Faulkner, or Hemingway,

---

toilers in the spirit of socialism", cf. *Problems of Soviet Literature* (New York, International Publishers, 1935), p. 220, cited by Victor Erlich, "Soviet Literary Criticism: Past and Present", *Problems of Communism*, No. 1, Vol. VII (USIA, Washington, D.C., Jan.-Feb. 1958), p. 39.

making statements like the following: "My pisateli sovetskogo obščestva. Naši zadači — ego zadači, ego žizn' est' naša žizn'." [3]

Regardless of Fedin's subjection to ideological pressure, the fact remains that this investigation has isolated and analyzed certain distinguishing features of his literary craftsmanship and, although evaluation has not been a primary objective, the data discovered in analysis does constitute evidence for appraisal. Kaplan, in attempting to reconcile the scientific method to art criticism, points out that "Every appraisal is a hypothesis, and the descriptive materials confirm or deny it. The description does not entail the appraisal, but it gives it more or less evidential weight." [4]

The hypothesis which suggests itself, previously accepted by stipulation, is that Fedin is an artist, and his artistry is the fundamental aspect of his literary gift. He hears the world like a musician, sees it like a painter, and feels it with the sensitivity of a sculptor. Nevertheless he controls his artistic impulse, subordinating it to his theme, to his central and guiding idea. Along with the insatiable demand that he study and analyze his environment, there exists in Fedin the capability to convey his experiences, be they rational or intuitive. Fedin could never be considered an author who writes for pleasure. He is an artist who studies, investigates, and, in his later works, pronounces judgment.

By way of conclusion, several comments are warranted regarding the contribution made by this study, its limitations, and what subsequent investigation appears warranted. The major contribution is considered to be the identification of the distinguishing features of Fedin's art free of Marxist bias; the analysis of these features should contribute to fuller understanding and appreciation. Any shortcomings of the investigation are attributable more to the inadequacies of the investigator than to any external cause. Some of the primary sources (such as earlier editions of Fedin's works), and secondary sources (such as the more than fifteen dissertations on file in the Lenin Library in Moscow and in various Soviet institutions of higher learning throughout the USSR) could not be procured, and Fedin himself refused to acknowledge any correspondence.

This investigation, however, was probably not hampered as much by the unavailability of materials as will be later efforts, which necessarily will delve into the subject in greater depth.

[3]　K. Fedin, "Čto že takoe sovremennost'?", *Čto takoe sovremennost'?* (Moscow, Izdatel'stvo Pravada, 1960), p. 279.
[4]　Abraham Kaplan, "On the So-Called Crisis in Criticism", *Journal of Aesthetics and Art Criticism*, Vol. VIII, No. 1 (September, 1948), p. 42.

It was noted earlier that this study was inspired by the investigation of Hongor Oulanoff of the literary achievements of the Serapion Brothers.[5] In evaluating the Serapion Brothers, Oulanoff concluded that

The final balance may appear somewhat disappointing. The achievement falls short of the initial purpose. *Except Fedin* (italics mine) and Kaverin of *Xudožnik neizvesten*, the Serapion Brothers did not attain the higher form of the "synthesis" toward which Lunc had urged them to strive.[6]

Oulanoff had also concluded that Fedin and Kaverin had achieved more than the others in plot construction. The present investigation, although not concerned with examining the structure of the works of the other Brethren, has isolated and analyzed the structure of Fedin's works in detail. Subject to particularly searching scrutiny was the inversion of chronology in *Goroda i gody*, and a hypothesis advanced to account for this device on literary grounds, which has not previously been undertaken.

Future investigators may wish to examine this problem using a comparative method, comparing the distinguishing features of Fedin's art on an individual basis with that of each of the other prose writers among the Serapion Brothers, specifically Zoščenko, Slonimskij, Kaverin, Nikitin, Vs. Ivanov, Lunc, and even Šklovskij and Gruzdev. Genre studies also appear warranted. Fedin has written in a number of different prose genres. These include short stories, novellas, novels, dramas, memoirs, theoretical articles, and propagandistic essays. Although he has realized his fullest capabilities in the short stories written during his early period, the first two novels, and the trilogy, investigations into the evolution of each of the genres would be useful. Changes in successive editions of Fedin's works warrant tracing, as well as the transition from small genres (short stories) to the long genres (novels), with emphasis on such features as *mise-en-scène*. Comparative analysis is also indicated in an effort to determine the influence of such pre-revolutionary writers as Puškin, Gogol', Turgenev, Gončarov, Dostoevskij, Čexov, and Tolstoj. The influence of Bunin and Remizov also merits study, as does that of Gor'kij. Finally, investigation of the influence of foreign authors, such as Thomas Mann (*Sanatorij Arktur* suggests the influence of *Magic Mountain*), Romain Rolland, and Stefan Zweig is warranted. As for the latest novel, *Koster*, it is a virgin field, awaiting the investigation of its sound structure (euphony, rhythm, meter), its linguistic structure (style and stylistics), and its use of image, metaphor, symbol, and myth.

---

[5]   H. Oulanoff, *The Theory and Practice of the Serapion Brothers* (= *Slavistic Printings and Reprintings*, 44) (The Hague, Mouton & Co., 1966).
[6]   *Ibid.* Prior permission to quote from the book was granted by Professor Oulanoff.

BIBLIOGRAPHY

This bibliography does not purport to be exhaustive, listing every work ever written by or about Konstantin Aleksandrovič Fedin. Neither is it so selective that it is limited to the books and articles which were used in this study. Other titles, which may prove of value to other investigators, are also included.

It was not possible in the present study to locate and consult all of the titles which were uncovered during the bibliographic search, nor was this attempted. Thus Fedin's early writings under the pseudonym Šved, as well as his publicistic articles, were not consulted, although they are listed in the bibliography. Conversely, when review of bibliographical guides, universal bibliographies, biblio-bibliographies, reference works, trade lists, encyclopaedias, dissertation lists, bio-bibliographies, periodical indices, learned journals, literary periodicals, Russian literary bibliographies, other national bibliographies, lists of work in progress, hidden bibliographies, and individual specific queries to Fedin or to Soviet and American libraries and universities failed to disclose any pertinent information, the sources consulted have not been listed. Of the listed sources, those consulted are identified by an asterisk.

The first section of the bibliography is devoted to the five collections of Fedin's works. The second section is devoted to separate editions in book form. Books which have appeared in several editions are identified only in the first edition, followed by the comment "plus later ed.". Prior publication in literary journals is normally not indicated, since this material is readily available in the back of each volume of the collected works. Primary sources are arranged according to date of publication; secondary sources are arranged alphabetically. Translations are arranged according to language. Translations into the non-Great Russian national languages of the USSR are those listed in *Index Translationum*.

I. COLLECTED WORKS

Sobranie sočinenij. 4 vols. (Leningrad, Priboj, 1927-28).
    Vol. I: *Pustyr'*. *Povesti i rasskazy* (Leningrad, 1927). Contents: Anna Timofevna. Rasskaz ob odnom utre. Sad. Pes'i duši. Konec mira. Staršij komendor. Ež. Blinki. Bakunin v Drezdene.
    Vol. II: *Goroda i gody*. *Roman* (Leningrad, 1927).
    Vol. III: *Transvaal'*. *Povesti i rasskazy* (Leningrad, 1927). Contents: Narovčatskaja xronika. Mužiki. Transvaal'. Tišina. Utro v Vjažnom. Abxaskie rasskazy (Bočki, Suuk-Su).
    Vol. IV: *Brat'ja*. *Roman* (Leningrad, 1928).
Sobranie sočinenij. 4 vols. (Moscow-Leningrad, Gosudarstvennoe izdatel'stvo, 1929-30).
Sobranie sočinenij. 4 vols. (Moscow-Leningrad, Gosudarstvennoe izdatel'stvo xudožestvennoj literatury, 1931-32).

Sobranie sočinenij. 6 vols. (Moscow, Godudarstvennoe izdatel'stvo xudožestvennoj literatury, 1952-54).*
Vol. I: *Goroda i gody. Roman.* Posleslovie k romanu *Goroda i gody* i avtobiografija pisatelja.
Vol. II: *Brat'ja. Roman.*
Vol. III: *Poxiščenie Evropy. Roman.*
Vol. IV: *Sanatorij Arktur* i *Pervye radosti. Romany.*
Vol. V: *Neobyknovennoe leto. Roman.*
Vol. VI: Povesti i rasskazy. Očerki. Literaturnye i publicističeskie stat'i. Literaturnye vospominanija.
Sobranie sočinenij. 9 vols. (Moscow, Gosudarstvennoe izdatel'stvo xudožestvennoj literatury, 1959-62).*
Vol. I: *Vstreča s prošlym. Povesti i rasskazy. Bakunin v Drezdene. Sceny* (1959).
Vol. II: *Goroda i gody. Roman* (1959).
Vol. III: *Brat'ja. Roman. Narovčatskaja xronika* i *Transvaal'. Povesti* (1960).
Vol. IV: *Poxiščenie Evropy. Roman* (1960).
Vol. V: *Sanatorij Arktur. Roman.*
Ispytanie čuvstv. P'esa.
Vojna i posle vojny. Očerki i stat'i (1960).
Vol. VI: *Ja byl akterom* i *Starik. Povesti. Pervye radosti. Roman* (1960).
Vol. VII: *Neobyknovennoe leto. Roman* (1961).
Vol. VIII: *Koster. Roman* (1962).
Vol. IX. *Pisatel', iskusstvo, vremja* (1962).

II. SEPARATE EDITIONS

Svetaet (Petrograd, Giz., 1921). Pp. 14 (also: Leningrad, Giz., 1924).
Contents: Velikoe tainstvo. Naučilsja.
Bakunin v Drezdene. Teatr v dvux aktax (Petrograd, Giz., 1928). Pp. 96.
Sad. (Petrograd, 1922). Pp. 31 (also: Leningrad, Giz., 1924).
Pustyr' (Moscow, Krug, 1923). Pp. 196.
Contents: Anna Timofevna. Sad. Pes'i duši. Konec mira. Rasskaz ob odnom utre. Staršij komendor. Ež. Blinki.
Goroda i gody. Roman (Leningrad, Giz., 1924). Pp. 384 (plus later ed.).
Rasskaz ob odnom utre (Leningrad, Krug, 1924). Pp. 32.
Contents: Rasskaz ob odnom utre. Pes'i duši.
Rasskazy (Moscow, Krug, 1925). Pp. 192.
Contents: Anna Timofevna. Sad. Pes'i duši. Konec mira. Rasskaz ob odnom utre. Staršij Komendor. Ež. Blinki.
Anna Timofevna (Leningrad, Giz., 1925). Pp. 113 (also: Leningrad, Priboj, 1928).
Fedor Lependin. Èpizod iz romana *Goroda i gody.* With introductory article by I. A. Gruzdev (Leningrad, Giz., 1926). Pp. 48 (also: Moscow, Žurgas-Biblioteka Ogonek, 1931).
Mužiki. Povest' (Leningrad, Priboj, 1926). Pp. 64.
Narovčatskaja xronika (= *Biblioteka sovremennyx pisatelej*) (Xar'kov, Proletarij, 1926). Pp. 196.
Contents: Avtobiografija. Narovčatskaja xronika. Transvaal'.
Rasskazy (Moscow, Izd. Ogonek, 1926). Pp. 56.
Contents: Tišina. Sad. Bočki.
Abxaskie rasskazy. Drawings by K. Erbštejn (Moscow-Leningrad, Giz., 1926). Pp. 28.
Narovčatskaja xronika (= *Deševaja biblioteka*) (Leningrad, Priboj, 1927). Pp. 64.

Transvaal'. *Rasskazy* (Moscow-Leningrad, Giz., 1927). Pp. 206.
Contents: Narovčatskaja xronika. Mužiki. Transvaal'. Tišina. Utro v Vjažnom. Bočki. Suuk-Su.

Transvaal' (= *Deševaja biblioteka*) (Leningrad, Priboj, 1928). Pp. 79.

Brat'ja. *Roman* (Leningrad, Priboj, 1928). Pp. 320 (plus later ed.).

Starik. Woodcuts by N. Alekseev (Leningrad, Izdatel'stvo pisatelej v Leningrade, 1930). Pp. 87.

Povesti i rasskazy (Leningrad, Izdatel'stvo pisatelej v Leningrade, 1933). Pp. 371.
Contents: Anna Timofevna. Narovčatskaja xronika. Transvaal'. Starik. Sad. Rasskaz ob odnom utre. Pes'i duši. Tišina. Mužiki. Ež. Blinki. Bočki. Suuk-Su.

Detstvo muzykanta (= *Biblioteka nachinajuščego čitatelja*) (Leningrad, Goslitizdat, 1934). Pp. 64.

Poxiščenie Evropy. *Roman* (Paris, Izdatel'stvo Zvezda, 1934). Pp. 256.*

Smert' Kvasta (= *Biblioteka Ogonek*) (Moscow, Žurgaz, 1934). Pp. 31 (also: Leningrad, Goslitizdat, 1936).

Poxiščenie Evropy. *Roman*. Book 1 (Leningrad, Izdatel'stvo pisatelej v Leningrade, 1934). Pp. 314.

Poxiščenie Evropy. *Roman*. Book 2 (Leningrad, Goslitizdat, 1935). Pp. 281.

Ja byl akterom (Moscow, Sovetskij pisatel', 1937). Pp. 66.

Risunok s Lenina (Leningrad, Goslitizdat, 1939). Pp. 16.

Novye rasskazy (= *Biblioteka Ogonek*) (Moscow, Pravda, 1940). Pp. 48.
Contents: Vstreča s prošlym. Risunok s Lenina. Člen delegacii.

Sanatorij Arktur. *Roman* (Moscow, Sovetskij pisatel', 1940). Pp. 188.

Malen'kie romany i četyre rasskaza (Moscow, Goslitizdat, 1941). Pp. 284.
Contents: Sanatorij Arktur. Ja byl akterom. Starik. Vstreča s prošlym. Risunok s Lenina. Rasskaz v pis'max. Člen delegacii.

Ispytanie čuvstv. *P'esa v 4 aktax* (Moscow, Vsesojuznoe upravlenie po oxrane avtorskix prav, 1942). Pp. 50.

Ispytanie chuvstv. *P'esa v 4 aktax* (Moscow-Leningrad, Iskusstvo, 1943). Pp. 116.

Gor'kij sredi nas. *Dvadcatye gody* (Moscow, Goslitizdat, 1943). Pp. 148.

Gor'kij sredi nas. *Kartiny literaturnoj žizni*. Part 2: *1921-28* (Moscow, Goslitizdat, 1944). Pp. 172.

Mal'čik. Drawings by A. Ermolaev (Moscow-Leningrad, Detgiz, 1944). Pp. 31.
Contents: Sazany. Vasja. Mal'čik iz Semleva. Komandir.

Svidanie s Leningradom (Leningrad, Voenizdat, Otdelenie pri Leningradskom fronte, 1945). Pp. 62.
Contents: Partizany na Nevskom prospekte. Živye steny. Vo vremena blokady. Rasskaz o dvorce. Den' nemca v Gatčine. Leningradskaja natura.

Davno i nedavno (= *Biblioteka Ogonek*). *Rasskazy* (Moscow, Pravda, 1947. Pp. 64.
Contents: Sazany. Garmon'. Vstreča s prošlym. Risunok s Lenina. Rasskaz v pis'max. Mal'čik iz Semleva. Časiki. Brat i sestra. Rasskaz o dvorce.

Izbrannye proizvedenija (Moscow, Goslitizdat, 1947). Pp. 712.
Contents: Brat'ja. Pervye radosti. Starik. Garmon'. Sad. Transvaal'. Vstreča s prošlym. Risunok s Lenina. Rasskaz v pis'max. Brat i sestra. Rasskaz o dvorce.

Pervye radosti. *Roman* (Moscow, Goslitizdat, 1946). Pp. 340 (plus later ed.).

Neobyknovennoe leto. *Roman* (Saratov, Saratovskoe oblastnoe izdatel'stvo, 1948). Pp. 692 (plus later ed.).

Pisatel', iskusstvo, vremja (Moscow, Sovetskij pisatel', 1957). Pp. 521.*

III. ARTICLES, SKETCHES, AND REVIEWS

Published in *Izvestija*, Syzran', 1919, under the pseudonym "Šved".

1. Šved. "Nu-ka!" (article), No. 80, Apr. 11, 1919.
2. Šved. "Graduščee sčast'e" (article), No. 95, May 1, 1919.
3. Šved. "O novyx akterax" (review), No. 100, May 8, 1919.
4. Šved. "Proletarskij teatr" (review of Najdenov's play *Deti Vanjušina*), No. 102, May 10, 1919.
5. Šved. "Dni našej žizni" (review), No. 104, May 13, 1919.
6. Šved. "Zarvalis'" (article), No. 107, May 16, 1919.
7. Šved. "Brat'ja-vragi" (article), No. 108, May 17, 1919.
8. Šved. "Versal'-ètap mirovoj revoljucii" (article), No. 112, May 22, 1919.
9. Šved. "Napirajut ..." (article), No. 115, May 22, 1919.
10. Šved. "Bolgary prosypajutsja" (article), No. 121, June 3, 1919.
11. Šved. "Udača" (sketch), No. 122, June 4, 1919.
12. Šved. "Cerkov' i bol'ševiki" (article), No. 123, June 5, 1919.
13. Šved. "Mir ili novaja vojna?" (article), No. 134, June 19, 1919.
14. Šved. "Bezopasnye komendanty" (article), No. 170, July 31, 1919.
15. Šved. "Trizna" (article), No. 171, Aug. 1, 1919.
16. Šved. "Poltava" (note), No. 174, Aug. 6, 1919.
17. Šved. "Vengriju dušat!" (article), No. 175, Aug. 7, 1919.
18. Šved. "Otstupajut" (article), No. 176, Aug. 8, 1919.
19. Šved. "Vokrug Vengrii" (article), No. 177, Aug. 9, 1919.
20. Šved. "Malen'kaja pobeditel'nica" (article), No. 178, Aug. 10, 1919.
21. Šved. "Ešče o sojuznikaz" (article), No. 180, Aug. 13, 1919.
22. Šved. "Vengrija v ogne" (article), No. 183, Aug. 16, 1919.
23. Šved. "Pis'mo Maklakova k Vinokuru", No. 195, Sep. 2, 1919.
24. Fedin, K. and Al. Roslavlev. "Čirok" (feuilleton), No. 197, Sep. 4, 1919.

IV. ARTICLES

Published in *Alyj put'*, originally called *Izvestija*, Syzran', 1919:

25. Fedin, Konst. "Ljubite knigu!", No. 1, n. d.
26. Fedin, Konst. "Vstranu-skažu!", No. 2, n. d.
27. Fedin, Konst. "Demokratija Černogo Neba", No. 3, n. d.
28. K. F. "Čto delajut sojuzniki", No. 6, n. d.
29. P. Sh. "V černom stane" (note), No. 7, n. d.

V. ARTICLES

Published in *Syzranskij kommunar*, formerly called *Alyj put'* and *Izvestija*:

30. Šved. "Smert' odnogo pravitel'stva" (article), No. 4 (210), Sep. 20, 1919.
31. Šved. "Korol' veselitsja", No. 1 (207), Sep. 17, 1919.
32. Šved. "Vse ponjatie" (article), No. 5 (211), Sep. 21, 1919.
33. Šved. "Sojuz krepnet" (article), No. 10 (216), Sep. 27, 1919.
34. Fedin, Konst "Leonid Andreev" (review), No. 10 (216), Sep. 27, 1919, p. 2.
35. P. Š. "Peredvižnye biblioteki", No. 10 (216), Sep. 27, 1919, p. 2.

36. P. Š. "Sovety, zaščiščajte vaši derevni!", No. 12 (218), Sep. 30, 1919.
37. Šved. "Čexi", No. 15 (221), Oct. 3, 1919.

VI. TRANSLATIONS

Albanian

Neobyknovennoe leto (Tirana, 1959).

Armenian

Pervye radosti (Yerevan, 1954).

Bulgarian

Pervye radosti (Sofia, 1947), *Neobyknovennoe leto* (Sofia, 1950), *Brat'ja* (Sofia, 1957).

Chinese

Goroda i gody (Shanghai, 1947; 2d ed., 1950; Peiping, 1954), *Pervye radosti* (Shanghai, 1953), *Neobyknovennoe leto* (Shanghai, 1953).

Chuvash

Mal'čiki (Cheboksary, 1960).

Czech

Goroda i gody (Prague, 1926; 1959), *Brat'ja* (Prague, 1929; 1951), *Transvaal'* (Prague, 1928), *Narovčatskaja xronika i drugie povesti* (Prague (1928; 1958), *Pervye radosti* (Prague, 1950; 1953), *Neobyknovennoe leto*, (Prague, 1951; 1953), *Ja byl akterom* (Prague, 1958), *Poxiščenie Evropy* (Prague, 1958), *Pisatel', iskusstvo, vremja* (Prague, 1958), *Goroda i gody* (Prague, 1959), *Sanatorij Arktur* (Prague, 1960).

Danish

Svidanie s Leningradom (Copenhagen, 1946).

Dutch

Goroda i gody (Zeist, 1930), *Poxiščenie Evropy* (Rotterdam, 1937).

English

Sad. May be found in E. Jolas and R. Sarge (ed.), *Transition Stories* (New York, Walter V. McKee, 1929), pp. 81-95. *Pervye radosti* (Moscow, 1948), *Pervye radosti* and *Neobyknovennoe leto* (dilogy in 3 vols., Moscow, 1950), *Sanatorij Arktur* (Moscow, 1957), *Pervye radosti* (New York, Vintage Books, 1960).*

Estonian

Neobyknovennoe leto (Tallin, 1954).

Finnish

Pervye radosti (Helsinki, 1956).

French

Goroda i gody (3d ed., Paris, 1930), *Transvaal'* and *Mužiki* (Brussels, 1927), *Pervye radosti* (Paris, 1949), *Neobyknovennoe leto* (2 vols., Paris, 1951).

German

Goroda i gody (Berlin, 1927; Berlin, 1948; Munich, 1948; Zurich, 1948; Berlin, 1954; Berlin, 1960), *Brat'ja* (2d ed., Berlin, 1928; Leipzig, 1954), *Pervye radosti* (Moscow, 1948; Leipzig, 1951; Berlin, 1955), *Neobyknovennoe leto* (2 vols., Berlin, 1950; Berlin, 1951), *Pervye radosti* and *Neobyknovennoe leto* (dilogy in 3 vols., Moscow, 1950), *Ja byl akterom* (Berlin, 1956), *Sanatorij Arktur* (Berlin, 1956; Berlin, 1958; Berlin, 1959), *Collected Works* (6 vols., Berlin, 1958; Vol. I: *Povesti i rasskazy*, Vol. II: *Poxiščenie Evropy*).

Hebrew

Pervye radosti (Tel Aviv, 1952), *Neobyknovennoe leto* (Tel Aviv, 1953).

Hungarian

Pervye radosti (Budapest, 1948; 1950; 1955), *Neobyknovennoe leto* (Budapest, 1949; 1950), *Sanatorij Arktur* (Budapest, 1954), *Poxiščenie Evropy* (Budapest, 1955), *Goroda i gody* (Budapest, 1955), *Brat'ja* (Budapest, 1959), *Pisatel', iskusstvo i vremja* (Budapest, 1960).

Italian

Goroda i gody (Turin, 1946), *Brat'ja* (2 vols., Turin, 1929), *Brat'ja* (1 vol., Rome, 1945).

Japanese

Pervye radosti (Tokyo, 1951; Kyoto, 1952), *Neobyknovennoe leto* (Tokyo, 1952; Kyoto, 1952).

Kazax

Neobyknovennoe leto (Alma Ata, 1959).

Latvian

Goroda i gody (Riga, 1956).

Norwegian

Pervye radosti (Oslo, 1949).

Polish

Goroda i gody (Warsaw, 1928; 1957), *Pervye radosti* (Warsaw, 1948; 1954), *Neobyknovennoe leto* (Warsaw, 1951; 1953), *Brat'ja* (Warsaw, 1956), *Poxiščenie Evropy* (Warsaw, 1957), *Sanatorij Arktur* (Warsaw, 1960).

Portuguese

Sanatorij Arktur (Sao Paulo, 1945), *Goroda i gody* (Sao Paulo, 1947), *Pervye radosti* (Rio de Janeiro, 1955).

224 BIBLIOGRAPHY

Romanian

Pervye radosti (Bucharest, 1949; 2d ed., Bucharest, 1951; Bucharest, 1957), *Neo-byknovennoe leto* (Bucharest, 1950; 1957), *Rasskazy v pis'max* (Bucharest, 1948), *Starik* (Bucharest, 1952), *Goroda i gody* (Bucharest, 1954), *Brat'ja* (Bucharest, 1954; 1955), *Risunok s Lenina* (Bucharest, 1955), *Poxiščenie Evropy* (Bucharest, 1956; 1959), *Sanatorij Arktur* (Bucharest, 1957).

Serbo-Croatian

Brat'ja (2 vols., Belgrade, 1939), *Mal'čiki* (rasskazy, Belgrade, 1945), *Pervye radosti* (Belgrade, 1946), *Neobyknovennoe leto* (Belgrade, 1956), *Goroda i gody* (Belgrade, 1956), *Sanatorij Arktur* (Belgrade, 1958).

Slovak

Brat'ja (Bratislava, 1950; 1951), *Pervye radosti* (2 vols., Bratislava, 1950), *Pervye radosti* (Bratislava, 1953), *Neobyknovennoe leto* (Bratislava, 1953), *Goroda i gody* (Bratislava, 1956), *Sanatorij Arktur* (Bratislava, 1958).

Slovenian

Goroda i gody (Ljubljana, 1931), *Brat'ja* (Ljubljana, 1955), *Neobyknovennoe leto* (Ljubljana, 1956).

Spanish

Goroda i gody (Madrid, 1927), *Goroda i gody* (Buenos Aires, 1944), *Brat'ja* (Madrid, 1930), *Transvaal'* (under the title *Neobyknovennyj čelovek*, Madrid, 1929), *Mužiki* (*Mužiki* titled *Pastux*, and *Transvaal'* titled *Mel'nik*, Madrid, 1928), *Sanatorij Arktur* (Moscow, 1958).

Swedish

Pervye radosti (Stockholm, 1954).

Uzbek

Pervye radosti (Tashkent, 1956).

VII. SOVIET DOCUMENTARY SOURCES

Godovščina social'noj revoljucii v Saratove (Saratov, 1918).
Pjat' let proletarskoj bor'by (Saratov, Gosudarstvennoe izdatel'stvo, 1922).
Revoljucionnoe prošloe Saratova (Saratov, 1930).
Pervyj vsesojuznyj s"ezd sovetskix pisatelej. Stenografičeskij otčet (Moscow, Gosudarstvennoe izdatel'stvo xudožestvennoj literatury, 1934).
Scott, H. G. (ed.), *Problems of Soviet Literature: Reports and Speeches at the First Soviet Writers' Congress* (Moscow-Leningrad, Cooperative Publishing Society of Foreign Workers in the USSR, 1935).*
Afanas'ev, N., *Bor'ba partii bol'ševikov za ustanovlenie i upročenie Sovetskoj vlasti v Saratovskoj gubernii* (Saratov, Saratovskoe oblastnoe izdatel'stvo, 1947).*

VIII. ARTICLES BY FEDIN

"Aleksandr Blok", *Kniga i revoljucija*, No. 1/13 (1921), p. 23.*

"Zamjatin", *Kniga i revoljucija*, No. 8-9 (1921), p. 85.

"Spor o social'nom zakaze", *Pečat' i revoljucija*, No. 2 (1929), p. 23.*

"Fel'eton o jazyke i kritike", *Zvezda*, No. 9 (1929).*

"Melok na šube", *Žizn' iskusstva*, Nos. 792-97 (1921).*

"Kak ja rabotaju", *Literaturnaja učeba*, No. 4 (1930), pp. 111-18.

"Stefanu Cvejgu: otkrytoe pis'mo", *Literaturnaja gazeta*, No. 59 (Dec. 14, 1930), p. 2.* Stefan Zweig's reply, as well as additional comments by Fedin, will be found in *Literaturnaja gazeta*, No. 9 (Feb. 14, 1931), p. 2.*

"U Rollana", *Izvestija*, No. 192 (July 13, 1932), p. 3.*

"Vstreči, vpečatlenija ... Priezd K. Fedina iz-za granicy", *Literaturnaja gazeta*, No. 58 (Dec. 23, 1932), p. 1.

"Èxo", *Izvestija*, No. 1 (Jan. 1, 1933), p. 5.*

"Jazyk literatury", *Literaturnaja učeba*, Nos. 3-4 (1933), pp. 110-115.

"Obladat' otvagoj Bal'zaka: odnodnevnika Len. Orgkomiteta VSSP", *Literaturnyj Leningrad*, Apr. 23, 1933, p. 1.

"O jazyke", *Literaturnaja gazeta*, No. 39 (Aug. 23, 1933), p. 3.*

"Vystuplenie na I vsesojuznom s"ezde sovetskix pisatelej", *Literaturnaja gazeta*, No. 109 (Aug. 23, 1934), p. 2.*

"Tema vtoroj knigi", *Literaturnyj Leningrad*, No. 57 (79) (Nov. 14, 1934), p. 1.

"Moja rabota nad romanom *Poxiščenie Evropy*",*Pravada*,No.313 (Nov.14,1934)p.4.*

"O rabote nad vtoroj čast'ju *Poxiščenija Evropy*", *Komsomol'skaja Pravada*, No. 87 (Apr. 15, 1935), p. 4.

"Ne snižat' urovnja svoego iskusstva", *Literaturnj Leningrad*, No. 17 (162) (Apr. 8, 1936).*

"O Puškine", *Zvezda*, No. 1 (1937), pp. 15-24.*

"O Romen Rollane", *Literaturnyj sovremennik*, No. 11 (1938).

"O Leskove", *Literaturnaja gazeta*, No. 48 (Sept. 15, 1940), p. 2.

"Pamjati A. S. Novikova-Priboja", *Krasnoflotec*, Nos. 10-11 (1944), pp. 43-44.*

"Buduščie knigi", *Literaturnaja gazeta*, No. 12 (Mar. 17, 1945), p. 4.*

"Pis'mo redaktoru", *Kommunist* (Saratov), Mar. 3, 1946.

"Vo imja sčast'ja narodov", *Pravda*, Aug. 4, 1950.*

"O bor'be za mir", *Literaturnaja gazeta*, Oct. 3, 1950.*

"Fakti istorii", *Pravda*, No. 1 (Jan. 1, 1951).

"Čudesnyj genij: o Gogole", *Pravda*, No. 64 (Mar. 4, 1952).

"Borec za sčast'e Germanii", *Ogonek*, No. 7 (Febr., 1953), p. 9.*

"Soveršenstvovat' masterstvo prozaikov", *Literaturnaja gazeta*, No. 30 (3214) (Mar. 11, 1954), p. 1.*

"Fuer die Kunst gibt's keine Rezepte", *Sozialismus; Monatschrift fuer Theorie und Praxis der Arbeiterbewegung* (Zurich), 1955, pp. 91-95.

"Na povodu dilogii", *Oktjabr'*, No. 8 (1955).

"Na literaturnom puti", *Oktjabr'*, No. 8 (1955).

"Pis'mo aspirantu", *Oktjabr'*, No. 8 (1955).*

"Konstantin Fedin beantwortet Fragen seiner deutschen Leser", *Schriftsteller* (Berlin), Nos. 11-12 (1955).

"Aus meiner Schriftstellerischen Arbeit", *Sowjetwissenschaft*, No. 4 (1956), pp. 31-40.*

"Die Tragoedie Stefan Zweigs", *Aufbau* (Berlin), No. 12 (1956), pp. 959-61.

"Begegnung mit Romain Rolland", *Aufbau* (Berlin), No. 12 (1956), pp. 1098-1104.

"Aleksandr Aleksandrovič Fadeev", *Ogonek*, No. 21 (1956), p. 25.*

"Der Schriftsteller und das Heute", *Sowjetwissenschaft* (Berlin), No. 5 (1957), pp. 903-909.*

"Den' s druz'jami", *Literaturnaja gazeta*, No. 96 (3752) (Aug. 10, 1957), p. 2.*
"Alexander Blok", *Sinn und Form* (Berlin), No. 9 (1957), pp. 1015-1020.*
"Roždennye oktjabrem: avtobiografičeskie zapiski", *Novyj mir*, No. 9 (1957), pp. 226-244.*
"Zwischen Resignation und Hoffnung. Zur mittleren Schaffensperiode von L. Frank", *Aufbau* (Berlin), No. 9 (1957).
"Mysli o masterstve", *Izvestija Akademii Nauk SSSR, Otdelenie literatury i jazyka*, XVIII, No. 1 (1959), pp. 3-8.*
"K obrazu Lenina v literature", *Novyj mir*, No. 4 (1959), pp. 241-247.
"Gedanken ueber die Meisterschaft", *Sowjetwissenschaft* (Berlin), No. 7 (1959), pp. 254-257.
"My Life and Work", *Soviet Literature* (Moscow), No. 1 (1962), pp. 144-152. Tr. by Eve Manning.*
"The Lofty Ideals of a new Epoch", *Soviet Literature* (Moscow), No. 4 (1962), pp. 127-130.*
"Kak my pišem", *Voprosy literatury* (Moscow), No. 7 (1962), p. 175.*

IX. SECONDARY SOURCES. BOOKS AND THESES

Akademija Nauk SSSR. Institut mirovoj literatury im. A. M. Gor'kogo. *Istorija russkoj sovetskoj literatury*. 3 vols. Vol. III: *1941-1957* (Moscow, Izdatel'stvo Akademii Nauk SSSR, 1961), pp. 212-234.*
——, *Očerk istorii russkoj sovetskoj literatury* (Moscow, Izdatel'stvo Akademii Nauk SSSR, 1954).*
——, Institut russkoj literatury (Puškinskij dom). *Voprosy sovetskoj literatury*. 9 vols. Vol. IX: *Sovetskij roman* (Moscow-Leningrad, Izdatel'stvo Akademii Nauk SSSR, 1961). Vols. I, III, IV, VI, and VIII also contain pertinent information.*
Analecta Slavica, A Slavonic miscellany, presented for his birthday to Bruno Becker, Professor of Russian History, Language and Literature in the University of Amsterdam (Amsterdam, 1955).*
Auerbach, E., *Mimesis* (Princeton, Princeton University Press, 1953).*
Bol'šaja Sovetskaja Ènciklopedija, Vol. XLIV, 2d ed. (Moscow, Gosudarstvennoe nauchnoe izdatel'stvo BSE, 1956), pp. 569-570.*
Borland, Harriet, *Soviet Literary Theory and Practice during the First Five-Year Plan 1928-1932* (New York, King's Crown Press, 1950).*
Brajnina, Berta Jakovlevna, *Konstantin Fedin* (Moscow, Sovetskij pisatel', 1951).*
——, *Konstantin Fedin* (Moscow, Sovetskij pisatel', 1952).
——, *Konstantin Fedin* (Moscow, Gosudarstvennoe izdatel'stvo xudožestvennoj literatury, 1953).*
——, *Konstantin Fedin*. Translated into German by Traute Stein (Berlin, Verlag Kultur und Fortschrift, 1954).
——, *Konstantin Fedin: Stenogramma publičnoj lekcii pročitannoj v Moskve* (Moscow, Znanie, 1954).*
——, *Tvorčeskij put' K. A. Fedina: posobie dlja učitelej* (Moscow, Gosudarstvennoe učebno-pedagogičeskoe izdatel'stvo, 1955).*
——, *Konstantin Fedin*. 4th ed. (Moscow, Gosudarstvennoe izdatel'stvo xudožestvennoj literatury, 1956).*
Brajnina, B. Ja., and E. F. Nikitina, (ed.), *Sovetskie pisateli: avtobiografii v dvux tomax*. Vol. II (Moscow, Gosudarstvennoe izdatel'stvo xudožestvennoj literatury, 1959).*
Brown, Edward James, *The Proletarian Episode in Russian Literature, 1928-1932* (New York, Columbia University Press, 1953).*

Bugaenko, P., *Masterstvo Konstantina Fedina* (Saratov, Saratovskoe knižnoe izdatel'-stvo, 1959).*

Butcher, S. H. (ed.), *Aristotle's Theory of Poetry and Fine Art* (New York, Dover Publications, Inc., 1951).*

Byčkov, S. P. (ed.), *L. N. Tolstoj v russkoj kritike*. *Sbornik statej*. 2d ed. (Moscow, Gosudarstvennoe izdatel'stvo xudožestvennoj literatury, 1952).*

Chiževskij, D., *Evgenij Onegin* (Cambridge, Harvard University Press, 1953).

Davidson, Donald, "The Inversive method of narration in the novels and stories of Joseph Conrad". Unpublished master's thesis, Joint University Libraries, Vanderbilt University, Nashville, Tenn. (May 15, 1922).*

Eastman, Max, *Artists in Uniform: A Study of Literature and Bureaucratism* (New York, Alfred A. Knopf, 1934).*

Erlauterungen zur Sowjetliteratur, Kollektiv fuer Literaturgeschichte (Berlin, Volk und Wissen Volkseigener Verlag, 1954).*

Erlich, Victor, *Russian Formalism* (The Hague, Mouton, 1955).*

Fadeev, A. A., *Za tridcat' let* (Moscow, Sovetskij pisatel', 1957).*

Forster, E. M., *Aspects of the Novel* (New York, Harcourt, Brace and Co., 1927).*

Gibian, George, *Interval of Freedom: Soviet Literature During the Thaw 1954-1957* (Minneapolis, University of Minnesota Press, 1960).*

Gorbačev, G., *Dva goda literaturnoj revoljucii* (Leningrad, Priboj, 1926).

——, *Sovremennaja russkaja literatura* (Leningrad, Priboj, 1928).

Gor'kij, M., *Sobranie sočinenij v tridcati tomax* (Moscow, Gosudarstvennoe izdatel'stvo xudožestvennoj literatury, 1949-1955).*

Grečnev, V. Ja., "Tema iskusstva v dilogii K. Fedina", *Voprosy sovetskoj literatury*. Vol. IX (Moscow-Leningrad, Izdatel'stvo Akademii Nauk SSSR, 1961).*

Gudzij, N. K., *History of Early Russian Literature*. Translated by Susan Wilbur Jones (New York, Macmillan Co., 1949).*

Gvozdov, A. N., *Očerki po stilistike russkogo jazyka*. 2d ed. (Moscow, Gosudarstvennoe učebno-pedagogičeskoe izdatel'stvo Ministerstva Prosveščenija R.S.F.S.R.).*

Hare, Richard, *Russian Literature from Pushkin to the Present Day* (London, Methuen and Co., 1947).*

Harkins, William E., *Dictionary of Russian Literature* (Paterson, N.J., Littlefield, Adams and Co., 1959).*

Jackson, Robert Louis, *Dostoevsky's Underground Man in Russian Literature* (The Hague, Mouton & Co., 1958).*

Jakimenko, L., "Pisatel' i stil'", *Masterstvo russkix pisatelej: Sbornik statej* (Moscow, Gosudarstvennoe izdatel'stvo xudožestvennoj literatury, 1959.*

Lenin, V. I., *Articles on Tolstoy* (Moscow, Foreign Lang. Publ. House, 1953).*

Lettenbauer, Wilhelm, *Russische Literaturgeschichte* (Wiesbaden, Otto Harrassowitz, 1958).*

Levinson, Z. I., *Konstantin Aleksandrovič Fedin: Bibliografičeskij spravochnik* (Tula, Izdatel'stvo Tul'skoj oblastnoj biblioteki imeni V. I. Lenina, 1958).

Libedinskij, J., *Sovremenniki: Literaturnye vospominanija* (Moscow, Sovetskij pisatel', 1959).

Lidin, Vl. (ed.), *Pisateli: Avtobiografii i portrety sovremennyx russkix prozaikov*. 2d ed. enlarged and revised (Moscow, Knigoizdatel'stvo sovremennye problemy N. A. Stolljar, 1928).*

Literaturnaja Ènciklopedija, Vol. XI. Edited by A. V. Lunačarskij (Moscow, Gosudarstvennoe izdatel'stvo xudožestvennoj literatury, 1929-1939).*

Lukin, Ju., *Romany Konstantina Fedina Pervye radosti i Neobyknovennoe leto: Stenogramma publičnoj lekcii pročitannoj v Moskve* (Moscow, Znanie, 1951).*

Makarenko, A. (ed.), *O pisatel'skom trude. Sbornik statej* (Moscow, Sovetskij Pisatel', 1953).*

Mathewson, Rufus W. Jr., *The Positive Hero in Russian Literature* (New York, Columbia University Press, 1958).*

Nikitina, E. F., *Russkaja literatura ot symbolizma do našix dnej: literaturno-sociologičeskij seminarij* (Moscow, Kooperativnoe izdatel'stvo pisatelej "Nikitinskie subbotniki", 1926).*

Novye uspexi sovetskoj literatury (Moscow, Sovetskij pisatel', 1949).

Oksenov, Innokentij, *Sovremennaja russkaja kritika: 1912-1924* (Leningrad, Gosudarstvennoe izdatel'stvo, 1925).

Oksenov, I. A., and V. Tarsis, *Sovremennye russkie pisateli* (Leningrad, Izdatel'stvo pisatelej v Leningrade, 1930).

Oulanoff, Hongor, *The Theory and Practice of the Serapion Brothers* (= *Slavistic Printings and Reprintings*, 44) (The Hague, Mouton & Co., 1966).

Ozerov, Vitalij Mixajlovič, *Obraz bol'ševika v poslevoennoj sovetskoj literature* (Moscow, Sovetskoj pisatel', 1950).*

——, *Obraz kommunista v sovetskoj literature* (Moscow, Gosudarstvennoe izdatel'stvo xudožestvennoj literatury, 1959).*

Palej, A. R., *Literaturnye portrety* (Moscow, Ogonek, 1928).

Percos, V., *Ètjudy sovetskoj literatury* (Moscow, Gosudarstvennoe izdatel'stvo xudožestvennoj literatury, 1937).

Poggioli, Renato, *The Phoenix and the Spider* (Cambridge, Harvard University Press, 1957).*

Pozner, Vladimir, *Panorama de la Littérature Russe Contemporaine* (Paris, Editions Kra, 1929).*

Rador, S., *Na postu: stat'i i zametki* (Moscow, Federatsija, 1931).

Reavey, George, *Soviet Literature Today* (New Haven, Yale University Press, 1947).*

Rolick, Alexander J., "Fedin and Soviet Criticism (1919-1926)". Unpublished Master's thesis, Columbia University, New York (1950).*

Rozanov, I. N., *Putevoditel' po sovremennoj russkoj literature* (Moscow, Rabotnik prosveščenija, 1929).

Scott, H. G. (ed.), *Problems of Soviet Literature* (Moscow-Leningrad, Society of Foreign Workers in the USSR, 1935).*

Setschkareff, Vsevolod, *Geschichte der Russischen Literatur im Ueberblick* (Bonn, Athenaeum Verlag, 1949).*

Shipley, Joseph T. (ed.), *Dictionary of World Literature* (Paterson, N. J., Littlefield, Adams and Co., 1960).*

Širmakov, P., "Tvorčestvo Fedina v period graždanskoj vojny i vosstanovlenija narodnogo xozjajstva". Unpublished Candidate's dissertation, University of Leningrad (1955).

Simmons, Ernest J., *An Outline of Modern Russian Literature* (*1880-1940*) (Ithaca, Cornell University Press, 1944).*

——, *Russian Fiction and Soviet Ideology* (New York, Col. Univ. Press, 1958).*

Slonim, Marc, *Modern Russian Literature: From Chekhov to the Present* (New York, Oxford University Press, 1953).*

——, *Outline of Russian Literature* (New York, Oxford University Press, 1958).*

Smirnova, Vera, "O romanax Konstantina Fedin", *Sovetskaja xudožestvennaja proza: Sbornik statej* (Moscow, Sovetskij pisatel', 1955).

Smirnova, Vera, "O romanax Konstantina Fedina", *O literature i teatre* (Moscow, Sovetskij pisatel', 1956).*

Stanislavskij, K. S., *On the Art of the Stage*. Translated with an Introductory Essay on Stanislavskij's System by David Magarshack (New York, Hill and Wang, 1961).*

Struve, Gleb, *Soviet Russian Literature 1917-1950* (Norman, University of Oklahoma Press, 1951).*

Struve, Gleb, *25 Years of Russian Literature* (London, George Routledge and Sons, 1946).*

Tamarčenko, D., *Put' k realizmu: O tvorčestve K. Fedina* (Leningrad, Izdatel'stvo pisatelej v Leningrade, 1934).*

Trifonov, N. A., and N. I. Kudrjašev, *Russkaja sovetskaja literatura.* 2d ed. (Moscow, Gosudarstvennoe učebno-pedagogičeskoe izdatel'stvo Ministerstva Prosveščenija R.S.F.S.R., 1958).*

Trotzky, Leon, *Literature and Revolution* (Ann Arbor, University of Michigan Press, 1960) (Ann Arbor Paperbacks).*

Upit, A., *Literaturno-kritičeskie stat'i* (Riga, Latvijskoe gosudarstvennoe izdatel'stvo, 1955).*

V literaturnix bojax: Sbornik statej (Moscow, Moskovskij rabočij, 1930).

van der Eng-Liedmeier, A. M., *Soviet Literary Characters: An Investigation into the Portrayal of Soviet Men in Russian Prose 1917-1953* (The Hague, Mouton & Co., 1959).*

Vernadsky, G., *A History of Russia.* 3d ed. revised (New Haven, Yale University, Press, 1951).*

Višnev, V., *Kniga xarakteristik* (Moscow-Leningrad, Gosudarstvennoe izdatel'stvo, 1928).

Voronskij, A., *Na styke* (Moscow, Gosudarstvennoe izdatel'stvo, 1923).

Warren, Austin, *et al.*, *Literary Scholarship* (Chapel Hill, University of North Carolina Press, 1941).*

Wellek, R., and A. Warren, *Theory of Literature* (New York, Harcourt Brace and Co., 1956).*

Zavalishin, Vjacheslav, *Early Soviet Writers* (New York, Praeger, 1958).*

Zelinskij, K., *Na rubeže dvux èpox: Literaturnye vstreči 1917-1920 godov* (Moscow, Sovetskij pisatel', 1960).

X. SECONDARY SOURCES. ARTICLES AND PERIODICALS

Abakumov, A., "Novinki xudožestvennoj literatury", *Rodnoj jazyk v škole*, No. 9 (1926).

Averbax, L., "Na rasput'i", *Na postu*, No. 1 (1926).

Berezkina, A. G., "Stanovlenie zamysla dilogii K. Fedina *Pervye radosti* i *Neobyknovennoe leto*", *Učenye zapiski Kujbyševskogo pedinstituta*, No. 19 (1958).*

Bojčevskij, V., "Konstantin Fedin", *Čitatel' i pisatel'*, No. 43 (1928).

Borodin, S., "Roman o velikoj sile bol'ševizma", *Znamja*, No. 2 (1949), pp. 177-181.

Bowling, L. E., "What is the Stream of Consciousness Technique?", *Publications of the Modern Language Association*, LXV (1950), pp. 337-45.*

Brajnina, Berta Jakovlevna, "Iskusstvo slova", *Oktjabr'*, No. 1 (1954).*

——, "Kompas istorii", *Zvezda*, No. 4 (1949), pp. 184-189.*

——, "Konstantin Fedin", *Novyj mir*, No. 11 (1947).*

——, "O svjazy vremen: zametki o tvorčestve K. A. Fedina", *Izvestija Akademii Nauk SSSR. Otdelenie Literatury i jazyka*, XXI, No. 2 (March-April, 1962), pp. 125-27.*

Bregova, D., "Konstantin Fedin", *Literatura v škole*, No. 2 (March-April, 1962), pp. 18-25.*

Brovman, N., "Zametki o xudožestvennoj proze", *Novyj mir*, No. 3 (1948).*

Bruening, Elfr, "Phantasie und Wirklichkeit. Konstantin Fedin: *Ungewoehnlicher Sommer*", *Schriftsteller* (Berlin), Nos. 21-22 (1954).

Craig, David, Letter to the Editor, *Soviet Literature* (Moscow), No. 7 (1962), pp. 174-75.*

Dobin, E., "Zaostrenie v sjužete", *Novyj mir*, No. 3 (1955), pp. 244-59.*

Dobranov, Ju, "Tvorčeskij put' K. Fedina", *Literatura i jazyk v politexničeskoj škole* (Moscow), No. 5 (1930).*

Dobrynin, M., "Èvoljucija tvorčestva K. Fedina", *Krasnaja nov'*, No. 9 (1929), pp. 231-243.*

Drozdov, A., "Vyxod v žizn'", *Novyj mir*, Nos. 4-5 (1946).*

Dynnik, V., "Perestavlennye glavy: O romane Konst. Fedina *Goroda i gody*", *Krasnaja nov'*, No. 9 (1925), pp. 270-76.*

Edgerton, William, "The Serapion Brothers: An Early Soviet Controversy", *The American Slavic and East European Review*, VIII, No. 1 (February, 1949), pp. 47-64.*

Fadeev, A. A., "Za vysokoe kačestvo literatury i principal'nuju kritiku", *Literaturnaja gazeta*, No. 64 (2551), (Aug. 10, 1949).*

Friče, V. M., "Literaturnye zametki: Sovetskaja derevnja ili *Transvaal*'", *Pravda*, No. 92, April 23, 1927, p. 5.

Gladkovskaja, L., "Sovetskij rasskaz", *Zvezda*, No. 3 (March, 1953), pp. 169-175.*

Goffenšefer, V., "Poxiščenie Evropy", *Literaturnyj kritik*, No. 4 (April, 1936), pp. 101-112.*

Gorbov, D., "Itogi literaturnogo goda", *Novyj mir*, No. 12 (1925), pp. 129-148.

Groznova, N. A., and A. I. Xajlov, "K 70-letiju K. A. Fedina", *Izvestija Akademii Nauk SSSR, Otdelenie literatury i jazyka*, XXI, No. 4 (July-August, 1962), pp. 370-72.*

Isakov, S., "Mecenat i xudožnik", *Krasnaja gazeta*, No. 9, Jan. 10, 1925, p. 5.

Ivanov, Vasilij, "Dva romana Konstantina Fedina", *Oktjabr'*, No. 1 (1949), pp. 168-174.*

Jurgin, N., "Masterstvo pisatelja: O romane Fedina *Goroda i gody*", *Žurnalist*, No. 2 (1926), pp. 53-54.

Kaplan, Abraham, "On the So-Called Crisis in Criticism", *Journal of Aesthetics and Art Criticism*, VII, No. 1 (September, 1948).*

Karasik, C. Z., "Problema iskusstva i revoljucii v dilogii K. Fedina *Pervye radosti* i *Neobyknovennoe leto*", *Učenye zapiski L'vovskogo universiteta im. Iv. Franko*, XXIV, No. 2 (1953).

——, "Tema iskusstva i revoljucii v romane Konstantina Fedina *Goroda i gody*", *Učenye zapiski Leningradskogo pedagogičeskogo instituta*, IV (1957), pp. 57-73.

Kedrina, S., "Auf dem Gutshof Leo Tolstois. Zu einem Kapitel aus Konstantin Fedins neuem, noch unvollendeten Roman", *Sowjetwissenschaft*, No. 4 (1956), pp. 834-37.*

——, "Tvorčeskij portret pisatelja", *Novyj mir*, No. 6 (June, 1951), pp. 251-53.*

——, "V svete *Kostra*: K 70-letiju so dnja roždenija K. A. Fedina", *Moskva*, No. 2 (1962), pp. 192-98.*

Kolesnika, A., "Goroda i gody", *Na postu*, No. 1 (1925), pp. 207-214.

Komina, R. V., "Dilogija K. Fedina *Pervye radosti* i *Neobyknovennoe leto*", *Literatura v škole*, XVII, No. 5 (September-October, 1956), pp. 18-27.*

Kovarskij, N., "Na znakomye temy", *Literaturnyj sovremennik*, No. 1 (1933).

Kozlos, I., "O sžatosti v proze", *Novyj mir*, No. 6 (1955), pp. 263-278.*

Kremen', A., "Goroda i gody", *Krasnaja gazeta*, No. 275, Dec. 2, 1924, p. 5.

Lelevič, G., "Jazyk literaturnyx faktov", *Leningradskaja pravda*, No. 180, Sep. 9, 1925.

Levidov, M., "Revoljucija čerez binokl'", *Večernaja Moskva*, No. 57, Mar. 10, 1925.

Lezinev, A., "Dejstvitel'no li oni brat'ja?" *Pravda*, No. 157, Aug. 8, 1928.*

Literatura i iskusstvo, Aug. 5, 1944, and Sep. 9, 1944.

Literaturnaja gazeta, Feb. 26, 1952.*

Literaturnye zapiski (Peterburg), Nos. 1-3 (1922).*

Lukin, Ju., "Ložnaja moral' i iskažennaja perspektiva", *Pravda*, No. 177 (9634), Jul. 24, 1944, p. 4.*

——, "Neobyknovennoe leto", *Pravda*, No. 65, Mar. 6, 1949, p. 3.*

Marchand, James W., *Prolegomena to a Theory of Literary Criticism*, an unpublished, undated paper distributed as a supplement to a series of lectures delivered at Vanderbilt University during the academic year 1961-1962 and 1962-1963.*

Marksistko-Leninskoe iskustvoznanie, Sep. 9, 1944.

Mironova, Anna, "About Konstantin Fedin's Collected Works", a review in *Soviet Literature*, No. 12 (1962), pp. 173-174.*

Nedobrovo, V., "Filosofija samobičevankja: O fil'me *Goroda i gody*", *Krasnaja gazeta*, No. 20 (1931).

Levin, F. "Ja byl akterom", *Literaturnoe obozrenie*, No. 6 (1938).

Nikitin, Nikita, "A. N. Tolstoj", *Zvezda*, No. 1 (1958), pp. 189-194.

Ogonek, No. 8 (February, 1962), p. 8.*

Oksenov, I. "*Goroda i gody*: Roman Konst. Fedina", *Leningrad*, No. 23 (1924), p. 13.

——, "Russkaja xudožestvennaja literatura v 1924 g", *Leningradskaja Pravda*, No. 1, Jan. 1, 1925, p. 6.

Ostrovskij, Ju., "Kniga o Fedine", Review of *Put' k realizmu*, by D. Tamarčenko, *Literaturnyj kritik*, No. 11 (1934), pp. 203-206.*

Paustovskij, K., "Zolotaja roza. Kniga o pisatel'skom trude", *Oktjabr'*, No. 10 (1955), pp. 67-68.

Pavlenko, P., "Vdoxnovljajuščaja sila", *Literaturnaja gazeta*, No. 88 (2471), Nov. 3, 1948.*

Penkin, M., "Neobyknovennoe leto", *Komsomol'skaja pravda*, No. 86, Apr. 13, 1949.*

Plotkin, L., "A. A. Ždanov i voprosy literatury", *Zvezda*, No. 1 (1949), pp. 109-121.*

Poljak, L., "Pervoèlement literatury", *Literaturnaja gazeta*, Sep. 15, 1955, p. 3.

Polonskij, Efrem, "Poxiščenie Evropy", *Literaturnaja gazeta*, No. 16 (1934), p. 2.*

Pravda, Summons to Soviet writers from Central Committee of the Communist Party of the USSR to perfect their craftsmanship, Dec. 7, 1948.*

Priležaev, M., "Služenie literature", *Literaturnaja gazeta*, No. 41 (3852), Apr. 5, 1958, p. 3.*

Pross-Weerth, H., "Konstantin Fedin", *Osteuropa* (Stuttgart), No. 9 (1959), pp. 693-700.*

Rossbach, Wolfgang, "Konstantin Fedin: Ein Repraesentant der Sowjetliteratur", *Der Bibliothekar* (Leipzig), XI, No. 13 (1959), pp. 1204-1209.

Safronova, O., "Problema iskusstva i revoljucii v romane Pervye radosti", *Učenye zapiski Kazanskogo pedagogičeskogo instituta, Kafedra literatury*, No. 12 (1958).

Samarin, P. M., "Konstantin Fedin i nemeckaja literatura", *Izvestija Akademii Nauk SSSR, Otdelenie literatury i jazyka*, XXI, No. 3 (May-June, 1962), pp. 226-233.*

Sergeev-Censkij, S., "Moja perepiska i znakomstvo s A. M. Gor'kim", *Oktjabr'*, Nos. 6-7 (1940), pp. 274-300.*

Severin, E., "Brat'ja Fedina", *Pečat' i revoljucija*, No. 7 (1928), pp. 92-99.

Šaginjan, M., "K. Fedin", *Rossija*, No. 2 (1924), pp. 213-214.

Šklovskij, V., "Serapionovy brat'ja", *Knižnyj ugol'*, No. 7 (1921).*

Smirnova, Vera, "Boevoj devjatnadcatyj god", *Literaturnaja gazeta*, No. 2 (2489), Jan. 5, 1949.*

——, "Neobyknovennoe leto", *Novyj mir*, No. 5 (1949), pp. 286-291.

Sobolev, Ju., "Literaturnye sovremenniki: Konstantin Fedin", *Večernjaja Moskva*, No. 193, Aug. 26, 1925, p. 2.

Spencer, Theodore, "The Critic's Function", *Sewanee Review*, 47 (October-December, 1939).*

Stewart, David H., "The Textual Evolution of *The Silent Don*", *American Slavonic and East European Review*, XVIII, No. 2 (April, 1959), pp. 226-237.

Struve, Gleb, "Constantine Fedin", *The Slavonic Review*, xiii, No. 37 (July, 1934), pp. 177-182.*

——, "Leonid Leonov and his Skutarevsky", *The Slavonic and East European Review*, XII, No. 34 (July, 1933), p. 190.*

——, "New Novels of Fedin and Leonov", *The Slavonic and East European Review*, XV, No. 45 (April, 1937), pp. 692-697.

Tal'nikov, D., "Literaturnye zametki", *Krasnaja nov'*, No. 9 (1928), pp. 245-273.*

Tamarčenko, D., "O kriterii xudožestvennosti. I. Postanovka voprosa. II. *Goroda i gody* K. Fedina", *Leningrad*, No. 8 (1932), pp. 76-87.

——, "Poxiščenie Evropy", *Literaturnyj Leningrad*, No. 6, Feb. 3, 1934, p. 2.*

Tarasenkov, An., "Poèzija velikix peremen", *Izvestija*, No. 3, Jan. 5, 1949, p. 3.*

Tereščenko, N., "Poèzija ostrix kontrastov: Konstantin Fedin", *Krasnaja gazeta*, No. 196, Aug. 11, 1925, p. 5.

Tixonov, N., "Na pod"eme: *Neobyknovennoe leto*", *Kul'tura i žizn'*, No. 35 (1948).

——, "O Konstantine Fedine", *Literaturnaja gazeta*, Feb. 23, 1952, p. 3.*

——, "V poiskax obraza vremeni: K 70-letiju so dnja roždenija K. A. Fedina", *Russkaja literatura*, No. 1 (1962), pp. 15-19.*

Upit, A., "Ob èstetike socialističeskogo realizma", *Literaturnaja gazeta*, No. 64 (2551), Aug. 10, 1949.*

Višnev, V., "Konstantin Fedin: Literaturnyj portret", *Novyj mir*, No. 9 (1925), pp. 113-127.

Voronskij, A., "Literaturnye otkliki", *Krasnaja nov'*, No. 2 (1923), pp. 333-346.*

Zelinskij, K., "Master slova", *Ogonek*, No. 7 (1951).

Žak, K., "K problematitse nektryx postav romanu Konstantina Fedina", *Chasopis pro slovanske jazyky, literaturu a dejiny* (Prague), No. 4 (1955), pp. 628-633.

Zonin, A., "O sub"ekte tvorčestva K. Fedina", *Pečat' i revoljucija*, No. 5 (1929), pp. 71-90.

INDEX